ABOUT THE AUTHOR

John Short has a BA (Hons) in Economics from the University of Stirling (in the first intake of students where he was the founding president of the Sports Union) and an MA in Economics from the University of Lancaster. He researched on the regional impact of public finance at the Universities of Aberdeen and Durham and at the Northern Region Strategy Team. He has been a consultant with IMF, World Bank, bilateral agencies and individual countries since 1982. He was a member of Gosforth RFC's cup-winning side at Twickenham in 1976 and was inducted into the Newcastle Rugby Hall of Fame in 2017.

This book is based on work carried out in the following countries:
Serbia, Belarus, Georgia, Moldova, Albania, Kosovo, Uzbekistan, Azerbaijan, Ukraine, The Gambia, Kenya, Uganda, Sierra Leone, Zambia, Zimbabwe, Sudan, Egypt, Mauritius, Rwanda, Seychelles, Ghana, Liberia, Malawi, Ethiopia, Niger, Nigeria, Namibia, Tanzania, Mozambique, Myanmar, Vietnam, Lao PDR, China, Papua New Guinea, Indonesia, Philippines, India, Bangladesh, Pakistan, Afghanistan, Yemen, Jordan, Palestine, Netherlands Antilles, Anguilla, Antigua, Barbados, Montserrat, St Helena, Pitcairn, Aruba, St Vincent and Grenadines, Grenada, St Kitts, Nevis, Jamaica, Dominica, British Virgin Islands, Falklands, Fiji, UK, Ireland.

DEDICATION

To my family members: those no longer alive, those present and those yet to be. Thank you for your support and inspiration.

John Short

APPLIED ECONOMICS: PUBLIC FINANCIAL MANAGEMENT AND DEVELOPMENT

Sixty Countries, Fifty Years' Experience

AUSTIN MACAULEY PUBLISHERS™

LONDON • CAMBRIDGE • NEW YORK • SHARJAH

ISBN 9781398444683 (Paperback)
ISBN 9781398444690 (Hardback)
ISBN 9781398444706 (ePub ebook)

www.austinmacauley.com

First Published 2022
Austin Macauley Publishers Ltd
1 Canada Square
Canary Wharf
London
E14 5AA

ACKNOWLEDGEMENTS

Thank you to Mark Brownrigg, Neil Walden, Mick Connarty and Neil Kay from my Stirling years for encouragement, comments and guidance.

CONTENTS

PREFACE

The genesis of this manuscript has been the frequent refrain from my offspring when I have commented on some news item and mentioned something about the place – you should write a book! COVID-19 and being in lockdown and almost full isolation has provided the opportunity to do that. After all, there is a point when taking up another book to read becomes a chore no matter how good they are – and I think I have exhausted the tales of John Rebus around Edinburgh, a city I know reasonably well from being the Third Man on the McEwan's' delivery trucks out of Fountainbridge brewery in 1967. No matter how good the books in the pile are. I also have to dispel the suspicion that I am a spy, which family and friends in Gosforth Rugby Club have long held – it has just been a coincidence that coups and assassinations have happened in countries that I have just left. I use "am" rather than "was" given the rumour of a coup in Fiji last September just as I was leaving Suva. The mention of Third Man is not going to help – maybe an early pointer!

Today we tend to store documents and material electronically but at the start of my journey as an economist this was not the case. Fortunately, I have retained hard copies of reports and other texts from early assignments, but often these do not contain all the names of those involved. So apologies if correct acknowledgement is not always given. Unfortunately, I have also lost some electronic files from the 1980s and early 1990s when my back up hard drive was damaged from an old computer so now I always have two backups – to be sure to be sure.

So for my family: Claire and Dan, Mary, Alexander and Leo; Christian and Miriam, Jonah and Isaac; Samantha and Duncan, Sophie and Emily; Amanda and Mikey, Elicia, Harrison and Evangeline; Juliet and Abi; and Rebecca; and also to Rana whose walks helped me to formulate and clarify my thoughts out in the Northumberland countryside.

An apology: there is an awful lot of "I" in this manuscript. Given the nature of the tome it may be inevitable, but nonetheless grating. One word of caution: the word mission is used a lot. In the context here, it is as an assignment/operation/work not as a calling/vocation!

ACRONYMS AND ABBREVIATIONS

ASIDES	Aberdeen Studies in Defence Economics
ASYCUDA	Automated System for Customs Data
CBA	Cost Benefit Analysis
CG	Central Government
COMESA	Common Market for Eastern and Southern Africa
CRPFM	Climate Responsive Public Financial Management Framework
DFID	Department for International Development
DRC	Domestic Resource Cost
EC	European Commission
EPR	Effective Protection Rate
ESAF	Enhanced Structural Adjustment Facility
EU	European Union
FRA	Fiduciary Risk Assessment
GDP	Gross Domestic Product
IFMIS	Integrated Financial Management Information System
IMF FAD	International Monetary Fund Fiscal Affairs Department
I-O	Input – Output
IPS	Integrated Planning System
IT	Information Technology
KPIs	Key Performance Indicators
KSU	Key Spending Unit
MoF	Ministry of Finance

MTBF	Medium Term Budget Framework
MTBO	Medium Term Budget Outlook
MTBP	Medium Term Budget Programme
MTEF	Medium Term Expenditure Framework
MTFF	Medium Term Fiscal Framework
NAO	National Audit Office
NOBL	New Organic Budget Law
NRST	Northern Region Strategy Team
PEFA	Public Expenditure and Financial Accountability
PER	Public Expenditure Review
PESC	Public Expenditure Survey Committee
PFM	Public Financial Management
PRGF	Poverty Reduction and Growth Facility
SD	Service Delivery
SDUs	Service Delivery Units
SNG	Subnational Government
SOE	State-owned Enterprise
SPEM	Strengthening Public Expenditure Management
TA	Technical Assistance
TSA	Treasury Single Account
USAID	United States Agency for International Development
VAT	Value Added Tax

1 INTRODUCTION

The initial aim of this document was straightforward – to put down in paper or at least in electronic format some semblance of what I have been doing over the past 50 years or so for my offspring and theirs. However, the more I put the proverbial pen to paper to achieve this initial aim, the more I also realised that there was material relating to the application of economics which may be of interest to those with a curiosity in public policy and how it is formulated and applied. It may even be attractive to those that are studying economics and want to pursue a career in the field as well as a tool to assist in learning. It might even encourage those studying economics to pursue a career as an economist rather than become an accountant! Indeed, it might stimulate my grandchildren to follow in their grandfather's footsteps.

Public policy is often decried and those who work in it are dismissed as "experts" which has taken on a derisory connotation in the political times of today, particularly since 2015. The scope and content of this manuscript are centred on Public Financial Management (PFM). PFM refers to the set of laws, rules, systems and processes used by sovereign nations (Central Governments (CG) and sub-national (SN) governments), to mobilise revenue, allocate public funds, undertake public spending, account for funds and audit results. What I hope to achieve is to present a picture of the reality of applying public financial management using warts-and-all examples from across the world from my own experiences – and, with a bit of luck, a smidgen of humour to lighten the load! After all, everything has to be evidenced-based and theory is dismissed without the verification of application. The book may be useful for those working in the public policy environment in central and local government who are focusing on the interaction of the planning and executing of budgets, and their financial control and audit, from both the revenue and expenditure perspectives. Hopefully, it demonstrates that they are not alone and the overall environment that they may be experiencing is not unique. The developments in public financial management that have taken place in the recent and not so recent past are presented with country examples taken from my own experiences.

The document can be divided into three interrelated parts. These parts are theme based and not in chronological order. Chapter 2 presents my apprenticeship years learning to and applying research in economics and public finance and some later intermittent follow up research. The second part from Chapters 3 to 8 covers budgeting and public financial management from both the expenditure and revenue perspectives as well as the assessment tools that have been developed to measure performance. I have sneaked private sector development in alongside taxation, both its policy and administration, in Chapter 7 as after all if taxes are at 100% there will be no private sector! Chapter 8 examines tax expenditures which is the revenue forgone or cost from giving tax breaks to achieve policy objectives. Capacity building experiences in these areas are presented in Chapter 9. The final part is Chapter 10 which attempts to draw some commonality from the previous chapters and assess what progress I have seen in the areas that I have worked in as an economist.

There are many colleagues that I have been fortunate to have worked with throughout my career. Their experiences are, in some cases, shared with me but they have many of their own. I have tried as far as possible to include our common experiences in the appropriate places to acknowledge their inputs to what I have been involved in. Some are frequent flyers. Where their experiences are wider I have referenced them wherever possible. I offer my sincere and grateful thanks to all of them and to the many others that I may have missed, who have contributed to this Short journey of an itinerant economist.

In the beginning

My journey as a practising economist started in my undergraduate years and could have easily been finished as soon as after I graduated. I applied to Stirling University early in 1967 for the academic year starting in September of that year. My memory is that I applied to Edinburgh and Stirling only as a late applicant and Stirling accepted me before Edinburgh so I chose Stirling which was a new university and was accepting its first students. Perhaps

I was the only Irish citizen applying and the university wanted to broaden its cultural mix! There were only 164 undergraduates and some postgraduates in the very first year.

Stirling's 2 semesters in an academic year system[1] helped me in settling down to economics as a subject rejecting along the way both history, which I nominally applied to study, and sociology. The lack of initial rigidity in having to specialise early was invaluable to me. The second great challenge that the university afforded was the formation of its institutions: in my case this was in the sporting sphere and I got myself tied into sports administration. I became the first Sports Union President (handing over to Vice President Jim Wylie at the end of my third year) and Chair of the Gannochy Sports Facility management committee (which I am sure would not have been chaired by an undergraduate in other places) as the Gannochy was a staff and student facility. There was no distinction between the species at that time in Stirling. As President I established the Sports Union and chaired the committee of all the sports clubs, represented them in dealings with the Students Union and the University Administration and attended meetings of the all the Scottish University Sports Unions and the British Universities Sports Association. A budgeting system had to be developed – agreeing with the Students Union on a budget, where a fixed percentage[2] (40% if I remember correctly) of the total Student Union Budget was negotiated and then distributed to member sports clubs based on need and availability.

So when I departed Stirling with a 2.2 majoring in economics, I also had gained valuable (and time consuming – was there a correlation?) experience in administration and budgets from scratch which has served me well since. Of those who continued into our fourth year[3] in economics I was the only one of the five to opt for the Money and Public Finance option with the rest doing Managerial Economics. Imagine one to one with Prof Andrew Bain and Prof Chuck Brown – nowhere to hide and looking back, daunting. Sometimes postgraduates were thrown in to help me out. Indeed I

---

1   Which was different from the other universities' 3 terms in a year system.

2   This was unique among the Scottish Universities and the envy of the other sports unions.

3   University Undergraduate Degrees in Scotland are over 4 years and secondary education was one year shorter relative to, say, England.

am grateful to one of the five, Neil Kay[4] for comments on my initial draft suggesting I separate out the non economic and economic components so that there would be two detached documents and adding in a lessons and observations final chapter.

I realised that I needed to improve on my class of degree if I wanted to work as an economist. I was fortunate to be accepted at Lancaster to do an MA. There is no doubt that the Stirling connection of Dr Ahmed El Mokadem who was now lecturing at Lancaster and had been a post doctoral research fellow at Stirling helped in getting me accepted. I had attended his seminars at Stirling.

Consultancy by its very nature is all about people – people you work with and the people you work for. I have been very fortunate to work with some great human beings right from the start. At Stirling lecturers Mark Brownrigg, Mike Greig, Les Simpson, and David Simpson and at Lancaster Jim Taylor and Ahmed El Mokadem guided me in the right direction. At the University of Aberdeen, David Greenwood, at the Northern Region Strategy Team Nick Segal and at the University of Durham Dick Morley continued to develop me.

Connections and luck were also important in my journey. After finishing in Indonesia (more of which later) in December 1985 I started out on my own with, it must be said, some trepidation. Having worked with Ray Goodman in Nigeria in 1984, I got a communication from him (phone call or letter? but certainly not an email as the internet was not as we know it now and email did not exist) saying he was leading a mission for the World Bank on behalf of the Dutch Government and would I be available to join him? At that time all such missions ended up back at Washington DC and I left with my next assignment as well as making more connections. Also by that time, Tom Allen and Charles Draper from the Australian company I had worked with in The Philippines and Indonesia had joined the Bank and became part of the West Africa team.

---

4   Neil is now Emeritus Professor in the Economics Department, University of Strathclyde, Scotland and has a stellar academic career: http://www. brocher.com/Academic/Academic.htm. Neil Walden also one of the five provided constructive comments. Neil became a specialist in marketing, tourism management and environmental studies and taught at the University of Strathclyde and Manchester Polytechnic as well as Jordanhill College. Mick Connarty, who took a sabbatical to be President of the Student Association in our final year, has also provided valuable comments. After graduation, Mick became leader of Stirling Council and was an MP from 1992 to 2015. https://en.wikipedia.org/wiki/Michael_Connarty

Having already worked in the region previously, I joined missions to Nigeria and Ghana. One of the missions was to Sierra Leone and my working relationship and friendship with Pirouz Hamidian-Rad (whom I had met on mission to Ghana) started which end up in Afghanistan via Papua New Guinea and on to Albania where he carried out a review of the Structure of the Ministry of Finance in the context of the Medium Term Budget Programme (MTPB).

Without these colleagues and experiences I suspect my career as an applied economist would have indeed be short-lived. There may be some lessons for an aspiring economist to draw from.

2 THE RESEARCH YEARS

I was incredibly fortunate in my foray into the research arena in the field of economics. I was studying for a Masters Degree in Economics at the University of Lancaster. Jim Taylor was a senior lecturer in the department and one of my lecturers on the regional economics module. He was carrying out research for his book Unemployment and Wage Inflation with special reference to Britain and the USA which was published by Longman in 1974. He invited me to work with him for my dissertation project which in the end turned out to be titled "An analysis of Earning Changes in the United Kingdom, 1960-71: expectations, Union Influence and Excess Labour Demand. A Fourteen Industry Study". Jim kindly used the results in Chapter 6 of his book and referenced it.

Looking back at the book and dissertation manuscript almost 50 years on, I am grateful that econometrics was one of the modules in the degree course. Not that I have ever used it since, but at least I can read a document containing equations and numbers. Nevertheless various thoughts come to mind. Jim fortunately had collected the raw data. However this was before computerization as we know it today. The university had a main frame computer and the data had to be punched onto cards to be inputted into the computer which then produced the ordinary least squares results. My job was to write this up in a full dissertation format describing the models used, the data and the variables, a discussion on the comparison of the performance of the models, the performance of the variables and on each of the 14 industries with an overall conclusion. Reading the manuscript after all these years I think I did a reasonable job! However the manuscript of 60 pages must have been a nightmare to type given the equipment then and I am extremely grateful to a family friend Norma Thompson for what must have been the hardest part of the dissertation.

The University of Lancaster offered a taught MA in Economics and also one in Regional Economics and Planning. While my MA was in Economics, I took, as one of my modules Regional

Economics and attended the whole of the lectures in the second Masters. Coming to the end of the MA I began to look for work and one of the posts I applied for was a research fellowship at the University of Aberdeen's Department of Political Economy which had received a Social Science Research Council grant to investigate the Regional Impact of Defence Expenditure. With my regional economic background as a postgraduate student and public finance specialism as an undergraduate I managed to get an interview. I was offered the post but often wonder to what extent bolstering the Department's football team to maintain its top position in the university staff games had played a role in being selected. I was happy to accept as I was acquainted with the City of Aberdeen as I had spent my secondary school years on the south side of the River Dee some five miles out at Blairs College.

And so my journey into gainful employment as an economist began first to the North East of Scotland, then onto the North East of England and then to the North East of Africa.

Research on Public Expenditure and the Regions

As in Lancaster, I was very fortunate to work with an experienced, encouraging and kind research supervisor. David Greenwood was a Senior Lecturer in Political Economy (Higher Defence Studies) who had produced "Budgeting for Defence" published by the Royal United Services Institute in December 1972. David became one of the most prolific commentators on defence economics in the UK and beyond. Indeed, David had a word ascribed to him. "Greenwoodery" is a term which has become popular in sections of the UK Ministry of Defence to refer to the distinctive approach of David Greenwood to the issues of defence budgeting in Britain and in particular to his contribution to the debate about "funding gaps" in the British defence budget in the late 1980s. ("Greenwoodery' and British defence policy" by John Baylis International Affairs, Volume 62, Issue 3, summer 1986, Pages 443–457.[5]

With my fellow research fellow, Timothy Stone, I embarked on working on different strands of investigation into the regional impact of defence expenditure. One of these assignments was to complete pieces of research that had already been started and

---

5   https://doi.org/10.2307/2617886 Published: 01 July 1986)

the work was subsequently published in the Aberdeen Studies in Defence Economics (ASIDES) series: Military Installations and Local Economies – A Case Study: The Moray Air Stations by David Greenwood and John Short (ASIDES No 4 Dec 1973) and Military Installations and Local Economies – A Case Study: Clyde Submarine Base by John Short, Timothy Stone and David Greenwood (ASIDES No 5 August 1974). It must be recognised that significant collection, collating and processing of data had already been undertaken and as the acknowledgements to the reports states "thus the authors were spared much laborious work". However, applying this valuable data to produce two analytical documents was not an insignificant effort.

David Greenwood and I worked on the Moray report while Timothy Stone produced an Analysis of the Regional Impact of Defence Expenditure: A Survey (ASIDES no 3). Most of my contribution to the Moray report was centred on estimating the income and employment impact of the military installations that were studied. A multiplier model was used which was based on Mike Greig (1972) "The Regional Income and Employment Multiplier Effects of a Pulp Mill and Paper Mill (Scottish Journal of Political Economy) and Mark Brownrigg (1972) The Regional Income Multiplier An Attempt to Complete the Model (Scottish Journal of Political Economy). As both Mike and Mark had taught me at The University of Stirling as an undergraduate student I was able to confer with them in the use of the multiplier model in the defence base areas and make the adjustments to fit the particular military, as opposed to the civilian, circumstances.

Both Timothy and I were given the task of writing up the Clyde Submarine Base Study. As David Greenwood wrote in the Preface "The task of presenting the material in a coherent form – with explanation, comment and analysis – fell to John Short and Timothy Stone, who worked on the preparation of the present paper, as their other commitments allowed. Both these authors are economists and their draft was, for the most part, written with professional readership in mind and with the emphasis on analysis and inference. This posed a problem when it came to editing their work for dissemination in the present format as a paper in the ASIDES series. The readership envisaged for these studies includes the "defence community" as well as our fellow economists. Moreover, because of the sparseness of the literature on the economics of defence, it is an aim of the series to present sufficiently comprehensive material to prompt other investigators to carry study further. In consequence extensive editing was required; in fact, several parts of the work were rewritten and the Editor's involvement so far exceeded the normal bounds of editorial licence that his assumption of formal responsibility through formal joint authorship was thought appropriate.

Indeed I feel I must go further than this for my colleagues' sakes though they have not insisted on it! Such was my insistence on having the last word on the composition of the paper as it now appears that the customary disclaiming formula needs to be recast. For whatever analytical merit this study may possess Messrs Short and Stone must take the credit: for the errors which remain and for infelicities of style and expression the responsibility is mine." The sentiment expressed in the Preface has been a useful lesson in making sure an audience is catered for and gobbledygook and jargon terms are omitted and concepts are presented concisely and clearly. Hopefully!

The new area of investigation in the defence sector that was carried out under the project was twofold (the other commitments alluded to above). The first was mapping the regional distribution of defence manpower which was conducted by Timothy Stone. I had the task of mapping the regional distribution of defence contracts. Neither of these efforts ended up in an ASIDES paper. Given the use of this information later (see below Northern Regional Strategy Team) I am certain that data were collected at least for 1972/73 as reference is made to unpublished work by D Greenwood, J Short and T Stone as the source of data on wages and salaries in the Northern Region and goods and services procured in the Northern region in the Defence programme. I do remember engaging with the departments responsible for defence procurement. I was able to return successfully to the topic at a later date and this is outlined below (see University of Durham).

My research experience at Aberdeen was invaluable in my development as an applied economist. I developed a willingness and determination to get involved with the laborious business of assembling, collating and processing data as well as having considerable patience in dealing with those from whom the project was trying to coax information (mainly Government Departments). I also developed a capacity for the careful work needed in calculations and in the use of data within a conceptual framework. However, as David Greenwood would comment I had been reluctant to exercise initiative and preferred to work as directed. My writing talent was limited with my strengths lying in the numerate rather than literary skills, but I was able to get across what I had to present! The experience of working with David Greenwood also provided me with contacts that I would be able to use in later research work.[6]

Given that my two year contract at Aberdeen was coming to an end, I successfully applied for the post of economist with focus on public expenditure at the Northern Regional Strategy Team (NRST) based in Newcastle upon Tyne. An outline specification for study of the Northern Region stated that the specification of the work was that it should not be envisaged as a "physical plan" for the region. Rather it should be a statement of realistic goals and related policies for the economy, social life and environment of the region which takes into account standards in the rest of the country. The regional study should highlight the major "national context" issues for the region and attention on these. It is important that these priority issues should be realistically defined having regard to past experience, knowledge of machinery, availability of information etc. This emphasis placed a need for the compilation of data on public expenditure in the regional context which previous regional strategies such as the Strategic Plan for the North West, and that of West Central Scotland had attempted. The latter had commented that the task of compiling the report has confirmed that the regional statistics of central government departments are not maintained in a form readily adaptable to regional boundaries. Both these strategies recommended that special measures should be taken for comprehensive statistics of past expenditure by region to be prepared on a systematic and routine basis.

The output of the NRST was a five-volume Strategic Plan for the Northern Region:

> Volume 1 Main Report
> Volume 2 Economic Development Policies
> Volume 3 Social & Environmental Policies
> Volume 4 Settlement Pattern & transport policies
> Volume 5 Public Expenditure Priorities

---

6   I once did a review of defence spending and David Greenwood provided me with much information that was not for publication which I used in the report stating that the material should not be quoted or publically used. It suited the organisation to do so which damaged my reputation!

Each of Volumes 2, 3 and 4 addressed public expenditure implication of all the proposed policies and recommended strategies.

A great deal of hard work and research underpinned the realisation of these outputs. Key to this was the composition of the team
which was made of economists with sector specialism in the main
and strategic planners. Critical input also was the leadership. Head
of the team was Bevan Waide who had previously been on the staff
of the World Bank with deputies on the economic side, Nick Segal
and on the planning side, Ian Crowther.

My job was to produce the public expenditure data and I worked
closely with Nick Segal who took over as Head near the end of
the work when Bevan returned to the World Bank. My first task
was to develop a methodology for the regionalisation of public
expenditure. The Public Expenditure Survey Committee (PESC)
approach to classifying the functional and economic classification was the logical approach. It provided the only comprehensive
method available for classifying public expenditure on a consistent programme-by- programme basis, both over time and across all
spending authorities. Using PESC also facilitated consultation with
government departments since this was the basis for their statistical
work. The next and more important step was to address how public
expenditure related to the regional context which had not been
previously considered. This was done by classifying programmes
and their components into those that supplied services to a region
(such as primary education) rather than to the nation as a whole
(such as defence). The term "regionally relevant" or "in and for"
expenditure was created which contrasted with expenditure "in"
a region which contributed to gross regional expenditure. Thus
expenditure "in" a region is an analysis of total public expenditure (including defence), while the expenditure "in and for" analyses that part of public expenditure which is relevant only to the
region which directly benefits in social welfare terms. Regionally
relevant expenditures were further separated into two categories:
A and B. Category A covered expenditure on goods and services in
a region as well as national transfer payments to that region, the
direct benefit of which accrue exclusively to the region (e.g. schools
expenditure or regional industrial aid). Category B covered expenditure on goods and services in a region, the benefits of which accrue
in and beyond the region concerned, but by reason of the nature
of the expenditure or particular locational linkages are propor-
tionally greater in the region in which the expenditures are made

(such as motorways). A further Category C covered expenditures in programmes that were national in character such as defence, the benefits of which cannot be attributed to a particular region but are fully and equally attributed to all regions.

It was recognised at the onset of the work that a comprehensive statistical breakdown of past public expenditure by region was not available. An essential step in the Team's public expenditure analysis required a special effort to compile such a statistical series. At the Team's request an ad hoc working group was set up by central government to assist the Team in assembling the data. The group comprised staff from the Department of the Environment, the Central Statistical Office and the Treasury who along with myself from the Team served on a regular basis on the working group. The data collection also benefited from other government departments that contributed to the working group's efforts and the other public bodies that supplied data directly to the Team. In the final compilation of statistics, approximately one-fifth was provided directly through the working group and nearly three-quarters was assembled by the Team from other sources (but no doubt encouraged by the existence of the working group) and the remaining five percent was estimated using proxy regionally-based indicators.

The output of this extensive data collection was the NRST Technical Report No 12 Public Expenditure in the Northern Region and Other British Regions. In the report, the distribution of regionally relevant expenditure was presented and analysed by total and by PESC programme for each of the eight regions in England, and Wales and Scotland covering the five-year period from 1969/70 to 1973/74 annually. Annexes presented each programme at the sub-programme level. As well, there was a separate section on the economic impact of public expenditure in the Northern Region based on the "in" classification of regional expenditure broken down by economic categories for 1972/73 for which the data on defence expenditure was supplied by my previous research project at the University of Aberdeen as noted earlier. A summarised version of the report was published as "The regional distribution of public expenditure in Great Britain, 1967/70 – 1973/74", *Regional Studies*, Vol. 12, 1978, pp. 499–510.

The Strategic Plan for the Northern Region was never implemented. There were two likely reasons. The first was that its emphasis on a public expenditure solution was too challenging to the Treasury which had a focus on the control of public expenditure which could have been undermined by loosening the allocation mechanism. In addition there was the introduction of the Barnett formula in 1978 which is a mechanism used by the Treasury in the United Kingdom to automatically adjust the amounts of public expenditure allocated to Northern Ireland, Scotland and Wales to reflect changes in spending levels allocated to public services in England, England and Wales or Great Britain, as appropriate. This formula is still in place in 2021 even though Joel Barnett himself deemed it a terrible mistake which should have been temporary solution in the run up to devolution in 1979 in Scotland, Wales and Northern Ireland. Adding a regional dimension to England based on allocation of public expenditure by perceived regional needed would have been a step too far. Secondly in 1979 there was a radical change of government. I remember going to a dissemination event at the University of Newcastle shortly after the election where it was made clear by someone from the new government that regional policy was no longer a priority.

Jumping forward to the present, the situation is really no different. There has been the creation of "The Northern Powerhouse" which seems to be focused on transport and high speed rail. It was set up by the then Chancellor Osborne who was an MP for Tatton near Manchester. The Northern Powerhouse is heavily focused on the Manchester and Leeds areas which are, in geographical terms, more north-west midlands and north-central midlands rather than the Northern Region that the Strategic Plan covered. There is some slight impetus that can be seen in the efforts of Onward a centre right think-tank which has the ear of some members of Parliament. Levelling up the tax system[7] looks at the regional dimension of tax policy and calls for a more transparent approach. The overall argument is that governments have done far less to understand the geographical distribution of the impact of different policies. In the paper on taxation, it argues that tax and spending choices are not geographically neutral. Tax and spending decisions can have quite different impacts even on places with similar income levels. It states that at every Budget, the Treasury publishes distributional analysis for households, to show how much more or less households in different income brackets will pay. However, the argument in the paper is that the Chancellor should go one further and publish a

---

7   In a paper released 18 January 2021 by Onward Levelling Up | ukon-ward.com

regional distributional analysis, to show how much more or less different regions are paying as well as how the tax system should be used to get private sector growth going in poorer areas. It argues that if it is only spending and not tax that is looked at there is a risk of trying to level up with one hand tied behind backs.

While still at the Strategy Team I was asked by Peter MacCormack, the Department of the Environment lead on the ad-hoc working group, if I would be interested in continuing the research, to which I replied in the affirmative! In effect I had a research grant for two years (with an option for a third year) and had to find a university who would accept me (and the grant). Fortunately, Dick Morley, who was Senior Lecturer in the Department of Economics at the University of Durham, was interested in the subject as he had used the regional public expenditure data that I had toiled over in his own work. He organised for me to be interviewed by the Vice-Chancellor and I was accepted (with grant) on to the staff of the Department of Economics. The grant also was sufficient to have a research assistant and secretarial support. David Nicholas was appointed as research assistant on the project.

The aim of the research was to generate a report, which was by design produced in a neutral vein, concentrating on the questions of the availability of data and the sources and methods employed to gather the data rather than analysing the data with respect to regional differences. In the final report A study of Money Flows in the Regions of the United Kingdom 1974/75 to 1977/78 the question of a suitable framework for the study of regional flows is tackled, with the detailed sources and methods confined to appendices. The research built upon the work undertaken at the NRST and updated the series on regionally relevant public expenditure. It expanded the data on "in" expenditures to cover all of the regions. In this aspect the work started on defence expenditure at the University of Aberdeen was extended and data on procurement and location of defence service and civilian personnel was supplied by the Ministry of Defence. This eventually resulted in 'Defence spending in the regions of the UK', Regional Studies, Vol 15, 1981, pp. 101–10. Reading that article again I cannot believe there was no acknowledgement by myself of David Greenwood and Timothy Stone which embarrasses me. As well as the expenditure side of government the Money Flows work addressed the revenue side of government in the regional context as well as the financial sector.

To illustrate the data collection efforts in the financial sector two examples are presented here which illustrates the level of support that the project enjoyed. The first is the Trustees Savings Banks and the second is the Building Societies. The Trustees Savings Banks were basically regional entities joined together in a confederation. Seventy-two banks had been amalgamated to 19 with a Central Board which was approached to supply statistics on the operations in the regions. A favourable response was received. While the 19 banks did not coincide with the 11 planning regions except for Northern Ireland, some could be added together to form one entity as in the case of Scotland. Others were wholly in one region, but some traversed regional boundaries. The Central Board provided details of these branches which had to be "moved" from one region to another to obtain the banks' operations classified by standard planning region. While a certain amount of data manipulation had to be carried out such as adjusting for different financial year end, tables were included in the report on the estimated Net Increase in Funds by Standard Planning Region for the 4 years from 1974/75 to 1977/78.

With respect to Building Societies, the initial approach was to the Building Societies Association which was helpful in providing information on its membership and in offering advice on the difficulties involved in any survey of the individual building societies. While not able to take part directly in any spatial exercise it did offer to act as a clearing house through which information would be channelled and aggregated whenever individual societies were concerned about confidentially. A survey of all 230 building societies was conducted with a letter going to each requesting information of that society's receipts (net of any repayments to depositors) and lending on property (net of any repayment of principal) for each and every planning region in which they conducted business. Follow up letters were sent to the top 17 (controlling 80% of assets in 1977) who has not responded by a certain date which proved fruitful. Living in Newcastle helped with Northern Rock (remember it?) and Leo Finn the chief executive was very supportive.

The Report contains a full discussion on the responses as well as other background research by the Building Society Association journal Facts and Figures. The following is a breakdown of the responses.

	Number	%	Assets £m	%
Societies contacted	230	100	28,199	100
Replies received	88	38.3	20,615	73.1
Without data	45	19.6	11,111	39.4
With data	43	18.7	9,504	33.7

The report contains reasons given by the 45 societies for not providing the data. The report also contains the sources for regional data by sector as summarized in the Data Availability Matrix opposite.

The original research funding was for two years with an option for a third. Unfortunately due to the changing priorities in the Department of the Environment, the third year option was not implemented despite the success of the project. An application was made to the Social Science Research Council but for only six months (in the hope of being accepted) and this was granted. This ensured that any outstanding data could be collected and the report could be completed. It would have been better to have asked for the full year as many of the journal articles were written after the six months at my leisure and the two books that were produced squeezed into the timeframe and secretarial support available.

As well as the Research Report two books were produced *Public Expenditure and Taxation in the UK Regions*, and *Money Flows in the UK Regions* both published by Gower in 1981. There were at least four books reviews. Graham Gudgen[8] concluded on reviewing the first book "There is a strange inversion of prestige in many disciplines by which painstaking work to produce statistics absolutely vital to intellectual progress is often given too little credit and reward. As a result many young researchers prefer other types of work. This book is to be greatly welcomed as a significant contribution to an increasingly important aspect of regional studies." R. J. Bennett[9] (University of Cambridge) wrote "When a new urge for regionalism emerges Short's work will provide an invaluable base of methodology and theory; in the meantime the tabulations provided in these two books present the researcher with an important and unique historical record which is of incalculable value".

---

8   Regional Studies Vol 15 No 5 1981
9   Progress in Human Geography, 1984

Data Availability Matrix (%)				
Sector/Source	CSO	Published	Direct approach to producers of data	Proxy
Private	100			
Company	100			
Public Sector Expenditure				
(a) Economic Category[1]		12	58	30
(b) Functional Analysis[2]		11	71	18
Revenue				
Central Government[3]				
Current		72		28
Local Authority				
Current			100	
Capital			100	
Financial Sector				
Banks				100
Building Societies			100	
Special Finance Agencies			100	
Dept. for National Savings				100
Trustee Savings Bank			100	
Shares, Unit Trusts etc				100
Finance Houses, Leasing				100
Other				100
EEC			100	

[1] Wages and Salaries, Transfers, etc.

[2] Education, Health, etc.

[3] 72% relates to adjusted published estimates

[4] Some flows in the financial sector are between supra-regional sectors and do not impinge on the regions directly (e.g. between the banking sector and government). These are not included in the matrix.

R J Johnston,[10] Department of Geography, University of Sheffield was of the view that "Neither book is compelling reading since their main aim is to outline how the data were collected and to present them. There is no analysis at all in Money Flows, and very little in Public Expenditure and Taxation: in the latter, the models tested are relatively simple, with only bivariate regressions used to estimate regional variations in spending. It is perhaps unfortunate that this analysis is not informed by the large literature on the determinants of spending patterns (for example Boaden, 1971; Johnston, 1980). As a result, Short's suggestions on why money is spent where it is are politically naive. Nevertheless, the extent of the task is breathtaking, and others will for long be indebted to Short and Nicholas. It would be easy to criticise these books for what they have not done, but this would be churlish. They have succeeded admirably in providing basic data for subsequent analysis, with a sensibly presented framework. The authors are to be congratulated on their achievement. Their books will undoubtedly become standard references (in all probability, long after their data are obsolete)." S. Dow[11] University of Toronto in a review wrote "This book (Money Flows) should be read by anyone interested in regional accounting. It represents a major contribution to the field in terms both of methodology and of new data. The most innovative feature is the compilation of regional financial sector accounts. The financial data they have gathered represents progress, but perhaps the most significant advance lies in their pinpointing precisely where regional data are lacking. The Appendices, which account for over two-thirds of the text, contain a gold-mine of data, some adapted from secondary sources and some new material, accompanied by a detailed commentary on sources and methodology. Short and Nicholas are however very reticent about delineating the ways in which their approach improves on the conventional approaches (Short's Public Expenditure and Taxation in the U.K. Regions provides a clearer account of the approach as applied to the public sector). A more explicit discussion of the reasons for choosing the money flows approach would have been helpful."

As well several articles were published: The Northern Region: Borrower or Lender?', *Northern Economic Review*, No 2, 1982. 'Public expenditure in the English regions', in Hogwood, B.W. &

---

10   Environment and Planning C: Government and Policy, 1983, volume 1
11   Urban Studies May 1, 1983

Keating, M. (eds.), *Regional Government in England*, Oxford, Clarendon Press, 1982, pp. 191–216. 'Public finance and devolution: money flows between government and regions in the United Kingdom', *Scottish Journal of Political Economy*, Vol. 31, 1984, pp. 113–29. 'Financial Flows in the Regional Context: the Experience of the United Kingdom in Situation and Outlook with Regard to Regional Accounts in the Community, Eurostat, 1984 (Seminar Proceedings from event held in Luxemburg, 30/11 to 3/12/1982).

As a postscript to the involvement in research in public finance in the regions the following experiences are of note. I was asked to work with the Centre for Urban and Regional Development Studies at the University of Newcastle in 1984 as part of the work on the ESRC Inner Cities Research programme. The purpose of the particular study was to focus on the importance of one function –general public expenditure in the inner city context. The sub-regional allocation of public expenditure was added to the regional context. With John Howard, I mapped out the programmes and their component parts to sub-regional and regional categories. When data were sought from government departments, the overwhelming response was that no data at sub-regional level were available and data at the regional level were significantly less than available than in the earlier work.[12] A conclusion of the report *The Developmental Role of Public Expenditure in Regions and Sub–Regions* was "…..regional and urban planning by the UK Government is seriously at fault. Only when it is fully recognised that effective decision making relies upon the availability of comprehensive information, and that economic development in regions and sub-regions is being determined – at least in part – by decisions taken outside the present influence of those responsible for planning, can planning itself become more effective. Further progress requires a raising of the status of regional matters within government, necessitating

---

12   R J Johnston in his review of the books on Public Expenditure and Taxation and Money Flows opined that "One major question mark must be put against them (the authors), however. Is the regional structure the most sensible? Clearly there is a need for data on Scotland, Wales, and Northern Ireland, but the use of the English regions, springs from their political use for regional strategies which have now been abandoned. Further spatial disaggregation (into urban/ rural components, for example) would have been more interesting, and in the development of any data set disaggregation is preferable to aggregation. But until a system such as that used in the USA is developed, perhaps the eleven-fold regional division for the United Kingdom is all that we can ask for." The answer was thus provided.

improved interdepartmental cooperation. The present study indicates that not only is that development far way, but that matters have deteriorated during the last decade."

In 2001 David Heald of the Centre for Regional Public Finance University of Aberdeen who has written extensively on public expenditure as a whole, the Barnett formula, regional aspects and devolution invited me to join him as a remote part time research fellow under the Devolution and Constitutional Change Research Programme of the Economic Social Research Council. One of the objectives of the work was to see if it were possible to recreate the regional public expenditure data of the late 1960s and early 1970s. One of the observations of the joint paper The regional dimension of public expenditure in England published in *Regional Studies*, Vol. 36, 2002, pp. 743–755 was "that better data will be required for a substantial number of years before the data infrastructure for the English regions compares with that which already existed in the three territories" (Scotland, Wales and Northern Ireland). The paper examines data published in 2001 and before 2001 and points to deficiencies of regional data in the public domain even though there are some regional public expenditure data in the annual Public Expenditure: Statistical Analysis published by Treasury. The problems identified in the Centre for Urban and Regional Development Studies report were still in place, but to a lesser extent. Certainly there was regional public expenditure, but not at the level to support that demanded by a regional planning agency in England (should it have existed) commensurate with what was provided in the other countries of the United Kingdom. I did however get to meet Joel Barnett at a workshop in Birmingham on January 16, 2002. I remember the day well as my first grandchild, Elicia, was born that day!

In order that this section is not locked into the situation of some 20 years ago, I have gone on to the Treasury website to bring the status of regional public expenditure data up-to-date. This has been quite illuminating and instructive as well as being very pleasing given the situation presented so far.

In order to provide information on the allocation of expenditure by country and region, the Treasury now asks UK government departments and devolved administrations to undertake an annual statistical exercise. This is based on expenditure data published in July each year in Her Majesty's Treasury's Public Spending Statistics release under a Country and Regional Analysis.

- The exercise is based on spending by the Devolved Administration and the subset of departmental spending that can be identified as benefiting the population of individual regions. It asks departments and Devolved Administrations to apportion that spending between countries and regions following guidance issued by the Treasury.

- The Treasury then collates departments' returns and combines these with the known spending of local government to produce the analyses of public expenditure by country and region that are published in this release.

The Country and Regional Analysis includes a wider coverage of expenditure for Scotland, Wales and Northern Ireland than that for which the devolved administrations and the Secretaries of State for Scotland, Wales and Northern Ireland are directly responsible.

A background methodology note accompanies the Country and Regional Analysis. It provides users with more information on the methods used to allocate spend between countries and regions and a methodology section is included.

For the country and regional analyses, expenditure on services is divided into identifiable and non-identifiable expenditure:

- Around 86 per cent of public sector expenditure on services is identifiable expenditure, which has been incurred for the benefit of individuals, enterprises or communities within particular regions. Examples are health, education, and social protection spending;

- Non-identifiable expenditure, constituting the remaining 14 per cent of total public sector expenditure on services, is deemed to be incurred on behalf of the United Kingdom as a whole. Examples include the majority of expenditure on defence, overseas representation, tax collection and debt interest.

Where precise accounting data on the recipients' locations are not available, allocation is based on other available information, following rules set down in the Treasury's guidance for departments. For example, administration costs incurred centrally in support of regional spending are attributed to regions in the same proportions as the spending that they support. In other cases, departments approximate regional benefits where the immediate beneficiaries' head office locations mask the final recipients' locations.

Expenditure financed by EU receipts can be classified as identifiable or non-identifiable depending on the characteristics of the expenditure itself. Receipts from the EU are treated as non-identifiable. Consequently, regional expenditure includes the expenditure financed by EU receipts. Payments to the EU are attributed to 'outside UK' as these are transfer payments that the EU then spends. In 2018-19 departments and devolved administrations were provided with funding for the purpose of EU Exit preparation. Although it is not possible to identify this expenditure separately in any of the tables or data published in the Country and Regional Analysis, it is included within the spending aggregates. The amounts allocated to individual departments have been published elsewhere.

Identifiable expenditure is attributed to a specific country or region using the 'for' basis wherever possible, which records the regions that benefited from the spending or whom the spending was for, rather than simply the location where the spending took place (the 'in' basis). Where it is not possible to allocate spending to regions on a 'for' basis, the 'in' basis is used instead. For most spending, the 'for' and the 'in' bases would in practice offer the same result.

A number of issues can be identified that limit the ability to offer a complete picture of 'who benefits?':

- practical difficulties: for example, schools are not used solely by the residents of the region in which they are located. Definitional and border problems become increasingly significant the smaller the geographical unit considered;

- conceptual problems: for example, agricultural support is treated as benefiting the farmers who receive subsidies, rather than the final consumers of food; and

- data collection issues: departments are encouraged, but not required, to allocate spending on the basis of 'who benefits?'. If spending is not significant (less than £20m annually on capital or current) or relevant information for allocating it to regions is not available, departments may use some statistical proxy instead. This might include using straight population shares, or the same allocation proportions as other related spending. It is neither considered practical nor cost-effective to collect local government spending data on the basis of 'who benefits?'. Instead, local government spending is assumed to benefit the area of the spending authority.

The tables present the spending attributed to the English regions alongside that attributed to Scotland, Wales and Northern Ireland. Although the figures are comparable, care is still needed when making cross-national comparisons because of the different scope of public sector activities in different countries. For example, water supply is a public sector function in Scotland and Northern Ireland, but is in the private sector in England and Wales.

The data cover central government, local government and public corporations. Excel tables are provided and the latest tables provide a time series from 2014-15 to 2018-19 for expenditure by function and data for 2018-19 by sub-function (which is also included in previous years so a time series can be generated). There is no doubt that since the pioneering work of the NRST on regional public expenditure back in 1974, the Treasury has mainstreamed and publishes the regionally relevant public expenditures with methodological background and in user friendly format for accessing the data. There is a degree of satisfaction that the terms and concepts that I developed back in the mid 1970s have finally seen the light in 2020 and the data are produced routinely and systematically. Regional planning as envisaged in the NRST could now be carried out on regular basis... if the political will was present. It will need more than the efforts of the Onward Think-tank.

The Calling of Cairo

After the research at Durham finished I spent a period "resting". However I was woken out of my slumber by a call from former colleagues in the Department of Political Economy at Aberdeen who has been involved in researching the economic impact of North Sea Oil on the local economy. Professor Donald MacKay (who had later moved to Heriot-Watt) and Tony MacKay had set up PEIDA an economic consultancy and along with Donald's successor at Aberdeen Professor David Pearce had been commissioned by the World Bank to carry out work on a petroleum products pricing study and a gas utilisation study. I was asked simply "would I like to go to Egypt for a year?" Now married with two young children, the family answer was a resounding yes.

The reason why I have included this work in the research chapter was that my job was to beaver away to produce the data particularly for the Petroleum Products Pricing Model. Early investigation indicated that there was a 1997 Input-Output (I-O) table which became the base for an extended Petroleum Products I-O table. Each petroleum product was incorporated as a separate sector and key energy using sectors such as cement, aluminium and fertilizers were developed as separate sectors. In all 35 sectors were developed to form a Petroleum Products I-O table. Much of my work was to contact companies in the sectors and use whatever sources of information that were available to extend the existing I-O table. The project had both Ron Edwards who was able to do the necessary mathematical inversion work to make use of the I-O table and David Pearce to make sense of it all. The output of that part of the overall consultancy work was a Petroleum Products Pricing Study that comprised the main report and two annexes which included the sectoral data and the I-O table. There was a separate internal document that documented the Energy Related Input-Output Table for Egypt. The overall project also delivered a report on Gas Utilisation Study which benefited from the work of Alex (Joe) Kemp, who became Professor of Petroleum Economics and Director of Aberdeen Centre for Research in Energy Economics and Finance. The project economist at the World Bank was DeAnne Julius who continues to have a stellar and distinguished career.[13]

I consider myself to be very privileged to have known, learned from and worked with David Pearce **https://en.wikipedia.org/ wiki/David_Pearce_(economist)** who was one of the pioneers, if not *the* pioneer in environmental economics, having written books on the subject as far back as 1989 with Blueprint for a Green Economy, and Economics of Natural Resources and the Environment. He also wrote several books on Cost Benefit Analysis. Sadly David died in 2005 aged 63.

I was fortunate that as an undergraduate I had been exposed to I-O methodology. Both my senior lecturers David Simpson and Jim McGilvary had been at Harvard and did research under Vassily Leontief the father of I-O analysis. During my final year, both

---

13   https://en.wikipedia.org/wiki/DeAnne_Julius

Vassily Leontief and Karen Polenske visited and conducted a workshop on I-O which I was lucky to attend and meet them.

3 FISCAL TABLES AND REVENUE ESTIMATION

My venture into working on public finance was not immediate after my Egyptian sojourn. When I did get opportunities, the work covered different, but not all, elements of the public sector which is outlined in Figure 1. Within this context the main area of my technical involvement was budgeting – both expenditure and revenue aspects – examining and analysing their distribution and trends but also the evolution of budgeting systems.

In the 1980s and for many years afterwards in many countries, budgets were typically cost based focusing on how much was allocated to wages and salaries, goods and services, transfers and capital items by functional administrative department (health, education, etc.) and not on what was to be achieved. The evolution of budget processes that stemmed initially from the reforms in New Zealand and Australia was in its infancy. Over time, analytical techniques such as public expenditure reviews and sector strategies were adopted and used which preceded Medium Term Expenditure Frameworks that evolved into Medium Term Budget Frameworks that encapsulate programme budgeting and budgeting for results.[14] However I am jumping ahead of myself and these developments are discussed in the next chapter. To get there, some scene setting is necessary and this is centred on a fiscal table and resource envelope.

Why is the Fiscal Table Important?

The formulation of any budget has to meet spending requests based on social needs and development goals within the availability of aggregate fiscal constraints. This maxim applies to the private as

---

14   Public Expenditure Management Handbook published by the World Bank in 1998 is a good primer on the subject.http://documents.worldbank.org/curated/en/489401468779669052/Public-expenditure-management-handbook

well as the public sector. This is the basic principle of the budget process – marrying the top-down/bottom up – the budget challenge.

Figure 1: The main components of the public sector, as defined in Government Finance Statistics[15]

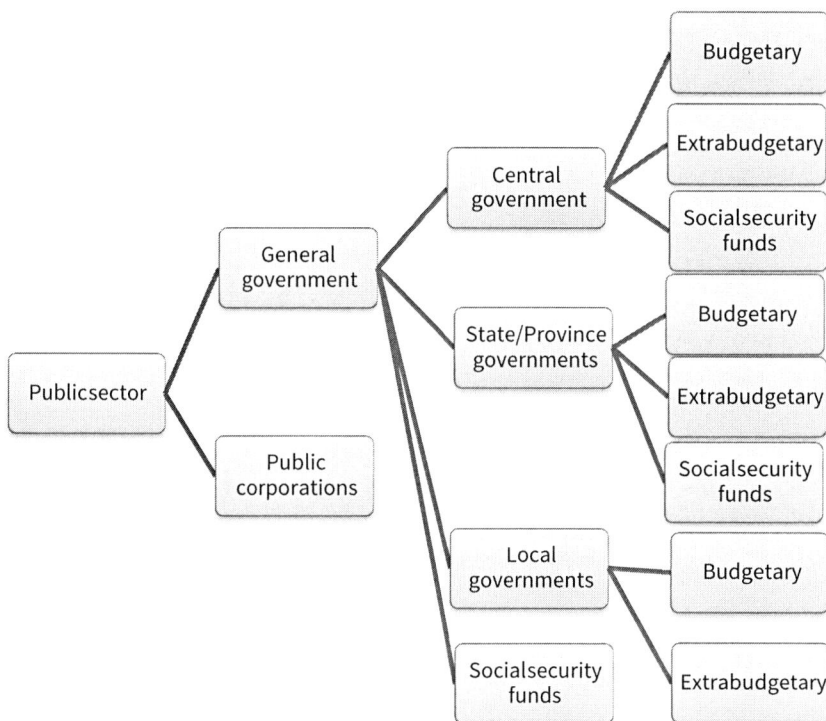

Only by having a Fiscal Table will the Government be able to plan and formulate a budget in the aggregate and convey to spending departments that the financial resources available to fund their desired spending objectives are not unlimited. Budgets have to be planned and formulated with a realistic understanding of what is available to be spent and not on the basis that there are no financial constraints.

---

15   International Monetary Fund, Government Finance Statistics Manual 2014, p. 25–27, provides a detailed explanation of the characteristics of central, state/provincial and local governments, including when more than three tiers of government are present. Budgetary units, extrabudgetary units and social security funds may exist in state/provincial, and local governments. Social security funds can be combined into a separate subsector as shown in the box with dashed lines. Figure has been taken from Guidance for Subnational PEFAs (pefa.org).

Aggregate Fiscal
Constraints
Limits imposed on
spending agencies' budget
requests

Agency spending requests
Social needs
Development goals

The fiscal table brings together the sources of finance and the associated expenditure that uses that finance (including savings). Elements of the fiscal table may be subject to rules – what is permissible – as a result of the country's legislation, membership of the EU if applicable, or if there is a programme with agencies such as the International Monetary Fund which may determine parameters for borrowing.

Many elements of the fiscal table pertaining to the budget being prepared and the following years are based on forecasts on their likely magnitude such as domestic revenues. Others elements such foreign grants and foreign borrowing for capital and non-capital projects are governed by agreements between a Government and the granting/lending agency. These funding agreements may have timing constraints that determines the time period that they can be included in the fiscal table.

Other elements such as recurrent expenditure may be a residual after domestic revenues have been estimated along with capital expenditure and its funding. Some elements of recurrent expenditure may be quasi-fixed such as wages and salaries and some transfers such as pensions and welfare payments as it may be difficult to change the numbers due to legal considerations.

Many of the elements of the fiscal table are based on agreements and fiscal rules. Others are based on rolling over existing aggregates based on increments for inflation. These expenditures are used to deliver services such as education, health, and security to citizens, but this aspect will be addressed in the next chapter.

A fiscal table is made up of the following components:

Component	Source of information
Revenue	
Domestic Taxes	Forecasting model
Domestic Tax arrears recovery	Recovery agreements and investigations
Domestic non tax revenue	
Fees and charges not retained by collecting agency	Forecasting model
Fees and charges retained by agency collecting	Forecasting model
Penalties and fines	Forecasting model
Interest received	Interest rates and principal
Dividends	Dividend policy
Current Grants	Agreement with Donors
Capital Grants	Agreement with Donors
Net Borrowing	Subject to fiscal rules
New Borrowing	Agreement with lenders
Repayment of existing borrowing	Repayment schedules based on agreements
Privatisation receipts	Privatisation schedule and likely receipts
Expenditure	
Capital	Funding agreements and fiscal rules
Recurrent	Residual from capital expenditure, domestic revenue and capital revenue subject to fiscal rules
Interest	Borrowing agreements
Wages and salaries	Existing wage bill plus inflation and other wage enhancements subject to policy changes
Transfers and subsidies	Existing regime subject to policy changes and increments based on elements such as inflation
Settlement of payment arrears (if any)	Stock of arrears and payments agreement schedules
Recurrent cost of completed capital projects	Project documents adjusted for inflation
Goods and services	Residual of revenue and quasi-fixed expenditure
Recurrent projects	Project agreements/residual particularly domestic funded projects
Contingency allowance for unforeseen events	May be subject to fiscal rules (% of revenue of expenditures) or final residual

The major element of the fiscal table that is based on the need for forecasting methodologies are domestic revenues.

Forecasting Revenues

Any model for forecasting revenues will depend on the conditions in a specific country. Typically the steps in forecasting will be dependent on available information that is relevant for the purpose – what is actually happening in revenue collection. A first step is to create a representative baseline for forecasting. This representative baseline will be conditioned by how stable the revenue base is for each of the components of tax type and non-tax type. If there is little or no change in tax policy over the years then a time series to determine relationships with tax drivers can be worked out. However, if there have been frequent changes in tax policy then the time frame will have to be shortened to reflect this instability. The second step is to understand the basic drivers of individual elements of tax and non-tax revenue. Typically this will be nominal Gross Domestic Product (GDP) for tax revenue. For non-tax revenue particularly fees and charges, the user population of the chargeable services will be the driver. Any policy of adjusting the level of fees and charges for inflation (or cost recovery) will also be important. Other factors that will be important are the degree that there is improvement in tax administration, resulting perhaps from a tax reform programme and changes in the structure of GDP which are tax generative.[16] However over the short to medium term, care has to be taken as to not overstate their impact as these will take time to be effective in increasing revenue collection totals. There may be an initial step increase from administrative reforms but this is unlikely to be repeated year on year. The determinants of revenue forecasting are thus:

- GDP growth

- Inflation

---

16   Such as subsistence farmers entering the cash economy and purchasing goods that had sales and excise taxes levied on them. Investment in rural roads widens the market for agriculture products and moves farmers out of subsistence production.

- The "X" factor – administrative gains/ change to structure of GDP

- New policy initiatives

The revenue side of the fiscal framework was an area that I have been involved in a number of countries – Uganda, Rwanda, Tanzania and Albania and more recently in Palestine.

Tax to GDP ratios – the percentage share of GDP that ends up in government revenue – differ quite dramatically often between countries with at what looks at first sight similar tax structures. Often this difference is ascribed to tax policy (including the scope and extent of exemptions) and tax administration, while not fully looking at the main tax driver, the economy itself. Indeed good tax policy and good tax administration should not distinguish between sectors in an economy with respect to how they are taxed.[17] Perhaps, then, the most logical explanation of this is the observation that these higher tax-to-GDP-ratio countries have a higher share of monetised economy in GDP through formal activity in industry, agriculture and tourism. Money means spending on taxed goods. Earning money leads to payment of direct taxes. Increased income means spending on excisable goods. The issue is not necessarily the composition of GDP but understanding how GDP is estimated.

I was able to demonstrate this hypothesis whilst working in Uganda. At the time tax policy and tax administration were fairly similar in Uganda and Kenya but Kenya's tax to GDP ratio was significantly higher than Uganda's but per capita income not significantly larger. Looking at how GDP was estimated in Uganda showed a significant non monetised share of the composition of total GDP. In order to demonstrate the importance of the monetised component of GDP in relation to the tax to GDP ratio, I modelled the impact of increasing the share of the monetised component over time keeping the tax policy and administration relationships constant. The growth in tax to GDP ratios was significant taking five year comparisons over a 30 year period.

Over the years I have modelled this hypothesis in work on revenue forecasting.

In 2000 tax to GDP ratio was 9.5% in Rwanda and 12.4% in Tanzania. Forecasts made in 2001 for tax revenue in Rwanda for 2015/16 were 16.5% of GDP and Tanzania 16.8% of GDP. For

---

17   Tax policy and tax administration are addressed in Chapter 7.

Rwanda the increases in forecasted ratios were due to GDP growth giving an 11.8% tax to GDP ratio plus 0.9 percentage points for a change in the composition of GDP and 3.8 percentage points for an accelerated change in the composition of GDP. The actual tax to GDP ratio in 2015 was 14.5%. For Tanzania the increases in forecasted ratios were due to GDP growth giving a 14% tax to GDP ratio plus 0.8 percentage points for a change in the composition of GDP and 2 percentage points for an accelerated change in the composition of GDP. The actual tax to GDP ratio in 2015 was 14.5%. It would be interesting to look at the actual composition of GDP in 2016 and what GDP growth since 2000 to examine what caused the models to be over by 12% in Rwanda and 14% in Tanzania over a 15 year period. I no longer have the Uganda report but it was not as detailed as the Rwanda and Tanzania reports but more a "what if" demonstration that increases in tax collections are related to the composition of GDP and its estimation.

In Albania the forecasts were done in two time periods which has allowed observation on the evolution of the estimation of GDP. The construction of Albania's GDP is made up two main elements: the observed value added and the non observed value added. In addition, agriculture has an own consumption element in its construction. It can be assumed that non observed value added is what could be termed the informal sector (which is perfectly legal but outside the formal tax system) and own consumption the non monetised sector – it is not sold for cash. The observed sector is the formal sector which is subject to registration for taxes. The relative sizes of each of these elements will impact on the Albania's tax base relative to GDP. Estimating GDP by value added by sector in 2010, 39% of agriculture value added is not sold i.e. is not monetised and 17.5% of value added in all sectors minus public administration is generated using the non observed technique for estimation. In 2004, comparable figures were 44% and 29%. This would suggest that in 2010, 7.9% of GDP by sector value added is non monetised, 13.7% is informal, 64.5% is formal with a further 14% in public administration. In 2004 the comparable figures were 11% of GDP non monetised, 23% informal, 58% formal and 9% in public administration. This indicates that Albania's tax base had expanded though still had room to grow further.

This construction is useful in an attempt to explain and forecast revenue, as the contribution of the formal monetised sector to the tax revenue is likely to be higher than the informal sector's. The informal sector is unlikely to be registered for Value Added Tax (VAT) so its value added will not be taxed (its inputs, however, are likely to be, if purchased from the formal sector). The surplus of the informal sector may be taxed through presumptive taxes if the authorities have been able to register the entities, whereas formal sector companies will be taxed on their profits. Formal sector companies' employees will be subject to Pay As You Earn tax, while informal entities will not. The non monetised element of GDP will be outside the tax base completely.

How the composition of GDP changes can have an impact on revenue without any changes in tax policy and tax administration, though in reality improvements in the latter two may well influence the structure of GDP through improving incentives and compliance. Since 2007 Albania has embarked on tax policy and tax administration reform that will have improved the incentive structure and these will have yielded some improvements in the tax to GDP ratio. Tax reform is seen as a spur to investment to generate the growth needed for structural change. However, significant improvements in the tax to GDP ratio will only be realised when the monetised formal economy has a significantly higher share of GDP than it presently has. Indeed since 2007, tax to GDP ratios have remained relatively constant while nominal tax rates have decreased for many taxes which suggests that the improved tax administration and higher share of monetised and formal activity in GDP has compensated for the impact of lower rates.

Based on these examples it is not unreasonable to formulate a simple medium term revenue forecasting model based on the tax to GDP relationships and the structure of GDP to show what would happen to the tax to GDP ratio given changes in the structure of the economy. Three basic relationships are modelled.

- GDP grows annually – the various sectoral components can grow at a uniform rate or by different amounts.

- With developments in the economy, there is a graduation from the non-monetised sector to the informal sector, and from the informal sector to the formal sector.

- As the size of the formal sector grows relative to the informal sector and the informal sector grows relative to the non-monetised, there is a greater contribution to tax per unit of GDP.

Sizable increases in revenue to GDP ratios from one year to another will only happen if the composition – the structure – of GDP changes in the manner addressed here. In 2013 the forecast of revenue to GDP in 2018 was 25% using the GDP growth model and 27% using the dynamic model. The actual revenue to GDP ratio in 2018 was 27.1%. The 2007 report's forecast was 30% for 2018 which suggested that the dynamic assumptions made using the earlier GDP composition data were slightly more ambitious which were dampened down using the later actual GDP composition.[18]

I also worked on a similar approach and developed a model for Palestine under the Department for International Development (DFID) PGF project although the assumption of the development of GDP with respect to informal/formal sector was not addressed due to lack of information on the structure of GDP in that regard. The model was based on monthly revenues by type and was more suited to a shorter time period. The model factored in growth rates for each tax based on the individual drivers. Monthly forecast data were replaced by actual data on a monthly basis which preserved the integrity of the seasonality of the data, although this could be compromised with regard to the timing of transfers of revenues collected on cross border transactions with Israel "clearance revenue". So long as these clearance revenues were received within the year, the model produced consistent annual forecasts. Assumptions contained in the model were clearly set out.[19] This was first produced in 2015 and updated in 2016 and 2017. The comparison with forecasts and actual was robust enough to justify the model to be used in the budget for the medium term.

The use of the movement from subsistence to informal to formal as determinant of revenue growth is supported in an IMF Blog[20] that shows rising tax revenues as a percentage of GDP in Malawi, Liberia, Nepal and Solomon Islands. The model in the accompanying

---

18   The Albania experience reports can be found on the PFMBoard website: https://pfmboard.com/index.php?topic=7707.0

19   Specifying clearly the assumptions made is important so that it is possible to carry out stress tests and assess fiscal risk. To score well on the PEFA indicator PI-14 Macroeconomic and fiscal forecasting underlying assumptions must be specified and included in the documentation. PEFA is discussed at length in Chapter 6. The IMF's 2018 Fiscal Transparency Handbook also reinforces this point.

20   https://blogs.imf.org/2020/09/25/mission-impossible-can-fragile-states-increase-tax-revenues/ September 25, 2020 by Bernardin Akitoby, Jiro Honda, and Keyra Primus

article[21] uses the share of agriculture in total output as one of the determinants of revenue growth over time. The article states share of the agriculture sector is statistically significant in Fragile and Conflict-Affected States (FCS). As FCS tend to have large informal sectors and a large share of agriculture in total output, this constellation of factors often pushes FCS towards a lower level of tax collection and a narrower tax base. In non-FCS, the results also suggest weaker tax performance with larger agriculture sector. However using agriculture per se is not a fully dependable proxy for the informal/subsistence component of GDP: over time the share of agriculture may stay the same but its composition may shift from subsistence to informal and to formal and as a result the contribution to revenue growth will be dependent on the size of the shift.

---

21 "Tax Revenues in Fragile and Conflict-Affected States —Why Are They Low and How Can We Raise Them?"

4 PUBLIC EXPENDITURE REVIEWS AND MEDIUM TERM BUDGET FRAMEWORKS

Public Expenditure Reviews

An accepted definition of a Public Expenditure Review (PER) is that it is a key diagnostic instrument used to evaluate the effectiveness of public finances. A PER typically analyzes government expenditures over a period of years to assess their consistency with policy priorities, and what results were achieved. A PER may analyze government-wide expenditures or may focus on a particular sector as Health Care, Education, or Infrastructure.

My first foray into public expenditure in the international arena was to Nigeria in 1984. The Nigerian Government had established a commission on public parastatals under Gamaliel Onosode towards the end of 1983, when **public confidence** in the economic direction of the country was eroded and accountability was lacking in government **subsidies** to public enterprises.[22] Along with Ray Goodman (a retired director at the World Bank), I was recruited to provide technical assistance to the commission. We examined major on–going projects in steel, pulp and paper, rice, and sugar with a view to recommending those projects to be mothballed or otherwise restructured, terminated or continued. This work involved extensive use of economic project evaluation, including Cost Benefit Analysis and Domestic Resource Costs measures. A ranking of projects for budgetary presentation and financial analysis was produced. The Onosode report was the first in Nigeria to tackle, comprehensively, the industrialisation drive and capital spending which dominated the oil boom of the 1970s and the early 1980s. The report identified five major defects in planning which it believed had become evident by the end of 1983:

---

22   https://en.wikipedia.org/wiki/Gamaliel_Onosode

- Public capital expenditure rose during the oil boom at a much faster rate than Nigeria's physical, technical or financial abilities.

- Huge expenditure on particular industrial projects did not yield expected returns because of inappropriate choices in their selection, size, design, location and management.

- Government policies laid too much emphasis on industrialisation, without regard to Nigeria's resource base and comparative advantage.

- Frequent changes in fiscal and monetary policies created planning problems for the private sector.

- The exchange rate of the naira was not managed to reflect the basic strength of the economy and the need to encourage domestic production.

I subsequently was a member of Public Expenditures Reviews in Nigeria, the first of which was the first ever Public Expenditure Review by the World Bank in its member countries which looked at all sectors. This was led by Joanne Salop. The areas that I examined were those that I had become familiar with on the work initiated in the Onosode Commission and to follow up progress which entailed visits to the establishments. Among those I visited was the Rolling Mill at Jos which was operating. There was a notice at the entrance welcoming the President of the World Bank: when I had finished it was downgraded to World Bank consultant! Other companies I visited were the Pulp and Paper Mill at Jebba and the Sugar factory close by at Bacita which were operational. I also visited a paper mill which was located near its supply of raw material – wood. What I remember was a building that was some four storeys high with floors – just the skeleton and no walls – with all the machinery still in boxes unpacked. I think it was the Nigerian Newsprint Manufacturing Company Limited at Oku-Iboku which eventually became operational.

Many governments made strides to include PERs as part of their budget planning cycle. Whether across the whole of government or focusing on a single sector, by examining how public expenditure was allocated and managed, governments and donors are better able to assess not only the impact of their investment, but also the effectiveness of budget planning and execution. PERs help diagnose spending problems and help countries develop more effective and transparent budget allocations. The objective is to establish a baseline understanding of key fiscal management and policy challenges, highlight priority reform areas for policymakers, and set the agenda for the next phase of budgetary planning.[23] Ideally any spending review should include tax expenditures – the realisation of policy objectives through the suspension of elements of the standard tax code – as part of the total resource allocation framework. Tax expenditures are addressed in Chapter 8 after the chapter on tax policy.

The inclusion of extra-budgetary organisations such as donor funded projects in PERs is critical to a successful PER. If they are not included the likelihood of decisions of governments to duplicate spending on a project is increased without that knowledge as part of the budgeting process. As well a donor may build a school or a clinic and hand it over to the responsible ministry in a flag waving ceremony but the ministry may not have included the school/clinic in its budget and allocated the running costs to make it operational. I have come across such cases. The need to include donor expenditure in a PER is illustrated by the PER in HIV/AIDs in Kenya that I worked on in 2005. Less than 1% of total expenditure was funded by the Government and 32% was funded by donors through the budget. The remaining 67% was funded by donors but off budget.

The HIV/AIDS 2005 PER was a follow up to 2005 Public Expenditure Review in Health, which had the theme *"Delivering Economic Recovery Strategy Priorities"*. The stated main objectives of the 2005 Ministry of Health Public Expenditure Review are to:

- Present the Government of Kenya's policies and objectives in the health sector, and the broad programmes and activities to achieve these over the next three years, annually.

- Evaluate the public health expenditures against budgetary allocations with emphasis on the composition of expenditure;

- Identify budget related constraints and resource use;

- Review the effectiveness of expenditures;

---

23   boost.worldbank.org/tools-resources/public-expenditure-review. This also includes a link to World Bank Discussion Papers No 323 May 1996 Evaluating Public Spending A Framework for Public Expenditure Reviews by Sanjay Pradhan whom I had the good fortune to work with in Uganda.

- Assess the extent to which the expenditures are aligned to policies and objectives in the health sector,

- Set out the broad annual financing requirements to implement planned activities using existing facilities and capacity, but removing short-term constraints while working to eliminate long- term constraints; and

- Establish priorities in recognition that there are constraints of financial, technical and physical nature that have to be addressed if the country is to improve its health outcomes.

The PER noted that it is compiled in the context of the Government's Economy Recovery Strategy, which sets out policies and programmes as well as measurable targets to alleviate poverty. The Review is thus, part of a continuing process that will over the years improve resource mobilisation from domestic sources as well as from the development partners, and its allocation to priority programmes between and within sectors. Consequently, it attempts to provide a base for decision-making, which can be expanded and built on in subsequent PERs.

This PER also drew from recent pertinent work that had been carried out on the health sector in Kenya including the 2003 Kenya Demographic and Health Survey; Kenya National Health Accounts; the Ministry of Health Human Resource Study; and Financial Disbursement Assessment, Ministry of Health Kenya. In particular, the Human Resource and Financial Disbursement Studies have provided answers to questions raised in past PERs on budget implementation.

A previous PER in 2004 (which I had also worked on) had demonstrated that while the policy direction is to increase provision for primary health care relative to curative care, examination of actual expenditure and budget allocations had indicated that the opposite had actually taken place. The 2005 PER has examined this finding in two ways. The availability of more detailed expenditure data for the four year period from 2000/01 to 2003/04 allowed more analysis than previously undertaken in PERs which pointed to the reason for this apparent failure to follow stated policy. In addition, the PER Team carried out an exercise to assess what proportion of the resources of the major hospitals were allocated to primary health care provision alongside their mandated curative care provision. By examining hospital expenditures in more detail (*albeit in a more cursory fashion given the limitations of time*), it became possible to understand what the impact of an underperforming primary health sector has had on the demand for services at the higher levels of provision.

The 2005 PER recognises that it had its limitations that had resulted from inadequacies of data, time and capacity. This was particularly so when officials had been requested to provide information in a timeframe that was unrealistic given their heavy and ongoing workload. In an ideal world, a PER would attempt to examine particular programmes by specifying activities and the physical inputs and associated costs required to implement these activities to deliver the outputs of the programmes. This means that PERs should be an activity built into the annual work programme of ministerial planning departments and should be initiated at the start of the budget cycle to provide sufficient time for them to be fully completed and discussed before budget formulation. A recommendation made was that subsequent PERs can and should strive in this direction.

The 2005 PER was updated in 2006 which I assisted with as part of a now established team comprising the director of Health Planning, Steven Otieno and his staff. Two additional sections were added. The first was an assessment of the implementation of the recommendations of the 2005 PER. The second included an analysis of ministry outputs and corresponding performance indicators as well as performance contract indicators for key management and agencies in the health sector.

As well as working on PERs in Nigeria and Kenya[24] over various years up to 2005, I was involved in PERs in Liberia, Rwanda, Zambia, Uganda, Papua New Guinea, Namibia, Ethiopia and Sudan in a variety of sectors. However, after the Kenya 2006 PER I became more involved in the application of a related but wider aspect of public expenditure methodology.

---

24   There were also PERs in Education (Paul Blay), Roads and Transport (Simon Groom), Agriculture (Paul Harnett) and Police (Tom Dolan) which I managed.

From Public Expenditure Reviews to Medium Term Expenditure Frameworks

In 1999 the IMF introduced the Poverty Reduction and Growth Facility (PRGF) to replace its Enhanced Structural Adjustment Facility (ESAF). While retaining its role of the guardian of macro-economic and fiscal stability, the core aim of the IMF under the PRGF was to arrive at policies that are more clearly focused on economic growth and poverty reduction and, as a result of better national ownership, more consistently implemented. One of the most significant aspects of the PRGF was the treatment of donor funding in recipient countries. Under the ESAF if a donor contributed to a country's budget it was considered as a "below the line" item in the fiscal table even if it were a grant. This reduced the need for borrowing but did not increase expenditure. As a result, donors provided off-budget support as they wanted to see tangible results in service delivery. The change to PRGF meant that donors could provide grants that could be included in the budget which increased public expenditure. Donors were able to switch from balance of payments support which was used to fund imports (often from the donor country so required evidence of such imports) to budget support.

Budget support is a form of aid where assistance is provided through the recipient country's own budget to support the implementation of its development programmes. General budget support is untied assistance which supports the country's national development plan as a whole. Sector budget support is provided for a particular sector or development programme so it is tied and earmarked to the sector as part of the expenditure allocation.

In this context, initiatives to improve the budget process from an annual standalone budget were developed and became the norm in many countries.[25] This was termed a Medium Term Expenditure Framework (MTEF) based on an initial annual budget and rolling baseline to the next two years (but could be more). Based on my contribution to a March 2014 IMF FAD Technical Assistance report

---

25   There is significant literature in on MTEFs for the interested reader including A Basic Model of Performance-Based Budgeting Marc Robinson and Duncan Last Fiscal Affairs Department https://www.imf.org/external/pubs/ft/tnm/2009/tnm0901.pdf. There is also Beyond the Annual Budget Global Experience with Medium-Term Expenditure Frameworks https://elibrary.worldbank.org/doi/book/10.1596/978-0-8213-9625-4 and OECD Best Practices for Performance Budgeting https://one.oecd.org/document/GOV/PGC/SBO(2018)7/en/pdf.

on Myanmar Strengthening Budget Formulation and Public Financial Management (PFM) Legal Framework, the following outlines
key features of an MTEF. Schematically an MTEF and rolling base-
lines can be depicted as follows:

Rolling Baselines and MTEF			
MTEF 2020 -2022			
Budget Allo-cation 2020	Forward Estimates 2021	Forward Esti-mates 2022	
For Approval	Roll over into indicative allocations based on existing policies and new policies if fiscal space permits		
	Budget Allocation 2021	Forward Estimates 2022	Forward Estimates 2023
	For Approval		
MTEF 2021-2023			

An MTEF is built around a Medium Term Fiscal Framework (MTFF)
which takes a medium term view on fiscal strategy: setting revenue,
expenditure, deficit and financing targets over a 3-4 year period.
In essence this is a fiscal table as outlined in the previous chapter
covering 3 – 4 years. Elements of the MTEF contain

- **Expenditure Ceilings:** Based on the agreed MTFF – near the
  start of the budget process – impose limits ("ceilings") that
  constrain the size of budget requests from spending agencies.

- **Multi-year budget**: Budget process produces annual budget
  and two-year "forward estimates" of the future impacts of
  current activities, policies, programmes and projects.

- **Baseline and rolling forward estimates:** Updating the costs
  of delivering existing policies/projects can be done at the
  start of the budget cycle – enabling the rest of the budget
  process to focus on what new activities and projects are
  possible within the resource constraints

"Forward estimates" are future expenditure plans prepared on the
basis of existing level of services. They capture the future funding
requirements of projects and activities included in the current year's
budget. A typical multi-year rolling forward framework includes

estimates for the current year and two to three outer years. At the start of a new year: (i) the forward estimates for the outer years are rolled forward with some technical adjustments; and (ii) one more year of forward estimates is added to maintain the multi-year characteristics of the framework. Thus, the estimates for the second year become the baseline or the starting point for the next year's budget. This process is repeated every year.

It is important though to distinguish between expenditures that are dependent on economic conditions and those that are planned allocations. Interest rate and debt repayment and social security payments that may be related to unemployment can be planned based on forecasts of exchange rate and GDP but may be subject to economic shocks more than planned allocations such as to schools (based on student numbers). Fiscal risk can be wide ranging including as contingent liabilities from State Owned Enterprises (SOE) and is always a factor that has to be addressed particularly if a country is subject to natural disasters which are becoming more frequent.

Illustrative figures demonstrate a "stable" process:

Baseline and Forward Estimates					
Establish the baseline cost of existing policy and projects for budget and + 2 years					
	2019	2020	2021	2022	
	Current Year	Budget Year	Outer Year Budget + 1	Outer Year Budget + 2	
Recurrent	65	65	67	70	
Capital	33	35	15	5	
Total	98	100	82	75	
	At start of next budget year 2021 becomes the budget year. Estimates already established for the cost of delivering existing policy in 2021 and 2022 become the baseline for the 2021 budget				
		2020	2021	2022	2023
		Current Year	Budget Year	Outer Year Budget + 1	Outer Year Budget + 2
Recurrent		65	67	70	73
Capital		35	15	5	1
Total		100	82	75	74

With estimates of revenue and borrowing this can translate into:

	2019	2020	2021	2022	2023
Budget Process 2019					
Budget allocation 2019 and forward estimates 2020 and 2021	98	100	82		
Budget Process 2020					
Baseline Forward estimates rolled over		100	82	75	
Approved new policy		10	15	15	
Approved savings		-5	-8	-10	
Approved wages and price increases		3	3	3	
Budget allocation 2020 and forward estimates 2021 and 2022		108	92	83	
Budget Process 2021					
Baseline Forward estimates rolled over			92	83	74
Approved new policy			10	15	15
Approved savings			-5	-10	-10
Approved wages and price increases			4	4	4
Budget allocation 2021 and forward estimates 2022 and 2023			103	92	83

The rolling forward of estimates allows the budget analysis and discussion to focus on new developments, such as new spending decisions, changes to the revenue policy, and savings in existing activities due to scaling back of operations or productivity gains. Indeed a policy and associated programmes may be ended if they have achieved their objectives such as a mass vaccination campaign. Only new vaccination for new-borne children would be rolled over. Establishing a baseline for funding the existing activities/projects at the start of the budget process simplifies the budget process and makes it easier to achieve aggregate fiscal discipline. However, the use of rolling forward estimates and "new initiatives" approach requires: (i) an ability to gain data on progress of projects soon after close of the last fiscal year; and (ii) a system to keep track of proposals and decisions regarding new initiatives. A computerized budget formulation system that enables on-line budget submissions by the spending units and specification of ceilings and processing of budget submissions by a Ministry of Finance is an important aspect of an MTEF.

There is, however, the linkage with budget execution and the medium term planning of the budget which is critical for delivery of the plans. Some countries that have a three year budget period will execute programmes over the three year period and account for expenditure annually in the budget execution reports. Spending is not constrained to a particular year within the three-year envelope.[26] Others will have an annual budget within the MTEF and allocate spending to a year and if a budget is not fully spent, the unspent element is cancelled. Vietnam, in contrast, carries over the unspent allocation to the next year and accounts for its execution separately from the next year's budget.

While not heavily involved in implementation, I carried out progress reviews of MTEFs in The Gambia, Sierra Leone, Georgia and Rwanda. I produced papers on the MTEF in Rwanda and Ghana (*Assessment of the MTEF in Rwanda*, Centre for Aid & Public Expenditure, Overseas Development Institute, London, May 2003 and *Assessment of the MTEF in Ghana*, Centre for Aid & Public Expenditure, Overseas Development Institute, London, May 2003). These contributed to A Review of Experience in Implementing Medium Term Expenditure Frameworks in a PRSP Context: A Synthesis of Eight Country Studies by Malcolm Holmes with Alison Evans published in November 2003.[27]

The case studies indicated that MTEFs were progressing in all countries, albeit at varying speeds and that in many cases they had

---

26   The UK Treasury makes a distinction between Departmental Expenditure Limits over the medium term which is the spending allocated to and spent by departments such as on the running of schools or hospitals and public spending on pensions, welfare benefits and debt interest which is termed Annually Managed Expenditure.

27   https://www.odi.org/sites/odi.org.uk/files/odi-assets/publications-opinion-files/2157.pdf

facilitated and were being strengthened by the then current empha-sis on implementing Poverty Reduction Strategy Programmes. In terms of MTEF development the case study countries were broadly categorised as follows: Maturing – South Africa, Uganda, Getting it together – Albania, Benin, Rwanda, Tanzania; Struggling – Burkina Faso, Cameroon, Ghana. The categories were based on a qualita-tive assessment of case study material. Each category indicated the direction rather than level of MTEF development to date.

Many factors underpinned the progress made, including the underlying political economy of the country. The case studies suggested that in countries where officials, particularly in the Ministry of Finance recognised the potential of a more medium term perspective to budgeting and were persistent in their advice to this effect at the political level, the prospects for the institutionali-sation of improved budgetary systems, processes and outcomes had been greatly enhanced. Equally, where conditions were not condu-cive and in place at the political level, the pace and nature of MTEF implementation proved to be very different. Political economy has to be recognised, therefore, and reform efforts need to work it. The more inimical it is to good budgetary outcomes, the more impor-tant it is that there are domestic champions about to argue its case. In a country like Sierra Leone, for example, the development of the MTEF had to contend with the ravages of a rebel war that devas-tated the country for many years and the disruptive impact it had on normal economic management. There was a backlog of six years of public accounts that were successfully completed by Cyprian Kamary when he took over as Chief Accounting Officer. Prior to this as Chief Budget Officer he provided leadership in the successful introduction and implementation of the MTEF process and assisted Ministries, Departments and Agencies in preparing their strategic plans and annual budget estimates within the MTEF Framework. In Georgia there was a focus on economic management after the split from the Soviet Union in 1990. The MTEF was developed as well as the downstream activities such as a single treasury account that incorporated extra budgetary units into it. This was supported by a home grown management information system. Despite the tension in 2008 onwards with Russia, the political willingness to prioritise development of economic and fiscal management has ensured that Georgia is now one of the top performers in the formulation and implementation of the budget and its various elements.

Medium Term Expenditure Framework to Medium Term Budget Programme

As noted Albania was categorised in the "getting it together" but the report also states that since the case study was prepared (it was published in 2002), progress had shown signs of stalling. It is in this context that the steps that were taken to transform the Medium Term Expenditure Framework into a Medium Term Budget Programme in Albania can be described. While the term Medium Term Expenditure Framework is widely used in English, the way this term had been translated into Albanian translates back onto English as Medium Term Budget Programme (MTBP). This is actually a clearer description of the MTEF that has been the starting point with the term MTBP as the end point!

The work in Albania on Strengthening Public Expenditure Management (SPEM 2[28]) by REPIM[29] started in May 2002 and ended in December 2004. SPEM 3 started in December 2005 and ended in January 2009. Both SPEM 2 and 3 were funded by UK DFID. A third contract funded by a World Bank Trust Fund Supporting the Ministry of Finance, Line Ministries and the Department for Strategy and Donor Coordination for Strategic Plans Development, the Implementation of Medium Term Budget Programme, Public Investment and Monitoring ran from October 2009 to September 2010.

While Albania had commenced work on developing the budget process as noted in the ODI paper, the initial review by the REPIM team of the situation was very revealing. An assessment of the then current budget process was carried out through:

- a review of existing documents related to the budget process (e.g. Organic Budget Law, budget guidelines documents from previous years, etc.);

- interviews with key officials in the budget process (e.g. the Budget Director and senior staff in the Budget Department);

- interviews with Sector Specialists in the Budget Department;

---

28 There had been a previous SPEM 1 support.
29 REPIM was formed in 1988 as a joint venture between me, trading as John Short Economic Services and Lancashire Enterprises.

- interviews with officers working in budget and planning units at the sector level;

- interviews with other key representatives in the budget process (e.g. senior officers from the Ministry of Economy, representatives from the Government Poverty Reduction Strategy secretariat, senior officers from the Treasury, etc.); and

- interviews with key people outside of Government (e.g. the major donor agencies).

One of the key findings was that the Ministry of Finance was ill prepared to carry out such work not because of its unwillingness but because of staff shortages and its ongoing work programme. In the process of developing an understanding of the functioning of the then present public expenditure management arrangements, the REPIM team met with sector specialists in the Budget Department to identify how their jobs were described, the functions they fulfilled, the training and management support they had received and their own assessments of how they would like to develop and enhance their roles in the system. This process was instrumental in revealing just how much of the time of Budget Department staff was spent managing virement[30] and the multiple reconciliation processes and how little time was devoted to public expenditure analysis. Indeed this virement management was extremely resource intensive, requiring several months' effort. The Budget Department appeared to be a *'Department of Minor Changes and Major Checking'* rather than a *'Department of Budget Policy for Outputs'*.[31] One of the first things that the project did was to design and implement software for the treatment of virement and ensure that the line ministries rather than the budget department took responsibility with the Treasury. In reality, the evidence showed that whatever Budget was initially established, many thousands of changes were made to this during the year. In other words, the *initial budget was effectively meaningless*. One conclusion was that the original Budget benefited from very little background work and planning.

----

30   The process of moving money from one financial account or part of a budget (a plan for how money will be spent) to a different one.

31   Phrase coined by Martin Johnston in a project quarterly report to DFID.

An output from this analysis was in addition to the virement software, the Budget Department was reorganised in a way that could allow sector specialists to focus on budget preparation and through training programmes to have the skills to:

- develop better links between policy, sector strategies and budgets;

- undertake cost analysis of expenditures and budgets; and

- improve their ability to manage public investment.

Given the shortage of staffing and staff diversion into management of virement, the production of the key MTBP 2004 -2006 document became a problem. The member of the Budget Department who had been primarily responsible for managing the previous MTBP was on study leave and his assistant had resigned and emigrated. The net result, therefore, was that the Budget Department, with responsibility for preparation of the 2004-06 MTBP, effectively had no staff with appropriate experience to carry out this function during the whole of the MTBP preparation period. Accordingly the MTBP issues paper, the Technical Notes, Sector Strategies that emanated from the National Strategy for Social and Economic Development and macro fiscal framework was prepared by the consultants on behalf of the Ministry of Finance (MoF). While this was clearly unsatisfactory, the Team Leader, understandably, had not realised by this time that the MoF expected the REPIM team to prepare the document in its entirety. This only became clear as the document was in the process of preparation and completion. The *preparation* of the MTBP document for and on behalf of the MoF was never envisaged in the SPEM 2 terms of reference (as prepared by the MoF) nor was such a role envisaged in the Work Programme.

Several factors resulted in the initial draft of the 2004-06 MTBP document being ready at end June rather than end May. This had implications for the ability of the MoF to go through a process of revision in time for the Minister to deliver a final version to the Council of Ministers at the beginning of July as originally timetabled. Clearly, a crucial factor in this was the absence of sufficiently qualified Budget Department staff throughout the whole 2004-06 MTBP preparation process. This had implications for the preparation of the document itself (with the initial draft being prepared entirely by external consultants). It also had implications for the management of the process (e.g. direct and practical actions to demand delivery of inputs from Government of Albania institutions that could not be taken by external consultants).

The effect of the staffing issue should not have been a surprise. Given the importance of the work of the Budget Department in general and the status of the MTBP process in particular, losing all middle-ranking specialists over an extended period was bound to have a substantial effect on the work of the department and the preparation of the MTBP document. Clearly there had been constraints in the appointment of staff that had been outside the control of the MoF (e.g. the availability of suitable candidates, protracted procedures for recruitment and lengthy procedures for transfer). Notwithstanding this, the experience of the 2004-06 MTBP showed that the failure to appoint and retain appropriate staff or transfer suitable replacements during 2003 could not and must not be repeated under any circumstances in the future. A repeated failure in this area during future MTBP preparation would inevitably call into question the Government's commitment to the process.

As noted above, (hopefully) extraordinary circumstances during 2003 resulted in the REPIM team engaging in direct preparation activities for the MTBP rather than focussing on supporting Government in its own preparation of the document. I can remember engaging with the Ministry of Health and the Tax Authorities. There was a risk of this extraordinary circumstance resulting in a general expectation that the role of the consultants under the SPEM 2 would be to prepare the MTBP from start to finish on behalf of the Government. It needed to be made clear at the outset of the process for the 2005-07 MTBP, to and from the highest position in the MoF that the consultants' role was to help in *strengthening* public expenditure management not *doing* public expenditure management. Whilst this was clear in the REPIM team's terms of reference and work programmes, it may not have been obvious to all parties. Unless this was clarified from the highest position in the MoF, there would continue to be a danger of limited engagement in the process by Government of Albania institutions. When the situation was in danger of being repeated for the 2005 2007 MTBP the then Minister of Finance complained to the UK Ambassador that the DFID consultants were not doing their job. The Ambassador, having being apprised of the situation, replied that the consultants were there to advise and not to do the work of his staff. The support of the Embassy, particularly Joe Preston was important in both the bad and good times. The 2005-2007 MTBP was produced entirely by the MoF.

The timetable and deadlines established by the MoF with regard to the responsibilities of departments, line ministries and other agencies in the 2004-06 MTBP preparation process were simply not respected. This was the major reason why the initial draft of the 2004-06 MTBP document was ready at end June rather than end May when it should have been ready. These delays occurred despite continued requests from the MoF for submission of information from other agencies and the continued offers of support by the MoF in preparing the information.

One of the benefits of the heavy involvement of the team in the MTBP preparation was the understanding of the capacity constraints in all of the ministries. As well, the deficiencies in governmental and legal framework were revealed in its entirety. These related to the development of a budget framework that linked the realisation of achievements in terms of outputs and goals to the inputs and their costs allocated to them. While perhaps labouring the point, the discussion is useful in being graphic about the reality of situations that, if glossed over, stymied any real achievement in relation to what was intended. This was not the case in Albania where by the end of total work programme much was achieved.

Key features and lessons in the realisation of a working MTBP during the support programme in Albania can be summarised as follows. The creation of the Integrated Planning System (IPS) in the Office of the Prime Minister as a document of the Council of Ministers ensured a strengthened political focus. The National Strategy for Social and Economic Development and other national strategies such as the European Integration Strategy took central stage. The MTPB was seen a key document that linked sector strategies into the IPS though the budget process and funding.[32] What is more illuminating to this story is the account of an integrated planning process in general but also in Albania in particular by Gord Evans.[33]

---

32   http://shtetiweb.org/wp-content/uploads/2014/05/IPS-handbook-2009. pdf

33   There is an excellent series by Gord Evans Professional Diaries #1: Integrated Planning: the Good, the Bad and the Ugly which gives a full account of an integrated planning system and his experience in the context of the MTBP in Albania. Gord also does justice to the subject in https://pfmboard.com/index. php?topic=7363.msg22086#msg22086 that reflects his vast experience in the interesting experiences section. See also Conversation with Marc Robinson on

In this description he alludes to his first meeting with Martin Johnston and me. "At some point, I started to do the rounds of whatever Technical Assistance (TA) was in town and agreed to meet a PFM team working with the Ministry of Finance on "Strengthening Public Expenditure Management" (yes, we tried, unsuccessfully, to convince them to add "revenue" as part of their project title just to flesh out the acronym). I met with the PFM consultants over a drink (well, maybe it was more than one) at the top of a revolving tower high over Tirana. Turns out they'd been working for some time in MoF to convert hardened devotees of incremental, line-object budgeting to an approach that would emphasize the policy assumptions underpinning expenditures. Now to a centre of government guy, to hear anyone on the PFM side use the word "policy," without it being circumscribed by adjectives such as macro, fiscal, structural, expenditure or wage, is siren-like. However, my PFM colleagues had a problem: lots of high-quality content, but nowhere to sell their wares." Needless to say, Gord formed a fruitful partnership with the SPEM 2 team that ensured that the IPS and the MTBP fitted together and was fully operational at that time.

The development of the MTBP gained traction by support from the new Minister of Finance, Arben Malay and, after elections, in a new follow up Government by Deputy Minister Sherefedin Shehu whose support was invaluable as was that of Arjana Cela and Mimoza Dhembi in the Budget Department and Gjergji Teneqexhiu, when he was General Secretary. When the Ministry of Transport, which was very powerful, turned up at Budget Hearing at the Ministry of Finance to present its proposals and had nothing to present, it was told that it looks like there would be no budget for Transport and the meeting ended immediately. Its attitude to the budget process changed. The budget reform process, albeit not planned as different consultants could have won SPEM 3 and the Trust Fund contracts, had the luxury of an extended timeframe and consistency of inputs from both international and local consultants. It benefited from consistent project direction and team leadership of Martin Johnston and Simon Stone whom I supported over the life time of the work.

---

performance budgeting https://pfmboard.com/index.php?topic = 6478.0 and the Conversation with Matt Andrews on limits to externally influenced PFM reform https://pfmboard.com/index.php?topic = 6075.0.

The Budget Department became focused on the changed agenda and was organised into Divisions to do this. One major change was that the responsibility for public investment was moved from the Ministry of Economy into a division in the Budget Department so that the whole of public spending was managed within the Budget Department.

In addition to these managerial aspects, there was a consistent approach to the technical aspects of the work across the whole of Government. A budget calendar was proposed, accepted and implemented that allowed sufficient time for all stages of the MTBP process to be completed in sequence. The budget calendar detailing all the steps and participants was made into a big wall chart and put on the wall on the ground floor of the Ministry of Finance so all were aware of its importance. This budget calendar is for whole of government with respect to development of sector strategies, issuance of hard budget ceilings, budget hearings on proposals and finalisation of the budget and its presentation to Council of Ministers and submission to Parliament.

A budget planning manual, budget preparation software and a New Organic Budget Law (NOBL) and procedures were developed and implemented. I was involved in the development of the investment selection procedures and produced Step-by-Step Guidelines for Allocating Core Investment building on earlier work on investment selection I had done in Ethiopia and Zimbabwe. However, before the manual, software and NOBL were finalised, the process and procedures were tested in a sample of key ministries so that any issues in application were ironed out and dealt with. The business case for the budget process was developed and tested and only then transformed into a software programme (entitled PSHIP) which was then tested before being rolled out under the watchful eyes of John Blissett.[34] The essential feature was the linkage between input

---

34 While this would appear to be logical this is not always the case. One instance I have experienced was the SIGBUD software in St Kitts where the specification of programs, performance indicators and activities were mixed up which rendered it ineffective. SIGBUD was produced by software engineers without reference to and understanding of a budget structure. When the Integrated Financial Management Information System (IFMIS) was being developed for the Treasury in Albania, the suggestion was made to the software engineers that an interface with the budget software would be useful so that the budget fed directly into it. The response was that it was not in their terms of reference so no! A good example of where a paper based budget execution accounting system process was in place which could be computerised was in Myanmar where there were very

costs and physical outputs by programme. A similar approach was taken for the budget planning manual. Only when this was seen to work was the NOBL drafted with the operational aspects included as Procedures which allowed flexibility should changes need to be made at a later date. This arrangement contrasts with many of the recent budget laws that I have seen in the some of the countries in the Caribbean where the law locks the government into fiscal rules that may be inappropriate in more straitened times such as in the current COVID-19 pandemic.

Training on all of this was conducted for Ministers, Parliamentarians (Public Accounts Committee), Sector Ministries, including the Ministry of Finance. The Budget Department was the recipient of significant training including the ability to train the sector ministries.

The linkages between the various components and stages of a functioning budget calendar are presented in the diagram.

Stages of a Budget Calendar

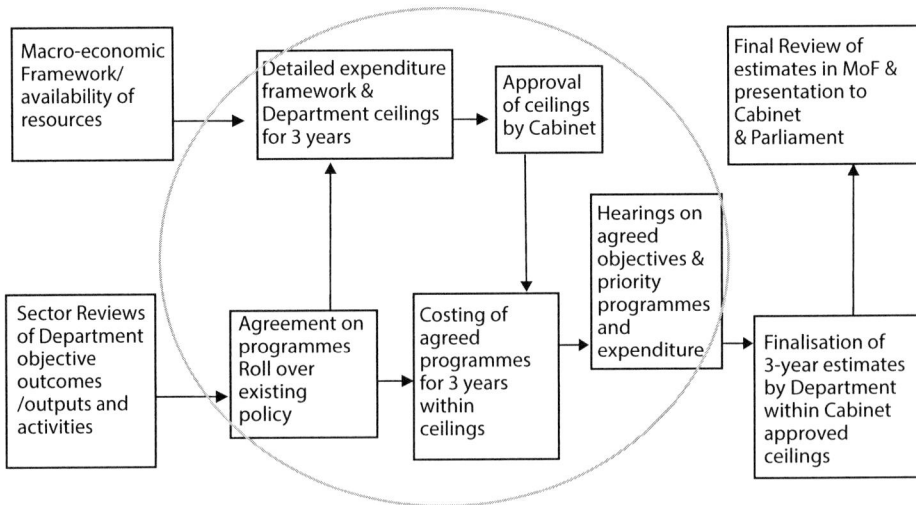

---

limited computers (at the time of the mission) and everything was written down in ledgers following logical processes and procedures.

Being SMART

The core concept behind the transformation of an MTEF to an MTBP – from an input based budget to a results based budget can be summarised using a programme tree that links inputs to an activity to generate SMART outputs to realise SMART objectives (goals). The MTBP programme tree is depicted in the diagram below as constructed by the SPEM team for the Albania MTBP.

SMART is an acronym that means Specific, Measurable, Achievable, Realistic, Time-bound. What this denotes is that any outputs and objective goals included in specifying a programme tree – known as key performance indicators (non financial) to be useful should be SMART.

Defining its components SMART is :

Specific: Information is sufficient to provide a clear and unambiguous understanding of what the Programme policy goal, objective or outputs that has been planned.

Measurable: information presented (number and measurement unit) is sufficient to provide a clear understanding of the quantity of the Programme policy goal, objective or outputs that has been planned.

Achievable: Technical capacities and financial resources are sufficient for the planned quantity of the Programme policy goal, objective or outputs to be successfully achieved or delivered.

Realistic: the Programme policy goal, objective or output is appropriate to the service delivery areas of the Programme it relates to.

Time-bound: The time period over which a Programme policy goal, objective or output is to be achieved or delivered is clearly spccificd.

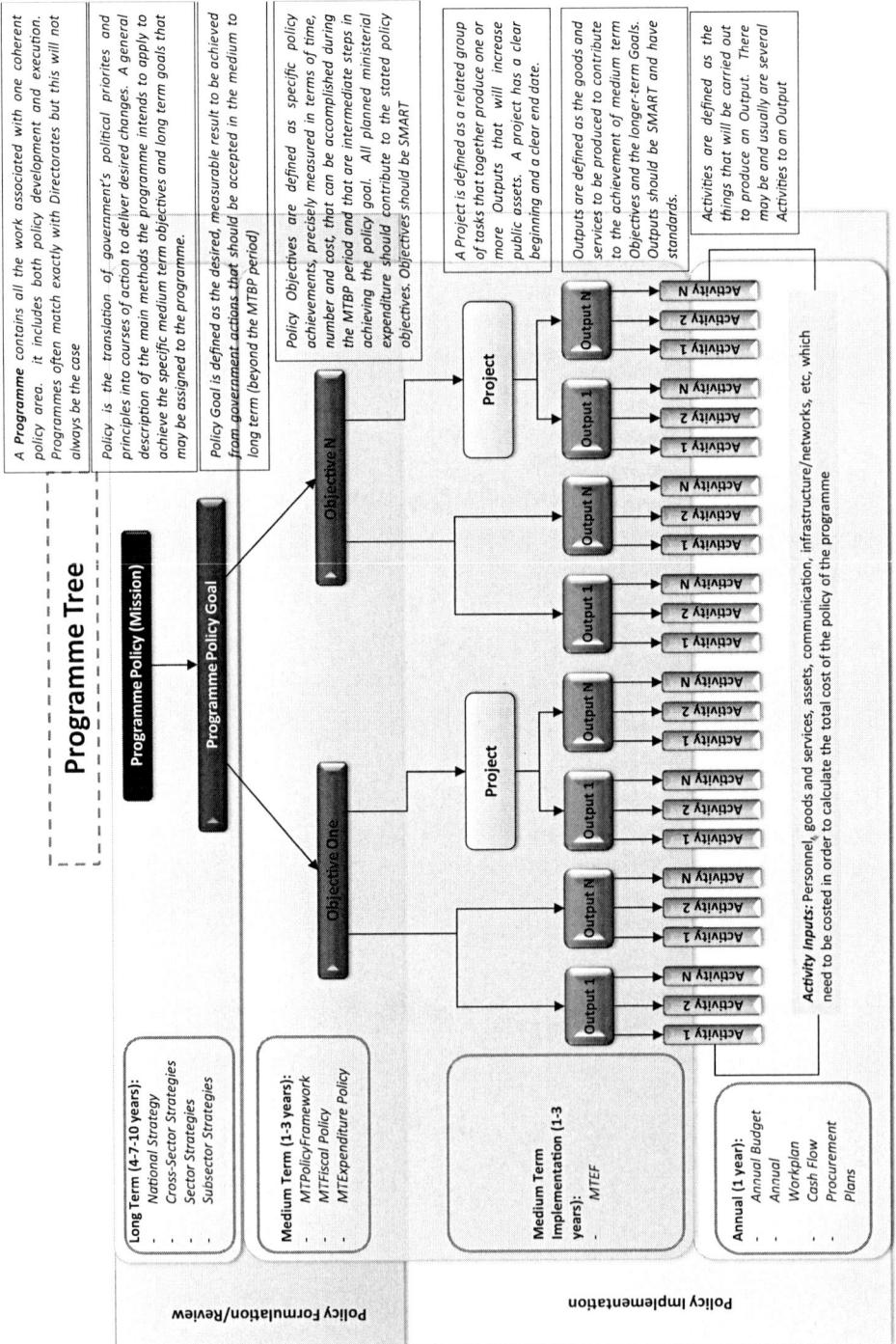

Programme Tree

A **Programme** contains all the work associated with one coherent policy area. It includes both policy development and execution. Programmes often match exactly with Directorates but this will not always be the case

Policy is the translation of government's political priorities and principles into courses of action to deliver desired changes. A general description of the main methods the programme intends to apply to achieve the specific medium term objectives and long term goals that may be assigned to the programme.

Policy Goal is defined as the desired, measurable result to be achieved from government actions that should be accepted in the medium to long term (beyond the MTBP period)

Policy Objectives are defined as specific policy achievements, precisely measured in terms of time, number and cost, that can be accomplished during the MTBP period and that are intermediate steps in achieving the policy goal. All planned ministerial expenditure should contribute to the stated policy objectives. Objectives should be SMART

A Project is defined as a related group of tasks that together produce one or more Outputs that will increase public assets. A project has a clear beginning and a clear end date.

Outputs are defined as the goods and services to be produced to contribute to the achievement of medium term Objectives and the longer-term Goals. Outputs should be SMART and have standards.

Activities are defined as the things that will be carried out to produce an Output. There may be and usually are several Activities to an Output

Programme Policy (Mission)

Programme Policy Goal

Objective One — **Objective N**

Project — Project

Output 1 — Output N (multiple)

Activity 1, Activity 2, Activity N

Long Term (4-7-10 years):
- National Strategy
- Cross-Sector Strategies
- Sector Strategies
- Subsector Strategies

Medium Term (1-3 years):
- MTPolicyFramework
- MTFiscal Policy
- MTExpenditure Policy

Medium Term Implementation (1-3 years):
- MTEF

Annual (1 year):
- Annual Budget
- Annual Workplan
- Cash Flow
- Procurement Plans

Activity Inputs: Personnel, goods and services, assets, communication, infrastructure/networks, etc, which need to be costed in order to calculate the total cost of the policy of the programme

Policy Formulation/Review

Policy Implementation

SMART objective-outcomes should have a baseline which allows for comparison over time so that progress in achieving the objectives can be ascertained.

A Programme Tree then is a diagrammatic way of describing the planned work of a programme to deliver services by a government. It shows how resources allocated to individual tasks (Activities) will eventually lead to the achievement of long-term policy ambitions (Goals). The sum total of the resources allocated to Activities will equal the total budgeted expenditure of the Programme. Or, to put it the other way round, it shows how a statement of a long-term policy ambition (Goal) is converted into a concrete set of tasks (Activities) that will be carried out year-by-year for which the outputs can be measured and monitored to ensure that the intended policy is implemented.

A Programme Tree incorporates every level of budget planning and analysis and covers every item of Programme expenditure. It is the most comprehensive representation of a Programme's link between policy and expenditures. The relationship of all Activities to the policy Goal can be traced through Outputs and Programme Objectives.

What is a Policy Goal?

A Policy Goal is defined as the desired, measurable result to be achieved from government actions that should be achieved in the medium to long term (beyond the MTBP period). A Goal is a long-term target for a Programme. It will be reached at some point beyond the medium term – that is in year 4 or later. Some policies have very long time horizons and these should be reflected in the description of the Goal. For example, implementing a complete anti-smuggling campaign may take a period of up to 10 years as key infrastructure and equipment are put into place and education campaigns are elaborated and rolled out to change perceptions by importers in particular as well as the general public, and so plans for anti-smuggling by the Customs authorities should ideally look up to 10 years into the future.

Goals should be measurable in some way or it will not be possible to know when, or whether, they are achieved. Continuing the anti-smuggling example, reducing smuggling is a goal, but it is difficult to quantify it as it is not specifically measurable. While the impact on customs revenue as a result of an anti-smuggling effort would normally be positive, attributing a share of the revenue increase solely to anti-smuggling is tricky, as there may be many reasons why customs revenue has increased. In this case an alternative measure needs to be sought. For example, the number of arrests and convictions[35] for smuggling is a specific goal related to the anti-smuggling policy and effort, and the increase in these in line with the increase in the anti-smuggling effort is a realistic measurable achievement. Nevertheless, it may be that the number of arrests and convictions will initially grow as the infrastructure for combating smuggling is put in place, but may decline over time as the education campaign becomes effective in tandem with the deterrent impact of the arrests and convictions. Clearly, some thought has to be given to the trajectory of the goal in both the immediate and long term. What are needed is a starting baseline and a realistic set of targets that reflect the anti-smuggling effort and its impact.

An alternative measure would be the value of the goods confiscated as a result of the anti- smuggling campaign and the associated revenues that should have been collected. The key is that the goal should be measured.

Work towards the Goal may already have started. Or it may begin in the medium term. In either case, there should be Objectives that will make progress towards the achievement of the Goal in one of more years in the medium-term. The medium term is the current year (year 0) and the next three years (years 1 to 3).

If a Goal has no Objectives that are linked to it then this means that work towards achieving the Goal will not begin until after the end of the mid-term plan – that is in year 4 at the earliest.

What is a Policy Objective?

Policy Objectives are defined as specific policy achievements, precisely measured in terms of time, number and cost, that can be accomplished during the MTBP period and that are intermediate

---

35   Having arrests solely as a goal is insufficient as arrests could be made without any legitimate justification to satisfy a target. Convictions as a result of an arrest would indicate that the arrest was justified.

steps in achieving a policy Goal. All department expenditures should contribute to the stated policy Objectives

The Objectives define the planned achievements in each year of the medium-term. The medium-term always keeps four years in view – the current year (year 0) and the next three years (years 1 to 3). An Objective may contribute progress towards the achievement of a Goal which will not be completed until the longer term. An Objective may describe the completion of action that was started some years previously. An Objective may describe work that is continued from year to year.

An Objective must state clearly what is planned to be achieved by the end of the year in question. It must be measurable so that it can be subsequently evaluated whether the Objective has been achieved. It is not a description of the means by which to achieve the Objective. The means will appear as Outputs and Activities.

Objectives should be independent of each other so that they can be measured separately without overlap or double counting. It will not be possible to define Outputs and allocate resources if the Objectives are not independent.

Objectives (and goals and outputs) should be SMART in relation to measurement of their objective-outcomes.

To continue the Customs example 'Increase of effectiveness in the collection of customs obligations and the facilitation of customs procedures' is a generalised Objective that cannot be measured. The Objective should show both the change in quantity and any change in quality that the vague 'increase of effectiveness' and 'facilitation" implies.

A more robust approach would be to have two Objectives, the first of which would have two parts. The first Objective would be "Increase effectiveness in the collection of customs obligations by selecting x% of customs entries that enter the country using the channel that only examines documentation and 100-x% that enter using the Channel where both documents and goods are inspected."[36] The number for x would be generated by the risk assessment module, which would reflect the assessed risk of import good categories and importers. A second part to this Objective would

---

36   Using the ASYCUDA software system, a yellow channel is where only documents are inspected while in the red channel physical inspection of good is also undertaken.

be to select y% of imports for post clearance audit. This would be compared to a base line of what was previously realised.

The second Objective would be 'Improve the facilitation of customs procedures by clearing Customs procedures for documentation inspection only imports in "x" minutes and for physical and document inspection channel in "y" minutes'. A standard can be established for the time to clear customs in both the channels. The progress over time will be clear from the change (or maintenance)[37] in time taken to clear customs by importers in each channel. The action necessary to achieve these changes will all appear as Outputs and Activities – new buildings, refurbished buildings, higher staffing ratios, better training for customs officers, installation of software and all its modules and associated hardware, better infrastructure and so on.

What is an Output?

Outputs are the goods and services to be produced to contribute to the achievement of medium term Objectives and the longer-term Goals. Outputs should describe the concrete actions that will deliver the Objectives. The ideal Output is SMART.

Outputs should describe, as far as possible, the situation that will exist when the Output has been implemented – at the end of the year in question or at some specified date during the year.

Example 1: Many Programmes include some kind of training. This might be a short course of a few days or a major degree Programme that takes years to complete; training might be provided in-house or commissioned from an external provider. In all cases, the aim is the same – the trainees/students should emerge with skills and/or knowledge that they did not have previously. And the successful trainees/students receive a qualification or certificate that provides evidence of their success.

Training needs trainers, training rooms and training materials. But these are inputs not Outputs.

The best definition, in this example, is the number of people who complete a specified course well enough to be awarded a qualification/certificate of attainment. This is a good indication of what the

---

37 If the standard has been achieved.

investment in training has produced. Because training courses can differ so much, each training course should probably be described in a separate Output.

Example 2: The annual budget process requires the production of documents to be considered and debated by the country's legislature. These are the draft Annual Budget Law that must pass into legislation before any spending can be incurred. It also may include the MTPB Document that sets out the overall policy and planning framework for the next three years, of which the annual budget is the first year. These are the two main outputs of the budget process.

The relationship between Objectives and Outputs

Each Objective will have one or more Outputs. One Output is unusual.

A common mistake is to confuse Objectives and Outputs. Workers with better qualifications, new buildings, improved technology and communications, the production of reports and surveys may all be very desirable. They may all be absolutely necessary. But achieving them is not an Objective. They are secondary to the policy Objective which might be to improve standards of service, or provide new services.

If there are more Objectives than Outputs, then something has gone wrong. It is probably a case of this confusion.

What is a Policy Standard?

Policy Standards are defined as the quantity and quality parameters that give the policy meaning. Objectives should be delivered to a certain Standard, which may be international, national, or other (such as European Commission (EC)).

Objectives and Outputs must be described in ways that enable the achievement to be measured against the plan. So Standards describe measures that can be used in that process. Every Objective will need Standards to be defined, unless the statement of the Objective (or Output) already contains a full definition of the Standards which apply to it.

The definition of Standards should set out the Standard in full or be summarised such that a non-specialist can understand them and otherwise be referred to in a public and accessible source where the full definition can be found. Public and accessible means a readily available document and/or a website. Users and potential users of services will want to know what to expect and they must be able to obtain the information.

What is a Project?

A Project is defined as a related group of tasks that together produce one or more Outputs that will increase public assets or capacity. The important aspect of a Project is that it has a clear beginning and a clear end and usually involves some transformation. Constructing and bringing into use a new building would be a Project; so would a major improvement in existing buildings. Projects often involve large sums of investment resources, though they usually include a mixture of investment and running costs expenditures. Projects usually need more than one year for their completion, but not necessarily so.

The fact that investment expenditure is involved does not automatically define a Project. There may well be projects that are not of a capital nature such as a training project. It is tempting to define Projects so that they last only one year. It makes it easy to define when a Project is regarded as complete. And it fits in with an annual schedule of contracting. But a Project should be defined in terms that match its own natural life from start to finish.

A Project has a clear end point when its work has been completed. But the end of the Project is not the end of expenditure. All Projects have consequences for the nature and cost of normal business and this must be reflected in the planned expenditure. Resources must be allocated to the Project and to the Outputs and/or Activities that will be needed if the Outputs of the Project are to be used effectively.

What is an Activity?

Activities are defined as the things that will be carried out to produce an Output. There may be and usually are several Activities to an Output. Activities are the basic building blocks in the plan for carrying out policy intentions. Resources must be attached to Activities by economic category (inputs such as wages and salaries, goods and services). So, Activities define the resources that must be assembled to carry out one task that will contribute to the delivery of the specified Outputs in the specified numbers to the specified Standard. In the specification of the MTBP there is no need to go into minute detail in defining Activities. At some point, the annual budget plan will be translated into individual work plans that show what must be done every month or, even, every week. But this degree of detail is needed only for a department's own internal management purposes. Small tasks of a similar nature can all be grouped together in one Activity.

However it is important not to confuse Activities and Objectives. Curriculum development in primary education and research into some aspects of tourism are activities in the primary school Programme and the tourism development Programme respectively.

Every Output must have at least one Activity directly linked to it. An Output with no Activities can have no resources attached to it. The Activities should be sufficient to achieve the targets set for each Output and the specified quality.

Checklists

The following provides a useful set of checklists in applying the elements of the Programme tree with questions to assist in clarifying that the concepts are being applied correctly.

Checklist for Policy Goals

- Does the definition clearly describe a desired policy achievement that will be reached in year 4 or beyond?

- Is the time horizon included in this definition appropriate to the nature of the policy?

- Does the definition include details of how the Goal is to be achieved instead of, or in addition to, the description of the policy achievement? If so, there may be some confusion between ends – which are described in Goals and Objectives – and means that are described in Outputs.

- Are there Objectives that will take forward work towards the achievement of the Goal in one or more of the mid-term years? If not, will the work only in year 4 or beyond?

Checklist for Policy Objectives

- Does each Objective describe the planned achievement of the policy at the end of (or during) the year in question? Do the Objectives describe ends and not means?

- Can the Objective be measured?

- Are the Objectives clearly different from each other?

- Are Outputs that relate to each Objective identified?

- Are the Standards that provide the quality measures defined?

Checklist for Standards

- Is there a quality measure for each Objective? This might be contained in the definition of the Objective itself, or in the Standards or in a combination of both.

- Is there data that will measure achievement of these Standards? If not, what steps must be taken to obtain appropriate data? And what proxy measures or performance indicators can be used meanwhile?

- Are the Standards quoted in full in the MTBP documentation? If not: are they summarised in the MTBP documentation so that a non-specialist can understand them; and are they publicly and easily available? Does the MTBP documentation identify this source?

Checklist for Projects

- Is it absolutely certain that the Project really is a Project? Could it be described more accurately as one Output of a larger Project? Or is it just buying things, which is probably not a Project at all.

- Are all the components specified that must be delivered if the Project is to be completed successfully?

- Are these components defined in Outputs?

- If there is a multi-year Project, can the position planned to be reached at the end of each year be defined?

- Have the running costs that will be incurred after the Project is over been identified?

Checklist for Individual Outputs

- Does the Output describe (more or less) identical entities? If the Output definition includes two or more different things, it cannot be measured or evaluated.

- Are the units in which the Output is measured described precisely? 'Number' is not sufficient. Number of what? – People? Documents? Clients? Audits?

- Is the name of the Output, the description or the unit of measurement includes abbreviations or acronyms, that are comprehensible to all? The content of the MTBP documents will be discussed by many people outside the budget institution itself. And the plans will become public documents because they are included in documents sent to the Legislature and they are published. Explain all abbreviations and acronyms when they first appear.

- If an Output definition was used last year, is it still appropriate? Some Outputs will be valid for several years because they describe accurately work that is continued in every year. Regular production of reports or statistics would be an example. Other definitions must change as other circumstances change. If it is not possible to monitor the Output, then the definition should be re-examined so that progress can be monitored.

- Does the Output definition include a quality Standard – either directly in the definition itself or indirectly by reference to a Standard?

- When the Output definition includes a change – a percentage, or a reduction or increase in numbers – is the baseline that will be used for comparison clearly described? So, 'Reduce absenteeism of full-time employees by 3 percentage points compared to the figure of x% in 2008' but not 'Reduce absenteeism by 3%'.

- Can the performance measure be interpreted unambiguously?

- When Outputs are profiled (over time) could it be done? Some Outputs are produced only once in the year and so only have to appear once in the profile. Most Outputs are produced in the majority, or all, of the months such as monthly expenditure and revenue statements, or in some cases daily, such as bank reconciliations. If progress is to be monitored, then there must be a plan for how many Outputs will be produced in each quarter. If this cannot be done, it is probably because the Output is not expressed in the appropriate units.

- Are data available that will measure an Output in the terms in which the Output is best expressed? For monitoring purposes, data will be needed at various points throughout the year. If implementation of the Output continues through the year, then quarterly data are needed. In other cases, data must match the profile of implementation as outlined above. If data are not available, what measures must be taken to create a regular supply of appropriate data? And what approximate measures can be used meanwhile? In the longer run, the definition of Outputs should not be distorted by the availability (or non-availability) of data. Statistics should be the servant of the policy, not the master, and should be adapted if necessary. This may take a while and pragmatism is needed in the meantime.

- Look at the trend over the 4 years of the MTBP. Does the pattern of units to be implemented, of total expenditure and of unit costs look plausible? Investment expenditure comes in big chunks in some years only and so the pattern of investment expenditure can be very variable. But variability is not expected in other expenditure. A trend should reflect expected levels of inflation, or planned changes in salaries or the running costs consequences of new work or other known changes that will influence the volume of work and/or the combination of resources needed to complete the work. The calculations on the report 'expenditure by Output' show the percentage changes from one year to the next. If variability is detected, can it be explained?

Checklist for Activities

- Can all the available resources be allocated to the Activities that have been identified?

- Is every task to be carried out included in an Activity somewhere? Are all the available resources are allocated to Activities? Anything that does not appear in an Activity does not exist in any practical sense. It may be mentioned scores of times in Strategies, policy documents. But if it has no money it will not happen.

An illustrative example

An illustrative example I often use in training is Agriculture Extension Services:

- Inputs – staff and equipment such as seeds

- Output – number of extension visits/number of hours on extension activity

- Objective-outcomes – increase in number of farmers exposed to "good" practice from baseline. *Exposed* is the objective rather than *using* good practice as the programme can only expose the farmers to good practice – it cannot force them to deliver but just train them to!

- Goal-outcomes – increase in quality and volume of crops from baseline. This cannot be the objective-outcome as there are many external factors such as weather than influence the achievement of the goal outside the control of the extension services programme.

The Budget Preparation Manual that was produced specified all the steps procedures and processes and thc institutional responsibilities to produce the annual budget and its roll over into the following two years.

One output of Trust Fund contract was the production for each ministry a Guide that contained advice on how to produce a good budget plan that can:

- Provide a comprehensive statement of how the Ministry intends to turn policy into action that will inform Government, the Assembly and the public.

- Provide a work programme for everyone who works in the Ministry.

- Be evaluated so that achievement can be compared to plan.

The Guides were designed to complement the Medium Term Budget Programme Operational Manual.[38] The Operational Manual is a detailed guide to the process of preparing a medium-term budget plan and of producing monitoring reports. The processes of planning and monitoring are assisted by the PSHIP software. The guide deals with the work that must be done before the PSHIP software can be used. It is a practical tool for the Ministry to use in defining the content of the plan – the way in which Programme Policies, Goals, Objectives, Standards, Projects, Outputs and Activities are defined and linked together so that they provide a clear narrative. The translation of policy Goals into practical action should be transparent.

The Guide provided definitions, illustrative examples of good and weak practice – all of which are taken from real life in Albania – and a checklist of points to review before the user approaches the computer. Where they are relevant, examples of good practice from other countries are included. One programme in the ministry was taken as an example to specify the inputs into the programme tree for that illustrative programme.

The guidebook was intended for anyone who is involved in the Medium Term Budget Programme in a budget institution. It was designed to be useful at all stages in the process, but in particular in the following circumstances:

- General Secretary/Director General – for monitoring implementation of the plan for the current year; for quality control of the plan for years 1-3.

- Group for Strategy Budget and Integration – for monitoring the plan for the current year and approving any changes that

---

38   All the Guides had been placed on the Ministry of Finance website but a search for this document could not locate them which suggested that they are no longer publically available.

might be necessary; for review of the draft plan for years 1-3 and considering any changes that might be necessary.

- Heads of Programme Management Teams – for monitoring the plan for the current year and deciding whether changes are necessary; for production of plan for years 1-3

- Members of Programme Management Teams – in producing detailed MTBP plans for years 1-3; for reviewing progress on the plan for the current year; and reviewing the effectiveness of definitions, measures and indicators being used.

- Newcomers to the MTBP and anyone involved in training people about the MTBP.

I produced the Guidebook for the Ministry of Finance following the structure that had been developed and outlined above.

The Climate Change PEFA fieldwork in December 2021 has provided an opportunity to assess progress. The linkages between the Integrated Planning process, sector strategies, the MTBP and the annual budget are coordinated and effective within the budget calendar particularly on the financial aspects. The process has been partially rolled out to the subnational entities. However there does seem to be lacunae regarding outputs and objectives as sector and budget staff members responsible for programmes do not always collaborate. Often indicators are specified for specification sake rather than reflecting realistic aspirations.

Beyond Albania

I contributed to the development of the budget process in other countries in the region. In Serbia I was asked along with Martin Johnston by DFID Serbia to review its project: Towards the more effective implementation of reforms. We carried out a review of the pilot stage and made recommendations for the 2006 work programme. This involved extensive consultation with participating institutions (both commissioning and recipients) including two workshops to discuss findings and recommendations to plan 2006 programme for Yearly Operational Plan of Action in recipient ministries for all participants. This review was followed up by Martin

Johnston advising the Ministry of Finance on the role of programme budgeting in the Public Expenditure Management process and the means by which programme budgeting may best be designed and implemented in Serbia. In Moldova I carried out a mid-term review assessment and evaluation for the Ministry of Finance of the PFM project that includes the introduction of an Integrated Financial Management Information System (IFMIS), improved budget preparation and execution, introduction of internal audit and the development of related training.

Apart from Albania, Kosovo was the country I was most active in the aspect of PFM covered in this section. However my involvement in Kosovo did not get off to an auspicious start. I was asked by DFID to work with the World Bank on providing support to the inter-ministerial team developing sustainable employment policy in the context of a multi-donor budget support operation led by the World Bank. I interpreted this as it was the inter-ministerial team that was preparing the policy and I pushed for hands-on support to the Government team. This conflicted with the way the World Bank saw the support and it was clear that there was an impasse as the World Bank was happy to produce and hand the policy documentation to the Government. I also was not convinced of the country's need to borrow in this way, given the alternatives which often were in the form of grants – the Bank was being a bank! I approached Valbona Bogujevci and Mark Poston of DFID Kosovo and reported that I thought it would be better if I did not continue and this was agreed (I suspect the Bank had also conveyed that message to DFID as well!) However, DFID Kosovo had other plans for me and I was assigned to work with the Ministry of Finance on the Central Government PEFA which is covered in the next Chapter.

Post Kosovo PEFAs I was involved in a series of interrelated areas. I assisted the Ministry of Finance with budget and MTEF reform through facilitating exchanges with the Ministry of Finance Albania in lesson learning from the reform process supported by presentations. Much of the support was enhanced by bringing in Albanian members (Sybi Hida, Saimir Sallaku and Arjeta Abazi) of the Albania MTBP Team and workshops were by and large conducted in Albanian. I was the team leader on the public expenditure review that examined Labour and Welfare, and Private Sector Development (Ministry of Trade and Industry) expenditures linking objectives to outputs for MTEF and annual budget with Paul Harnett and our Albanian colleagues and Alban Kaçiu our local Kosovar consultant.

I then became the team leader for DFID's support to reformulation of the MTEF leading inputs into the production of and training on a policy costing manual, template and manual on linking strategic planning to MTEF and impact analysis of new policy initiatives and associated training, including a training programme for inductees into budget departments. The training aspect is covered in detail in Chapter 8.

Kosovo's Ministry of Finance had had support over the years from the United States Agency for International Development (USAID) and had developed an impressive budget execution system built around a Treasury Single Account and an Integrated Financial Management Information System (IFMIS). The IFMIS project was started with installation of initial modules (General ledger, Appropriations, Expenditure controls) and training on applications with addressing change management as a key element. The underlying philosophy was Think BIG, start small: the project was developed in phases ensuring successful implementation at each stage before moving on to new modules (Purchasing, Revenue, Assets, Inventory) and further ministerial roll out. It has been a success and the impact can be seen on commitment control and in-year reporting of budget execution and annually, leading to audited accounts within the year.[39]

The budget preparation process and associated software were much behind Albania even though the downstream aspects were much more advanced. There was a MTEF and indeed the PFM Law was such that it supported an MTBP. Yet despite an experienced USAID Advisor (initially Kris Kauffman and then Bruce Reid) in situ in the Budget Department sharing an office with the Director, the next step of budget reform was not undertaken. It can be concluded that for whatever reason the Director was resistant to change even though in the Prime Minister's Office a fledging Integrated Planning System was beginning to take shape into which the planning manual and associated training that was produced by the DFID project that I led contributed.

Both Albania and Kosovo made significant investment in motorways during the time I was working in both countries which is a good example of the prioritisation of investment expenditure that both countries channelled through the budget process. These investments opened up both countries internally and ensured that

---

39   https://pfmboard.com/index.php?topic=106.0

the time taken to travel by road from Pristina to Tirana was cut to less than three hours. The motorway on the Albanian side through the mountains with its bridges, viaducts and twin tunnels is a feat of engineering which brought the relatively isolated Kukes in touch with rest of the country. This was followed on the Kosovo side by the Pristina to the border motorway skirting Prizren. Prior to these motorways, the route between Pristina and Tirana was through what is now North Macedonia and around Lake Ohrid and through Pogradec and Elbasan.

In 2017 I was asked by Sandeep Saxena of IMF FAD whom I had worked with in Myanmar and the Caribbean to use my experiences to assist the Department for Budget Management in the Philippines in reviewing budget preparation practices and translating them into a manual to guide the various agencies. I produced a manual based on the Albania and Kosovo material covering the budget calendar, fiscal table, taxation and revenue estimation, costing analysis, and applying the programme tree to the existing programme structure.

Sequencing

The realisation of an MTEF/MTPB has to be placed in the context of sequencing of PFM reforms. Jack Diamond in Good Practice Note on Sequencing PFM Reforms[40] states that "sequencing decisions should focus on three main PFM priorities determined by the principle deliverables of a PFM system. Historical experience suggests that reform actions should focus on three main PFM deliverables in the following order: first, ensuring some minimal level of financial compliance (fiscal control); secondly, improving fiscal stability and sustainability; thirdly, improving the efficiency and effectiveness in service delivery. These top level priorities, determining the overall sequencing strategy, should be the same for all countries. Within this strategic view, it is argued, specific reform actions can be taken to achieve a top-level priority, determined and sequenced based on country circumstances. At this lower level there is no universal ideal sequence for PFM reforms. A hierarchy in prioritization should be recognized at the top level. For example, a core level of compliance with budgetary legislation, financial regulations and

---

40   Commissioned by the PEFA Secretariat. It can be downloaded from https://pfmboard.com/index.php?topic = 6475.0

procedures is required to attain the planned fiscal deficit, an important requirement for ensuring macroeconomic stability. Compliance and macroeconomic stability in turn support efficient and effective service delivery. Attempting to leapfrog this hierarchy in the top PFM priorities will likely lead to unsuccessful reforms. For example, attempting to improve service delivery, say by introducing results-based budgeting reforms, when adequate financial control is lacking or there is undue instability in resource availability, is unlikely to be successful, and could prove counterproductive".

The diagram below shows that programme budgeting is at the end of a long line of reform actions. Everything in the fifth column encapsulates the holy grail of a full MTEF/MTPB. The fourth column was in place before the fifth column was embarked upon in Albania and Kosovo even though some of the first three columns such as full accrual accounts were not in place.[41] Indeed I used this diagram in a presentation in September 18th 2012 titled Public Financial Management: Where is Kosovo today and where is it going? And named it: The Road to Nirvana with the explanation of Nirvana as – Paradise, Heaven, Illusion, Fantasy! An MTBF as depicted is thus strictly linked to policy and is anchored in sector MTEF/MTBPs. It is developed at a more detailed level, with full integration of recurrent and investment costs of programmes projected in the outer years of the budget cycle. The associated fiscal strategy should also include non-financial performance ("results based") information linked to programme budgets. This programmatic approach represents the highest level of budget planning, and should be viewed as the furthest stage in the evolution of PFM towards greater emphasis on efficiency and effectiveness in resource use.

The Kosovo presentation highlighted that the MTEF/MTBP is usually associated with a more decentralized budget management regime, relying heavily on agencies' capacity to fully harmonize strategic planning and budgeting activities, and where they are expected to operate in a performance management regime. The overall focus on the presentation was on the systemic risks relating to the overall reform environment; the institutional factors that

---

41   The debate on accounts – cash, modified or accrual is outside my scope of competences or, more to the point, interest. The IMF has a How to Note: Implementing Accrual Accounting in the Public Sector Prepared by Joe Cavanagh, Suzanne Flynn, and Delphine Moretti (who led the Antigua PEFA I worked on and with whom I did the PEFA training) https://www.imf.org/external/pubs/ft/tnm/2016/tnm1606.pdf

determine how well reforms will be received and implemented; and the organizational factors and Human Resource factors that often impose constraints on the extent of implementation of reform. The factors influencing risks were addressed including the number of institutions involved; the time required for implementation; scope of reform actions; the degree of behavioural change implied; and the degree of visibility in the final results. Not an easy and quick task to undertake, but well worthwhile when realised. Gëzuar!

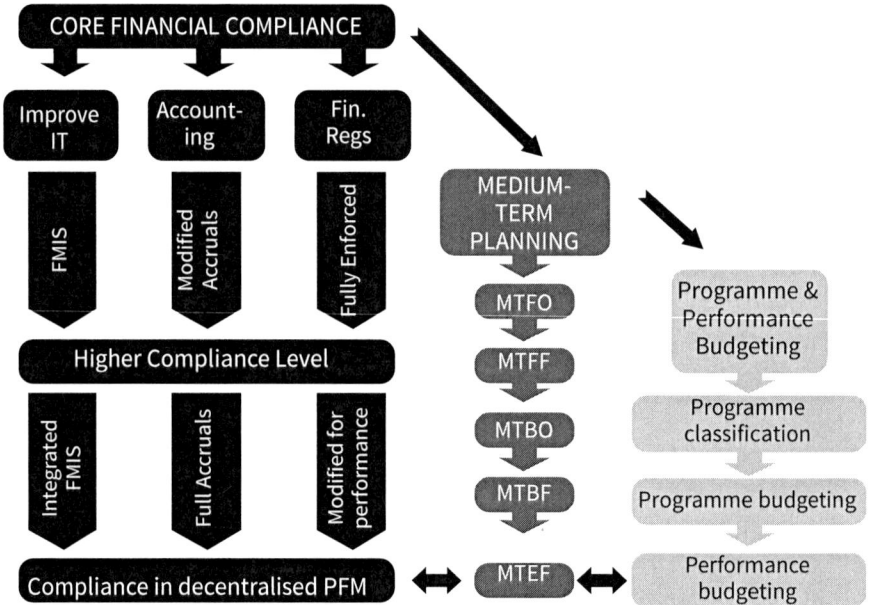

MTFO is medium term fiscal outlook. MTFF is medium term fiscal framework. MTBO is medium term budget outlook. MTBF is medium term budget framework.

5 THE COSTING OF PROGRAMMES

Rolling over existing programmes and new initiatives

One of the major differences between existing programmes that are rolled-over and new policy initiatives is that existing programmes by dint of being already in the budget should have been specified in terms of activities and inputs and should have been costed appropriately.[42] New policy initiatives need to be costed. While costing is a topic in its own right and may well require a manual or manuals for individual departments there are some general processes and procedures that can be applied to costing. For the work I carried out in Kosovo a costing manual was produced to guide the development of programme budgeting and I used this for the budget preparation manual that I worked on in the Philippines. The Albania sector planning guides referred to costing of activities in each guide.

In the context of this document costing has to be factored in relation to the linkages already outlined in earlier chapters so as to complete the picture.

- Policy initiatives are proposed to deliver elements of the government's programme that was presented to an electorate, included in any National Development Plan or are in response to changing circumstances caused by events.

- Policy initiatives are best addressed in terms of what they aim to achieve in the present, the near and medium term and the long term.

- What is to be achieved should be concrete and measured and related to time so it can be assessed in terms of delivery.

- How it is achieved is best related to specific outputs or accomplishments that can also be measured and related to time.

---

42   If this has not been done or has been done superficially the rolling over process should address this.

- The realisation of the policy deliverables – both measurable policy objectives and the associated outputs – can only be achieved through a set of activities or actions.

- These activities require resources – inputs for their realisation.

- These inputs are purchased and have an associated cost.

- Government assigns expenditure to allow their purchase.

- Expenditure has to be budgeted in terms of affordability – how much revenue is available.

The issue of costing is centred on answering the question:

Are all the resources that are appropriate to the development and implementation of the programme tree related to the policy initiative included in the specification of the activities? These should include:

- expenditures on all the personnel associated with the activities

- all the other expenditures associated with the activities

- all Projects that are concerned with this policy.

Inputs and their cost of policies will be driven by attributes of what the policy is attempting to achieve and the associated standards. The specification of these inputs is best determined by the specialist in the individual Departments and any sector specialists in a Budget Department as a full understanding of the drivers of inputs and costs is required. If these skills are not available in-house they should be imported on a consultancy basis.

Drivers of Cost

Cost drivers will vary from Department to Department and even within Departments depending on the policy initiative. For example for Education Services, the numbers of students at each level of education will be critical and these numbers are mainly derived from demographic projections. But also important will be the standards such as pupil teacher ratios, book/computer to pupil ratios etc.

For Health Services the numbers of potential users requires demographic projections and analysis of the standards of health and incidence of sickness. However, it is important also to distinguish between curative and preventive health services as the drivers of the latter may well be different from the former.

For Social Services, the number of claimants is the cost driver. Claimants include pensioners, unemployed, the poor and disabled. The number of pensioners can be derived from demographic projections, the number of unemployed from projections of the unemployment rate, and the number of poor from projections of poverty levels.

The requirement for police services depends on the potential amount of crime and antisocial behaviour as well as the desired level of action. The requirement for prisons depends on the number of prisoners, though the relationship is one of interdependence. The requirement for justice services can be divided into the requirement for commercial and criminal justice services. The former requires an analysis of the legal environment with regard to commercial activities. The latter is partially derived from the requirement for police services.

Road Transport Services are driven by the numbers of cars and other vehicles. Projections of these derive from estimates of demand, based on demographic trends and income levels. The higher are incomes, the higher the demand for cars, and the greater the demand for road space. Growth in the economy will likely give rise to more commercial traffic as goods are sold domestically and are exported and imported. In road building standards will be an important determinant of costs and these should be clearly set out in the specification which will require detailed analysis and indeed policy debate. Lower standards at the building stage may well mean increased maintenance costs on an annual basis in the recurrent budget which have to be included in the forward estimates.

Agriculture services are largely defined through agricultural policy. The number of farmers, the size of farms and the types of crops and livestock are obvious cost drivers and these should be projected. If policy is to give production subsidies, then the type of crop or livestock that is being subsidized is a key factor. If it is publicly provided, such as extension services or research, requirements from farmers as a whole can be estimated through analysis of their needs. The estimated requirements are the cost drivers.

Industry and the services sector may also benefit from public funding designed to help overcome initial barriers to entering business; assistance to small businesses is an example. The requirements must first be identified and projected, and these are the cost drivers. Similarly with investment and export promotion, assessing target areas and what is needed for their penetration will drive the cost.

For Public Finance Management Services, Department of Finance and Budget Department tasks are the main cost drivers; as well as that, is the work of the revenue collecting agencies. These are in the areas of tax and macro/fiscal policy formulation, annual budget preparation, revenue collection, budget execution according to the budget plan, and accounting for spending. These tasks are the cost drivers.

All of these will be described in an activity which will in turn be broken down into their component inputs and the cost of the inputs. A detailed project structure will be needed to generate the programme tree in terms of each Department. Having a list of activities enables Departments to identify the resources needed to complete them. There are several types of resources that need to be identified: staff, materials and services, and equipment.

The time frame should also be assessed. If the policy is completed in less than one year, one year or more than one year – the contributing activities needed to be costed over the relevant time period.

People-related Expenditures

People are the most valuable resource that a budget institution has. In some budget institutions, salaries and related costs form a very high percentage of total expenditures. But the fact that they are precious and expensive resources does not make paying people an Output. People are a necessary contribution to the achievement of an Output, not an Output in their own right. So, mostly, salaries and other people-related expenditures are included within Activities where they are clearly identifiable in the appropriate expenditure classification.[43]

---

43   It is possible that the recruitment of new personnel might be an Output within a Project – that is, recruitment is one component necessary to the successful completion of a Project. After the end of the Project, paying salaries becomes a normal part of everyday business and is treated as described above.

For a given activity, the Department needs to identify which staff category people should work to complete it, and for how much time. This will enable the ability to calculate the cost of wages and salaries for the activity. For a leaflet design, for example, a designer is needed, which may be a member of staff, but if it is done through a contractor, it would be included in goods and services. For certain tasks, existing staff may need to be trained in order for them to contribute to the realisation of the policy. This will count as additional cost to performing the activity, but if the training is done in-house it will be included as staff costs but if it is contracted out the cost will be included under goods and services.

So clear specification is important! The key factors are:

- Specify number of people to deliver the policy – in as much detailed as possible breaking down by categories such as management, technical, support

- Specify salary – average for each category based on existing scales

- Specify associated personnel cost, such as pensions related to each category based on existing scales.

- There may be legislation adopted or in the process of being adopted which may impact the cost of personnel costs, therefore this type of information needs to be factored into the process of estimating costs.

Goods and Services as Inputs

Some activities also require material to be expended in order to complete them. Examples may be office material, construction material, etc. For each activity identified, the amount of material required to complete it should be calculated. Use the same logic for calculating purchase of services.

Again clear specification is important! The key factors are:

- Specify the goods and services required to deliver the policy

- List items and amount

- Prices of items

Allocate a portion of total costs of utilities to the activity, on basis of an estimate or proportional allocation of total costs that may be incurred for normal operations of the Department or organization.

There may be legislation adopted or in the process of being adopted which may impact the cost of resources. An increase of VAT, for example, may drive prices upwards; therefore this type of information should be collected and factored into the process of estimating costs.

Transfers

The treatment of transfers is centred on their purpose. Are there transfers to certain groups to deliver the policy? What is the basis for the transfers? How are they measured? What is the number of recipients?

So, clear answers to these questions are needed for specification. If the policy is to increase support to farmers by providing production subsidies, then the likely number of recipients, the amount that they produce of the subsidized item and the unit subsidy amount is required. If it is the introduction of a welfare scheme, the number of likely recipients and the unit payment is required.

The Treatment of Investment Expenditure

Major capital works, such as new building or large-scale refurbishment, are Projects. They meet the definition of a Project as a set of actions with a clear beginning and a clear end that together bring about some transformation.

Other investment expenditure is not a Project. Buying things – furniture, equipment, and vehicles – is part of normal business and continues in every year, or in most years. It is just like buying other goods and services. The purchase is a necessary contribution to the achievement of an Output and is therefore an Activity.

Some activities require purchase of equipment, such as any machinery, vehicles, etc. Cost is to be calculated in the same way as the use of other materials. If the activity requires use of capital equipment that already has been purchased, and the equipment will be consumed and needs to be replaced at the end of the planned initiative, the cost should be calculated in terms of replacing the equipment. If, however, existing equipment is being used which will be used further after completion of activities, the cost should not be taken into account, unless the use has seriously impaired the life-time use of the equipment. Clearly some judgement has to be made. However, if a cash budget is in operation rather than an accrual budget only if direct expenditure is made on capital items would they be included as a cost and only in the time period that the payments have been made.

As noted the development of the MTBP as a budgetary tool along-side the annual budget has implications for the investment process. Not only should the capital cost of a project and the timescale of its expenditure implementation annually be a consideration but also should be the recurrent cost of implementation once the capital phase has been completed. Both of these need to be included in the forward projections of expenditure so as to ensure that these can be accommodated within the forward fiscal table and resource forecasts. It should be a must that the financing of a project over its lifetime is catered for – if it is not, the project should not be included in the annual budget and MTBP. However it is also essential that the recurrent cost of implementing a project, say a school or hospital, are catered for as well. The investment costs may well be funded by a donor but the recurrent costs are likely to fall on the Government. These must therefore be included in the affordability of the investment decision.

The implementation of an MTBP necessitates that all agencies develop estimates of not only the annual expenditure on projects to completion but also the running (O & M) expenditure once a project is up and running.

The generation of the cost of an activity from the bottom-up is depicted in the Figure 'Calculating the Costs for an Activity'.

Apportionment

Inputs appropriately costed – must be allocated to Activities and thus to Outputs and these would then be the expenditure on that activity and the output. Much of the time, this allocation of expenditures is straightforward. When a clearly identifiable agency is wholly responsible for the delivery of one Activity, and one Activity only, then the resources needed to deliver the Activity will be easily identifiable.

Calculating the Costs for an Activity

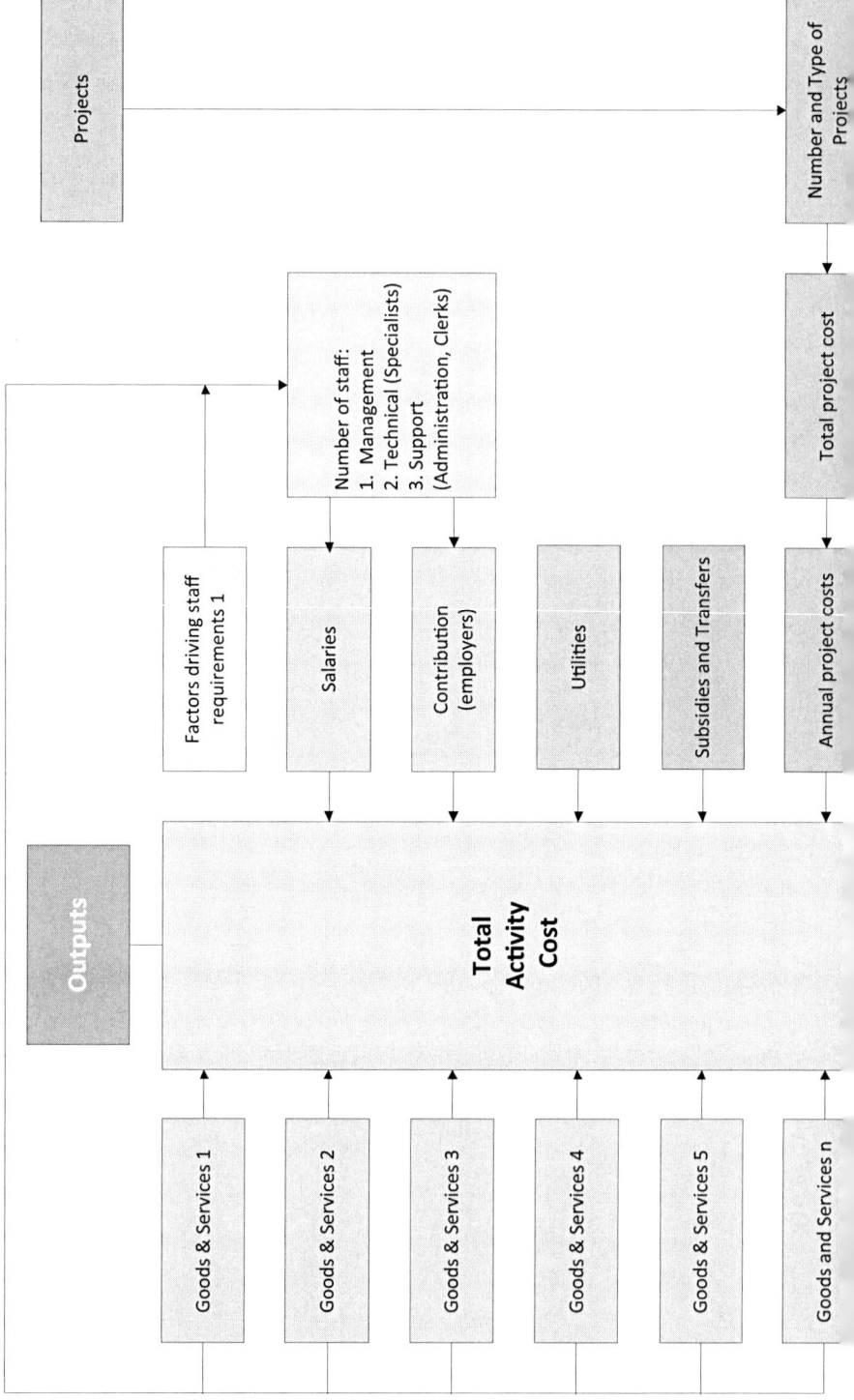

Projects → Number and Type of Projects → Total project cost → Annual project costs

Factors driving staff requirements 1

Number of staff:
1. Management
2. Technical (Specialists)
3. Support (Administration, Clerks)

Salaries

Contribution (employers)

Utilities

Subsidies and Transfers

Total Activity Cost

Outputs

Goods & Services 1

Goods & Services 2

Goods & Services 3

Goods & Services 4

Goods & Services 5

Goods and Services n

It is less straightforward when the same group of resources (people, equipment, etc.) is used to deliver two or more activities. In this case, the resources must be divided among the Activities as accurately as possible. This is apportionment. It is the process of estimating what proportion of the total expenditures should be allocated to each Activity. This has to be clearly specified by carrying out some analysis of the time spent on each activity, noting the marginal nature of the input.

Minor Items: It is possible to allocate all costs among Activities and Outputs. But sometimes the sums involved are so small that it is not efficient to spend a lot of time making the calculations.

Example: cars. Where a person, or a Department, has the exclusive use of a vehicle, then the cost of that vehicle, including fuel and the cost of the driver, can easily be allocated to a specific activity. Where a fleet of cars is maintained for use, as required, by everyone in the budget institution, and the usage of motor vehicles is not a major requirement of any Department's activities then it is probably not worthwhile to separate out the expenditures into all activities provided the New Policy Initiative's staffing requirements are minimal.

Example: electricity. If a building is occupied by a single Department or by a single subordinate institution, then the expenditure on maintaining the building, including the expenditure on electricity, can easily be allocated to a Programme. It may be straightforward to apportion the costs to activities using the percentage of total workers employed on the Activity. If a building is occupied by many Departments and sectors, working on lots of different Activities, then this procedure is too time-consuming to be worthwhile provided the New Policy Initiative's staffing requirements are minimal.

Contingency: For certain projects or initiatives, there may be some uncertainty as to the exact number of units of inputs required to deliver an output. There may also be a degree of uncertainty on the price of these units particularly if they are subject to world markets and currency fluctuations particularly if priced in US$ or sourced from countries with a different currency. It is advisable to calculate a contingency sum for each of the inputs. The assumptions underlying the contingency should be clearly specified and be defended.

Sources of Information: Organizations should have a base of information regarding historical costs of materials, staff, contracts, equipment etc., which they can obtain from previous project or programme operations files. Historical price quotations and contracts can be used, project reports which indicate the amount of resources used for certain initiatives, historical financial reports which provide ideas as to how much certain activities cost in the past. Be aware that historical information needs to be adjusted to current and future conditions. Keep in mind the time schedule of the project and the likely increases in prices or any other external conditions that may impact cost of activities.

Simple market research can be performed to obtain prices for the materials or services necessary for completing the cost of activities. It may be possible to reach out to vendors and obtain some price quotations for cost estimating purposes. The Procurement Unit could be a source of prices for certain common services.

Distinguishing between Unit Input Costs and Unit Output Costs

Often there is the temptation to apply a unit cost to a number such as a related output to generate a total cost, but it important that care is taken applying unit cost from another source to an existing situation. For instance, it is likely that a cost per kilometre of road may be available from a road that was constructed previously. In examples of roads, mention has been made of different types of roads and standards; however, using a unit cost from one situation to another may well be fraught with danger as like must be compared with like. At best an indicative cost might be obtained. The cost of roads is usually calculated at the end of a long study by engineers and transport planners who will specify and design the characteristics of the road including standards. And even then it will be subject to a competitive bidding process and contract.

Indeed in discussing unit costs, it is important to distinguish between unit input costs and unit output costs. Unit output cost is the cost of the outputs that the policy intends to deliver divided by the number of units delivered. In a primary education example, the unit output cost would be the total cost of primary school enrolment divided by the number of students enrolled.

A simple unit output cost would be insufficient of itself, however, to be the basis for an unambiguous costing of policies or programmes. It would need to be accompanied by a range of policy standards which would describe the quality parameters for the delivery of the output. These would include in the case of primary education, for example, the average pupil-teacher ratio, the nature and quantity of teaching equipment (books, pens, computers, etc.), the standard to which primary school teachers are to be trained, average school size, and so on.

Unit input costs are the unit costs of the various inputs that are required to fund the activities for a particular programme or sub-programme. Unit input costs in primary education would include, for example, average teacher wages, average cost of a set of school textbooks, etc. This concept is the focus of this section on costing.

Once a particular policy and its associated output have been defined, a given set of activities will be required to deliver this policy output as discussed. These activities would include in the case of primary education, for example, the training of primary school teachers (to maintain the current numbers of trained teachers in the sector or to expand this number as required depending upon policy objectives), and the teaching of primary school children.

In turn, a given quantity of unit inputs will be required to deliver the requisite level of activity in each area for the policy goal to be achieved. A given number of teachers would need to be employed (subject, for example, to physical constraints on supply) to deliver primary school teaching services to the required number of students according to a given pupil-teacher ratio. The unit cost of primary teachers (i.e. average primary school wages) multiplied by the required number of teachers would then describe a significant component of the total cost of delivering the policy goal.

Multiplying each unit input cost by the number of units required will determine the total cost of the desired policy output. Dividing this total cost by the target output gives the target unit output cost. The underlying unit cost model can then be used to modify policy objectives as appropriate. This may involve, for example, estimating the cost of expanding the target output (e.g. primary school enrolment, kilometres of road construction, etc.) by 10 per cent.

Or, for example, it may involve estimating the extent to which the existing policy would have to be scaled back if the unit cost model were to reveal a financing gap between the total cost of the policy and the total resources available to fund it (or, the resources that would need to be switched out of other uses to maintain the policy commitment under this circumstance.)

For many policy objectives, factors influencing the demand for a given service will have implications for the scope of the associated policy. In the case of primary education, for example, the number of students requiring primary education services is a function of the number in the primary age group (i.e. the cohort of students), the number repeating and the number dropping out during the progress of the cohort through the system. As this number changes the number of students that need to be catered for under the policy target will change also. With knowledge of the unit output cost (as derived from a unit cost model for example), the change in funding requirements under the budget and the MTBP resulting from changes in the scope of the policy would be known also.

A unit costing model would also permit the funding consequences of other underlying changes to the scope of the policy to be estimated. If policy standards change, this is likely to affect the total cost of the policy. An active policy to lower the primary school dropout rate, for example, would increase the projected numbers in the cohort, with consequences for the total cost of the policy. Another example (from a different sector) would be the standard width of trunk roads. As this width varies, the unit output cost of a kilometre of road construction would vary also.

6 FIDUCIARY RISK ASSESSMENTS AND PEFAS

The move from balance of payment support to budget support changed the partnership relationship between the suppliers and recipient of financial support. The financial support was not tied to any transaction or support to a particular project but was akin to general taxation receipts that financed the budget as a whole (general budget support) or a specific sector (education/health sector budget support).

Most, if not all, budget support operations were part of a Structural Adjustment Programme and had conditions attached usually related to policy and institutional reform in the recipient country. These conditions were negotiated prior to the finalisation of the agreement and transfer of the funds. Often conditions were designed to help a Ministry of Finance implement policies that it wished to enact but found difficult to get wider political acceptance. This certainly was the case in Uganda on the adjustment programmes that I worked on. As budget support was usually released in tranches, the releases were tied to meeting conditionality, but often that was fudged! Those policies that were forced on a government tended to be problematic. I remember being part of team in Ethiopia and the team leader attempted to change the agreed conditions on investment promotion policy and the Minister of Finance stood up, said no, and left the room. The conditionality was not altered.

Over the years, I was a team member on structural adjustment programmes in Nigeria, Uganda, Sierra Leone, Rwanda, Zambia, Malawi, Papua New Guinea and Vietnam for DFID and the World Bank and carried out evaluations of the EC programmes in Tanzania and Malawi.

However, the focus of this Chapter is on the tools that have been developed to ensure that funds supplied enter the budget and are accounted for and not diverted to other uses. The ones that I have worked on are DFID's Fiduciary Risk Assessment (FRA) and the multi country Public Expenditure and Financial Accountability

(PEFA) Assessment and its predecessor the Public Expenditure Management Country Assessment and Action Plan. There are others.[44]

Fiduciary Risk Assessment

In the pre-PEFA days DFID assessed the formulation of the budget, payment control, accountancy and auditing arrangement in a country as part of its budget support assessment. I carried out such an analysis in Kenya in 2001 for Nick Dyer who was in the DFID regional office in Nairobi. As there was no standard methodology as well as documented procedures, the work was very demanding of officials particularly tracing payment procedures and decisions from authorisation to approval and their verification process. DFID started in 2002 to produce direction on Fiscal Risk and issued Guidance Notes and How to Notes in 2004 with updates in 2006, 2008, 2009. In June 2011 DFID issued a detailed and extensive How to Note Managing Fiduciary Risk when Providing Financial Aid. This note defines fiduciary risk as the risk that funds are not used for the intended purposes; do not achieve value for money; and/or are not properly accounted for. The realisation of fiduciary risk can be due to a variety of factors, including lack of capacity, competency or knowledge; bureaucratic inefficiency; and/or active corruption. The Note distinguished between a PEFA and a FRA in that the PEFA Framework was seen as an indicator-based evaluation which provides information about the current strengths and weaknesses of the national PFM system. The DFID FRA uses this and other information to inform judgements about the levels of fiduciary and corruption risk in using national PFM systems and records how risks are being managed. The Note specifies that a PEFA assessment should be the main mechanism for gathering data on PFM performance, and provides important input for discussions with government and other partners on PFM reform priorities. In the absence of a PEFA assessment, the Note specifies that a FRA should follow the

---

44   Such as IMF's Fiscal Transparency Code https://blog-pfm.imf.org/files/ft-code.pdf and joint World Bank and IMF Report on the Observance of Standards and Codes (ROSC) https://www.worldbank.org/en/programs/rosc. The Department of Foreign Affairs and Trade of Australia's (DFAT) approach is similar to that of DFID.

8 Good Practice Principles and 15 benchmarks (that are set out in an Annex) that cover the same ground as a PEFA.[45]

As well as the FRA in Kenya, I carried out FRAs for DFID in Palestine in 2004, Moldova in 2006, 2008 and 2009, Serbia in 2009 and Kosovo in 2009. As specified in the How to Notes the main source of PFM information is the PEFA assessments which was started in 2005. The sources of information on corruption have to be indirect as a consultant cannot go up to someone who is rumoured to be on the take and ask questions![46] Surveys by various agencies in a country are essential in this regard. Surveys carried out by Transparency International are a useful source. Transparency International produces an index of corruption perception annually which scores and ranks countries in terms of the degree to which corruption is perceived to exist among public officials and politicians. It is a composite index drawing on corruption-related data in expert surveys carried out by a variety of reputable institutions. It reflects the views of business people and analysts from around the world, including experts who are resident in the countries evaluated. Transparency International also produces a Bribe Payers Index. It also produces the *Global Corruption Barometer* which presents the main findings of a public opinion survey that explores the general public's views of corruption, as well as experiences of bribery around the world. It assesses the extent to which key institutions and public services are perceived to be corrupt, measures citi-

---

45   The How to Note Guide can be found at
https://www.gov.uk/government/publications/
how-to-note-managing-fiduciary-risk-when-providing-financial-aid

46   The only time I was ever confronted for a payment in all the countries visited was in Lagos. I was at the airport returning home and, as was the norm, all bags were searched. There was a few old Naira in my case left over from a previous trip as the Government had changed the notes in the meantime. These should have been destroyed so were confiscated. I was sitting on the British Caledonian (BCal) plane when the bag searcher came on board and told me to follow him. The BCal crew told me to take my carryon bag with me indicating that if I was not back by the time they were due to leave – tough! I was taken through the airport to a supervisor who shook his head and told the guy to get me back on the plane. I took this guy by the arm and dragged him through security and made the flight! He was clearly after a bribe which he did not get. Given the number of times I visited Nigeria this suggests that its reputation is perhaps not as bad as it is made out. No other examples also point to positives in other countries. The excellent communicator on economics and statistics Tim Harford in Chapter 8 Why Poor Countries are Poor in his book The Undercover Economist makes an understandable issue of bribes in his discussion of development, if with a little too much emphasis relative to other issues such as bad policy.

zens' views on government efforts to fight corruption, and includes questions about the level of state capture and people's willingness to pay a premium for clean corporate behaviour. The Barometer is designed to complement the expert opinions on public sector corruption provided by the *Corruption Perceptions Index* and the views of senior business executives on international bribery flows reflected in the *Bribe Payers Index.*

The European Bank for Reconstruction and Development – World Bank Business Environment and Enterprise Performance Survey examines corruption in interactions between the state and firms. The survey asks enterprise managers about a broad range of issues, of which corruption is a small sub-set. Rather than giving an assessment of "corruption," the Business Environment and Enterprise Performance Survey asks firms about many dimensions of corruption that they encounter in their interactions with public officials, how frequently bribes are paid, how large they are, how problematic they are for the operation and growth of the firm. The survey also asks how much the firm is impacted by other firms using corruption to shape laws, rules, and decrees to their advantage.

From FRA to PEFA

The European Commission uses PEFA as its FRA in a country that it has a budget support programme. I carried out an EC FRA in 2004 in Anguilla and for St Helena, the Falkland Islands and the Pitcairn, but remotely for the latter three! In these I used an assessment tool that the IMF and the World Bank have developed together – the Public Expenditure Management Country Assessment and Action Plan[47] mentioned above and I was part of a team that applied it in Kenya.[48] The approach and methodology in the assessment in Kenya impressed me compared to the relative haphazard approach I had to take in the FRA I had conducted in Kenya in 2001. Conse-

---

47   Useful documents in this area can be located at http://www1.worldbank. org/publicsector/decentralization/March2005Seminar/Background%20Readings/ World%20Bank%20IMF%20FinalHIPCAAPGuidance2003-04.pdf.
http://documents1.worldbank.org/curated/en/157391468764376114/pdf/multi-0page.pdf http://documents1.worldbank.org/curated/en/678011468328164960/ pdf/32116.pdf

48   The full team was E. Hawthorn (WB), D. Last (IMF – East AFRITAC), M. Ngari (IMF, Nairobi), Guy Jenkinson (EC), C. Pretorius (UK DFID), J. Short (EC/ WB, Consultant)

quently I used the new methodology in the EC FRAs which was a new development in conducting EC FRAs as far as I am aware.

The aim of this new approach by the IMF and the World Bank was to guide an assessment of the quality of the public expenditure management systems in each Heavily Indebted Poor Country and reflect this in the public expenditure management assessment and action plan, and the 16 key indicators. These assessments were to serve three main purposes:

- to assess the existing capacity for the identification and reporting of budgeted and actual outlays included in overall public spending, including poverty-reducing spending

- to create an understanding of risks associated with implementing poverty-reducing spending in, especially, but not solely, the context of receiving debt relief; and

- to clarify what donor and technical assistance should be provided to improve systems for managing poverty-reducing and other public spending.

Public Expenditure Management Indicators

	BUDGET MANAGEMENT
Formulation	COMPREHENSIVENESS 1. Budget reporting follows GFS definition of consolidated general government. 2. Government activities are not funded through extra budgetary sources to a significant degree. 3. Budget outturn data (levels, functional allocation) are quite close to that of the original budget. 4. Budget includes capital and current expenditure financed by donors. CLASSIFICATION 5. Budget classified on an administrative, economic, functional basis. 6. Poverty-related expenditure clearly identified in the budget. PROJECTION 7. Multi-year expenditure projections integrated into the budget cycle.

BUDGET MANAGEMENT		
Execution	INTERNAL CONTROL 8. Small stock of expenditure arrears; little accumulation of new arrears over past year. 9. Internal audit is active. 10. Tracking surveys supplement internal control. RECONCILIATION 11. Fiscal and banking reconciliation undertaken routinely.	
Reporting	REPORTING 12. Internal budget reports from line ministries/Treasury received within four weeks of the end of the relevant period. 13. Functional classification is reflected in the in-year budget reports. FINAL AUDITED ACCOUNTS 14. Closure of the accounts occurs within two months after the end of the fiscal year. 15. Audited account presented to the legislature within 12 months of the end of the fiscal year.	

An additional indicator on procurement was added.

	16. Efficiency and effectiveness of the public procurement system. The procurement system promotes efficiency and effectiveness in the expenditure of public funds through clear and enforceable rules that promote competition, transparency and value for money.

These assessments and the ensuing action plans will focus on the primary dimensions of PEM performance:

- Budget formulation, covering the design of basic budgetary institutions and aspects of the process to prepare the annual budget;

- Budget execution, covering core aspects required to implement the budget; and

- Budget reporting, covering in-year, and end-of-year financial statements.

This document provides 16 core questions to probe the standard of PEM in a country, and to inform the judgment about the correct assessment for each of 16 key indicators. Each indicator is described. In each case the requirements for meeting a reasonable performance against the indicator is described as a benchmark with one of three scores: a, b or c attributed against established criteria. The benchmarks are struck at a level to indicate reasonable, rather than world-leading, practice.

While PEFA has been mentioned extensively so far without any level of detail I will now address that omission. PEFA has its genesis from dialogue between donors from which the Strengthened Approach to supporting PFM reform was developed. The joint World Bank IMF assessment tool detailed above is, in my mind, the parent of PEFA! Indeed I no longer had the Kenya report and the "manual" as they had been lost and in trying to track them down I kept referring to them as an earlier testing version of PEFA 2005. Duncan Last came to my rescue as he had the Kenya report!

The Strengthened Approach to PFM

The purpose of the Strengthened Approach is to achieve better public financial management systems in countries through effective engagement and support over PFM reforms with a focus on results. The lessons of where reform had progressed furthest and had been more sustainable were taken as its basis. The objectives shifted the emphasis from diagnosis of the problems to implementation of capacity development within countries, adopting a country-tailored approach to diagnostics and capacity development, reducing the transactions costs for countries while meeting donor information needs,[49] and ultimately increasing the effectiveness of PFM reform efforts. The increased emphasis on country ownership and transpar-

---

49   There has been development of further drill down assessment tools on Tax (TADAT), Investment (PIMA), Procurement (MAPS), External Audit (SAI PMF) which needs to be managed alongside PEFAs if this aim is to be realised. Other guides such as Public Investment Management Reference Guide https://openknowledge.worldbank.org/handle/10986/33368 by Jay-Hyung Kim, Jonas Arp Fallov, and Simon Groom (who has worked on Albania and Kenya with REPIM) are also invaluable for drilling down. The complementaries of MAPS and PEFA tools are the subject of a webinar summary of the joint webinar organised by the MAPs and PEFA Secretariats which can be found on the PEFA website https://www.pefa.org.

ency aimed to promote greater accountability and public oversight of PFM.

PEFA was created out of this Strengthened Approach – the monitoring of results through a common information pool through a PFM Performance Measurement Framework.[50] The Framework was designed to be an objective, indicator-based assessment and monitoring tool to provide a common information pool on PFM performance for government, donors and other stakeholders at country level. The Framework focuses on the results of PFM reforms in terms of actual improvements in systems performance.

Since its inception the PEFA Framework for assessing public financial management has undergone improvement changes with the latest in 2016 being to a degree relatively substantial.[51] The first PEFA Framework Guide was published in June 2005 with 28 government indicators and 3 donor indicators. A revised version was produced in January 2011 where 3 indicators were modified based on the experience of actual PEFAs. In 2015 an extended methodology was tested in various countries[52] and the results were used to formulate the 2016 (and current) Framework with 31 indicators relating to government and no donor indicators which were subsumed into the relevant government indicators.

In outlining and explaining the detailed PEFA structure, I will focus on the 2016 version.[53] What does PEFA assess? The purpose of a good PFM system is to ensure that the policies of governments are implemented as intended and achieve their objectives. An open and orderly PFM system is one of the enabling elements needed for desirable fiscal and budgetary outcomes:

- Aggregate fiscal discipline requires effective control of the total budget and management of fiscal risks.

- Strategic allocation of resources involves planning and executing the budget in line with government priorities aimed at achieving policy objectives.

---

50   There is a Conversation with Frans Ronsholt, who at the time was Head of PEFA Secretariat at https://pfmboard.com/index.php?topic = 148.0 which is a good reference point on PEFA.

51   https://www.pefa.org/

52   I was a member of the CARTAC team that used it on Grenada.

53   https://www.pefa.org/sites/default/files/resources/downloads/PEFA%20 Framework_English_Web_Dec18_Second%20Edition.pdf.

- Efficient service delivery requires using budgeted revenues to achieve the best levels of public services within available resources.

PEFA identifies seven pillars of performance that in an open and orderly PFM system are essential to achieving these objectives. The seven pillars thereby define the key elements of a PFM system. They also reflect what is desirable and feasible to measure. The pillars are as follows:

I. Budget reliability. The government budget is realistic and is implemented as intended. This is measured by comparing actual revenues and expenditures (the immediate results of the PFM system) with the original approved budget.

II. Transparency of public finances. Information on PFM is comprehensive, consistent, and accessible to users. This is achieved through comprehensive budget classification, transparency of all government revenue and expenditure including intergovernmental transfers, published information on service delivery performance and ready access to fiscal and budget documentation.

III. Management of assets and liabilities. Effective management of assets and liabilities ensures that public investments provide value for money, assets are recorded and managed, fiscal risks are identified, and debts and guarantees are prudently planned, approved, and monitored.

IV. Policy-based fiscal strategy and budgeting. The fiscal strategy and the budget are prepared with due regard to government fiscal policies, strategic plans, and adequate macroeconomic and fiscal projections.

V. Predictability and control in budget execution. The budget is implemented within a system of effective standards, processes, and internal controls, ensuring that resources are obtained and used as intended.

VI. Accounting and reporting. Accurate and reliable records are maintained, and information is produced and disseminated at appropriate times to meet decision-making, management, and reporting needs.

VII. External scrutiny and audit. Public finances are independently reviewed and there is external follow-up on the implementation of recommendations for improvement by the executive.

The 7 pillars are linked as follows

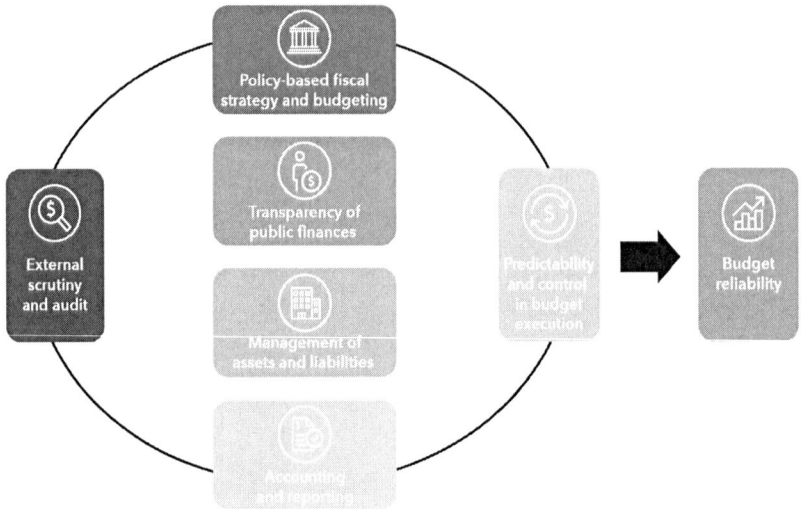

Within these seven broad areas, PEFA defines 31 specific indicators that focus on key measurable aspects of the PFM system. PEFA uses the results of the individual indicator calculations, which are based on available evidence, to provide an integrated assessment of the PFM system against the seven pillars of PFM performance. It then assesses the likely impact of PFM performance levels on the three desired budgetary outcomes: aggregate fiscal discipline, strategic allocation of resources, and efficient service delivery. Each of the 31 indicators can have up to 4 dimensions and in total there are 94 dimensions.

Scoring of the 31 performance indicators is the heart of the PEFA process. For each indicator, the score takes into account the dimensions in each indicator, which are aggregated according to the methodology which is prescribed for the specific indicator either the average of the dimensions or the weakest link (the lowest scored dimension). Each dimension is scored separately on a four-point ordinal scale: A, B, C, or D, according to precise criteria established for each dimension. In order to justify a particular score for a dimension, every aspect specified in the scoring requirements must be fulfilled. If the requirements are only partly met, the criteria are not satisfied and a lower score should be given that coincides with achievement of all requirements for the lower performance rating. A score of C reflects the basic level of performance for each indicator and dimension, consistent with good international practices. A score of D means that the feature being measured is present at less than the basic level of performance or is absent altogether, or that there is insufficient information to score the dimension.

The scoring criteria are established in the Framework for each and every dimension. The Quality Assurance process provided by the PEFA Secretariat is designed to ensure that there is consistent scoring against the evidence collected and presented in a PEFA report. It also ensures that the process of carrying out a PEFA from the production of Concept Note and participation of involved agencies through to publication is followed. This Quality Assurance though the PEFA Check was not in place prior to the 2016 PEFA. Some PEFAs were carried out without any significant peer review. They may have been of dubious quality as the rigorous reviewing of scores may not have been carried out. Reports had not always been submitted to the PEFA Secretariat for review as this was not a requirement in the same way as it is today.[54]

---

54   I remember being on one PEFA in 2014 where the score of A and evidence on the 2008 PEFA for indicator PI-23 Availability of information on resources received by service delivery units did not match what was being provided in 2014. The 2008 evidence can be summarised as "everyone knows the information is in the library". So the 2014 team went to the library (it was a small island) and looked for the necessary documentation and found nothing! The 2014 evidence was No comprehensive data collection on resources to service delivery units in any major sector has been collected and processed within the last 3 years. There is no information available in the budgeted and actual resources received by operational units. In the budget nomenclature, the expenditure is not broken down to operational units, and the ministries do not maintain any register on resources given to health clinics or primary schools. As well, the operational units do not maintain any financial reports, and no special survey was realized during the last years.

PILLARS	INDICATORS	DIMENSIONS
I. Budget reliability	1. Aggregate expenditure outturn	1.1 Aggregate expenditure outturn
	2. Expenditure composition outturn	2.1 Expenditure composition outturn by function 2.2 Expenditure composition outturn by economic type 2.3 Expenditure from contingency reserves
	3. Revenue outturn	3.1 Aggregate revenue outturn 3.2 Revenue composition outturn
II. Transparency of public finances	4. Budget classification	4.1 Budget classification
	5. Budget documentation	5.1 Budget documentation
	6. Central government operations outside financial reports	6.1 Expenditure outside financial reports 6.2 Revenue out side financial reports 6.3 Financial reports of extra-budgetary units
	7. Transfers to sub-national governments	7.1 System for allocating transfers 7.2 Timeliness of information on transfers

		8.1 Performance plans for service delivery
	8. Performance information for service delivery	8.2 Performance achieved for service delivery
		8.3 Resources received by service delivery units
		8.4 Performance evaluation for service delivery
	9. Public access to fiscal information	9.1 Public access to fiscal information
III. Management of assets and liabilities	10. Fiscal risk reporting	10.1 Monitoring of public corporations
		10.2 Monitoring of sub-national governments
		10.3 Contingent liabilities and other fiscal risks
	11. Public investment management	11.1 Economic analysis of investment proposals
		11.2 Investment project selection
		11.3 Investment project costing
		11.4 Investment project monitoring
	12. Public asset management	12.1 Financial asset monitoring
		12.2 Non-financial asset monitoring
		12.3 Transparency of asset disposal
	13. Debt management	13.1 Recording and reporting of debt and guarantees
		13.2 Approval of debt and guarantees
		13.3 Debt management strategy

IV. Policy-based fiscal strategy end budgeting	14. Macroeconomic and fiscal forecasting	14.1 Macro-economic forecasts 14.2 Fiscal forecasts 14.3 Macro-fiscal sensitivity analysis
	15. Fiscal strategy	15.1 Fiscal impact of policy proposals 15.2 Fiscal strategy adoption 15.3 Reporting on fiscal outcomes
	16. Medium-term perspective in expenditure budgeting	16.1 Medium-term expenditure estimates 16.2 Medium-term expenditure ceilings 16.3 Alignment of strategic plans and medium-term budgets 16.4 Consistency of budgets with previous year's estimates
	17. Budget preparation process	17.1 Budget calendar 17.2 Guidance on budget preparation 17.3 Budget submission to the legislature
	18. Legislative scrutiny of budgets	18.1 Scope of budget scrutiny 18.2 Legislative procedures for budget scrutiny 18.3 Timing of budget approval 18.4 Rules for budget adjustment by the executive
V. Predictability end control in budget execution	19. Revenue administration	19.1 Rights and obligations for revenue measures 19.2 Revenue risk management 19.3 Revenue audit and investigation 19.4 Revenue arrears monitoring

20. Accounting for revenue	20.1 Information on revenue collections
	20.2 Transfer of revenue collections
	20.3 Revenue accounts reconciliation
21. Predictability of in-year resource allocation	21.1 Consolidation of cash balances
	21.2 Cash forecasting and monitoring
	21.3 Information on commitment ceilings
	21.4 Significance of in-year budget adjustments
22. Expenditure arrears	22.1 Stock of expenditure arrears
	22.2 Expenditure arrears monitoring
23. Payroll controls	23.1 Integration of payroll and personnel records
	23.2 Management of payroll changes
	23.3 Internal control of payroll
	23.4 Payroll audit
24. Procurement	24.1 Procurement monitoring
	24.2 Procurement methods
	24.3 Public access to procurement information
	24.4 Procurement complaints management
25. Internal controls on non-salary expenditure	25.1 Segregation of duties
	25.2 Effectiveness of expenditure commitment controls
	25.3 Compliance with payment rules and procedures

	26. Internal audit	26.1 Coverage of internal audit 26.2 Nature of audits and standards applied 26.3 Implementation of internal audits and reporting 26.4 Response to internal audits
VI. Accounting and reporting	27. Financial data integrity	27.1 Bank account reconciliation 27.2 Suspense accounts 27.3 Advance accounts 27.4 Financial data integrity processes
	28. In-year budget reports	28.1 Coverage and comparability of reports 28.2 Timing of in-year budget reports 28.3 Accuracy of in-year budget reports
	29. Annual financial reports	29.1 Completeness of annual financial reports 29.2 Submission of reports for external audit 29.3 Accounting standards
VII. External scrutiny and audit	30. External audit	30.1 Audit coverage and standards 30.2 Submission of audit reports to the legislature 30.3 External audit follow-up 30.4 Supreme Audit Institution independence
	31. Legislative scrutiny of audit reports	31.1 Timing of audit report scrutiny 31.2 Hearings on audit findings 31.3 Recommendations on audit by the legislature 31.4 Transparency of legislative scrutiny of audit reports

The format of a PEFA report is set out in the Framework and the Guidelines and the report format has recently been revised in 2020. As well as assessing PFM at central government level, PEFA is also used to assess subnational governments (SN) – states/provinces and local authorities. In addition to the 31 indicators, there is one additional indicator with three dimensions that measures the effectiveness of transfers from a higher level of government to the entity being assessed. (HLG-1 Transfer from a higher level of Government). An updated version of the SN PEFA methodology is currently being finalised.

The Core PEFA Central Government and Subnational PEFA assessment tools have been expanded in 2020 to include three separate thematic assessments:

- Service Delivery https://www.pefa.org/resources/guidance-sng-pefa-assessments-service-delivery-module-piloting-phase

- Gender responsive public financial management frameworkhttps://www.pefa.org/resources Supplementary Framework for Assessing Gender Responsive Public Financial Management | Public Expenditure and Financial Accountability (PEFA)

- Climate Responsive Public Financial Management Framework (PEFA Climate) https://www.pefa.org/sites/pefa/files/resources/downloads/PEFA%20Climate%20Framework%20from%20August%204%202020%20Final.pdf

All of these are in the pilot stage with the Service Delivery and Gender Responsiveness assessments added on to the CG and SN assessments. The Vietnam SN PEFA which I worked on added on a Service Delivery assessment and the Moldova CG which I have worked on also added on a Gender Responsive PEFA. The PEFA Climate is more a standalone exercise and I worked on the Albania assessment.

Applying PEFA

PEFA has been a huge part of my PFM work experience. Using the 2005 and 2011 methodology I was involved in PEFAs either as team leader or team member in Moldova (CG twice) Sierra Leone (CG twice plus SN management), Serbia (CG plus 6 SN), Kosovo (CG and 11 SN), Anguilla, Antigua, Barbados, St Vincent and the Grenadines, Palestine and peer reviewed reports on Azerbaijan, Indonesia and Mozambique. I was part of the CARTAC team that used the 2015 testing methodology in Grenada and used the information to rescore using the 2016 methodology. Matthew Smith and Celeste Kubasta of CARTAC were PEFA adopters in their work plan in the Caribbean Islands and I was fortunate to work with them on many occasions. Sadly Mathew is no longer with us and he is much missed.

I applied the 2016 methodology in Georgia, (CG and 3 SNs with Lasha Gotsiridze and Papuna Petriashvili), St Lucia, Jamaica, Dominica, British Virgin Islands (BVI), Ukraine (CG and 2 SNs) and Moldova (CG and 4 SNs) and peer reviewed Uganda. I was also asked to take a draft of the PEFA in Lao PDR and the CG and 2 SN PEFAs in Pakistan and redraft and quality assure them to the PEFA Check level. I was part of the PFTAC team led by Celeste Kubasta that carried out the Fiji PEFA in 2019 and was the first to apply the new report format. In addition I was commissioned by the PEFA Secretariat to critically review the draft of the revised SN PEFA Framework.

I carried out both a FRA in 2004 and a PEFA in 2013 in Palestine. In 2004 Ramallah was a relatively small town but by 2013 it had grown significantly to a city. However the logistics of travelling from West Jerusalem where the DFID and the World Bank offices were located required travelling through security checkpoints that separated the two jurisdictions. The FRA also covered Gaza as it was possible to travel there provided the correct travel documentation was presented at the checkpoint and the last part of the journey was by foot. By 2013 Gaza was not a place that could be easily visited and the focus was on the part of Palestine under the government in Ramallah.

Illustrating PEFA in action

Most PEFA reports are public documents and can be found on the PEFA website. I am including here the write up of three indicators from PEFAs that I have been involved in to illustrate the scoring and data requirements. These three indicators demonstrate the way indicators and their dimensions are scored and the information needed to do this. These particular indicators have been chosen as they are linked and there is also a relationship to the previous chapter on PERs and MTPB. PI-8 and PI-16 are taken from the same country Ukraine and PI-11 is from a subnational PEFA in Batumi, Georgia.

PI-8. Performance information for service delivery

General description of the characteristics of the indicator within the scope covered. This indicator examines the service delivery performance information in the executive's budget proposal or its supporting and documentation in year-end reports. It determines whether performance audits or evaluations are carried out. It also assesses the extent to which information on resources received by service delivery units is collected and recorded. The time period covered: dimension 8.1: performance indicators and planned outputs and outcomes for the next fiscal year; dimension 8.2: outputs and outcomes of the last completed fiscal year; and dimensions 8.3 and 8.4 last three completed fiscal years. The coverage is CG, including services managed and financed by other tiers of government where the CG significantly finances such services through reimbursements or earmarked grants, or uses other tiers of government as implementing agents.

Under the adopted programme budgeting regulations and methodology, performance information is a mandatory part of a budget programme and integrated in the annual budget planning and reporting cycle. The Budget Code requires all stakeholders in the budget process to plan and execute budget programmes upholding the principles of efficient and effective delivery of public services throughout all budget stages. There were around 550 service delivery and administrative budget programmes from 83 Key Spending

Units (KSUs) presented in Annex 3 to the 2019 Law on the State Budget.

Key Spending Units plan and report on programme implementation annually.[55] Budget programmes are formulated and submitted by KSUs as a part of budget programme requests, which must be aligned with the budget declaration and the KSU's medium-term action plans, as per Article 22 of the Budget Code and thus ensure a link with the fiscal framework and sectoral policy objectives, respectively. Within 45 days from approval of the annual budget, KSUs propose and the MoF approves individual Budget Programme Passports. Each programme is managed by a chief programme manager responsible for in-year monitoring and annual evaluation in line with the MoF Decree no. 608 that sets out the methodological guidance for evaluating budget programme efficiency. Resources available to service delivery units (SDUs) are comprehensively recorded and information about their collection and expenditure is available through the government accounting system. Performance of each programme is reported annually. Independent evaluation and performance audit are being introduced, but further technical capacity is needed.

In agreement with the MoF, the assessment and scores for this indicator are based on the sample of KSUs. This sample includes the Ministry of Education, Ministry of Health, Ministry of Youth and Sports, and Ministry of Social Policy. The following table illustrates availability of performance information on planned and executed service delivery (SD) programmes for the sampled KSUs.

---

55   In line with the MoF Decree no. 1098 [of 29.12.2002].

Table 8.1: Performance data on planned service delivery and reporting on actual delivery for the sampled KSUs

KSUs	Budget allocation (in UAH billion) SD programmes	SD programmes (total programmes)	Performance data for service delivery programmes		Planned and reported performance		
			Programme Objectives	KPIs	Outputs	Outcomes	Activities
MoH (2300000)	42.2	36	Yes	Yes	Yes	Yes	Yes
MoES (2200000)	39.4	40	Yes	Yes	Yes	Yes	Yes
MYS (3400000)	3.0	8 (11)	Yes	Yes	Yes	Yes	Yes
MSP (2500000 and 2500001)	236.1	38	Yes	Yes	Yes	Yes	Yes
Total	320.7	122 (125)					
Percentage of SD programmes compliant (%)		100	100	100	100	100	100

(Sources of information: Annex 3 to the 2019 Budget Law, MSP and MYS data, publicly available budget programme passports and programme budget passport reports, assessment team calculations.)

Summary of scores and performance table

Indicator/Dimension	Scoring Method M2 (Average)			
	Current assessment		Previous assessment (PEFA 2016 framework)	
	2019 Score	Brief justification for score	2015 Score	Explanation of change (including comparability issues)
PI-8: Performance information for service delivery	A		C+	
8.1 Performance plans for service delivery	A	Key Spending Units (KSUs) annually publish information on planned programme objectives, and KPIs outputs and outcomes.	B	Methodology refined, and with improvement in actual performance.
8.2. Performance achieved for service delivery	A	Reports on performance achieved are published annually but deviations from the plan are not always explained and reports do not include basis for comparability over time.	C	Methodology refined, improvement in the amount of information generated.

8.3. Resources received by service delivery units	A	Information on all resources disaggregated by sources of fund received and used by service delivery units across sectors are recorded and available from in-year and annual budget execution reports of each service delivery unit.	A	No change in performance.
8.4. Performance evaluation for service delivery	B	Independent evaluations and audit of programmes have been carried out and published.	D	KSUs have started publishing assessment results of programme performance. Spending reviews have been introduced for the first time in 2018. Efficiency audits are carried out and published but the degree of conformance with the relevant ISSAIs could not be confirmed due to insufficient evidence.

8.1 Performance plans for service delivery

Performance level and evidence for scoring the dimension
KSUs publish disaggregated data on planned performance for each programme upon MoF approval of the individual Programme Budget Passports. The Passports are delivered on a standardized template which requires the KSUs to include information on the programme-related state policy goals, budget funds use direction, objectives and key performance indicators (KPIs). Methodology prescribed under the MoF Decree no. 1536 for preparation of the quantitative and qualitative KPIs, requires the KSUs to develop indicators of cost (input), product (output), performance (efficiency) and quality (effectiveness) in service delivery, which cover KSUs' and their subordinate spending units' activities, outputs and outcomes. As of recently, the documents include gender considerations and sex disaggregated KPIs. The score for the dimension is A.

8.2 Performance achieved for service delivery

Performance level and evidence for scoring the dimension
Information on each budget programme performance for the previous year is reported annually by 15 March in the respective Budget Programme Execution Report. All KSUs formally comply with the reporting requirement and this information reaches the Parliament as an integral part of the overall annual budget execution report. Contents of budget programme execution reports correspond to the information that is presented in budget programme passports, allowing the comparison of performance achieved against the annual plan. Realization against specific KPIs is to be fully disclosed in Section 8 of the individual programme report. As of 2015 amendments to the Budget Code of Ukraine, KSUs are also required to publish their budget programme execution reports separately. For 2018 fiscal year reporting period, these reports were published by most KSUs on their websites and included the information about quantity of outputs produced and outcomes achieved, disaggregated by programmes. As required by a unified template adopted by the MoF,[56] the presented information was consistent with annual planned outputs and outcomes as set forth in budget programme

---

56   In line with the MoF Decree no. 1098 [of 29.12.2002].

passports and if any deviation in the actual performance that is explained in the most cases. The score for this dimension is A.

8.3 Resources received by service delivery units

Performance level and evidence for scoring the dimension
Comprehensive coverage of the Treasury Single Account (TSA) includes all of the accounts operated by SD Units, regardless of the sector (i.e. health, education, infrastructure, and others). Specific own-source revenues collected and external grants received, in-kind contributions by SD Units are planned and recorded under the Special Fund of the State Budget. Their use is earmarked and the actual spending is tracked by the Treasury territorial units.

Accounting information on all financial resources received and executed by the SD Units is available from in-year and annual budget execution reports of each service delivery unit disaggregated by budget programmes and sources of fund. Each SD Unit submits reports on revenues and expenditures disaggregated by budget programmes and types of financial sources on monthly, quarterly and annual basis.[57] Those reports consist of the information on non-financial resources in kind[58] and associated with them expenditures. Moreover, SD Units submitted to the Treasury a specific statement on natural earnings disaggregated by budget programmes and sources of fund on monthly basis. The source of funds includes budget, own sources and any external funds, including but not limited grants and natural earnings. Information from interviews and available evidence confirms that this is all implemented as planned. The score for this dimension is A.

8.4. Performance evaluation for service delivery

Performance level and evidence for scoring the dimension
The Budget Code promotes a target-based approach to budgeting and requires budget programme managers to monitor and assess budget programmes at each stage of the budget process. Targeted performance is monitored and evaluated through data on

---

57   MoF Decree no. 44 [of 24.01.2012].
58   MoF Decree no. 1407 [of 24.12.2012].

performance indicators from official statistics, government reports and internal managerial systems. The methodological background for annual assessment of programme efficiency is contained in Ministerial Order no. 608. Ministry of Social Policy, the Key Spending Unit (KSU) which accounts for 74.2 percent of the total sample by budget size (table 8.1), published the evaluation results in 2018. Interviews with development partners indicate that monitoring and evaluation practices vary across government KSUs.

Budget programmes and their performance metrics are refined each year, but analysis of specific Budget Programme Passports suggests there is room to improve coherence between purposes, goal, objectives, measures, and KPIs. Whereas all KSUs in the sample annually publish information on planned service delivery, the volume of reported information and its internal coherence reduces the possibilities for performance-based analysis and allocation decisions.

In early 2018, the Cabinet authorized a spending review exercise in five service delivery KSUs and the results have been published (including Ministry of Social Protection and Ministry of Health which stand for 87 percent of the total sampled KSUs). Reviews of programmes were conducted by inter-sectoral working groups with representatives of the reviewed KSU, MoF and other sector-specific KSUs. Cabinet Decree no. 101 provided procedural instructions and some methodological guidance on conducting the exercise. A second round of spending reviews for five different KSUs is scheduled in 2019 in line with a new methodological guidance note.

There is an adequate legislative framework for performance audit of government operations. In the period covered by this dimension (2016 to 2018), the Accounting Chamber carried out and published the results of nearly 200 audits of efficiency. Plans are in place to develop a dedicated performance audit methodology with technical assistance support. The State Audit Service has the mandate and could offer additional capacity for audit of programme performance through its combined audit approach. There is insufficient evidence, however, to confirm the degree of conformance with the relevant performance auditing international standards.

Finally, the Government benefited from a number of independent reviews and evaluations in key service delivery sectors. The most notable of these independent reviews was the World Bank's Public Expenditure Reviews in health and four more sectors in 2016. The score for this dimension is B.

Performance change since the previous assessment

Structurally, performance of the Ukrainian PFM system on PI-8 remains largely unchanged relative to the previous assessment. Individual budget programmes continue to correspond to organizational structures and/or the legal mandate of the KSU. Quality of programme objectives, KPIs, outputs and outcomes differs across individual programmes and KSUs but there have been notable improvements in performance metrics achieved in part with external technical assistance. Available information suggests that there is room to further improve the coherence of programme structure and strengthen the links between objectives, goals, measures and KPIs (i.e. between Form 1 and Form 2 of the budget request). Horizontal and vertical alignment and coordination of activities under budget programmes (among KSUs on CG level and between CG and SNG programmes, respectively) continues to pose a challenge.

Recent or ongoing reform activities

The State Budget Department at the MoF is undertaking a comprehensive review exercise of the main Decrees that regulate programme budgeting with a view to align them with the most recent amendments to the Budget Law and introduction of the Medium-term Budget Framework (MTBF) approach. Decrees 1098 and 1536 have been updated and amendments to Decree 608 are pending (by end 2019). New requirements, effective as of 2019, call for publication of realized programme metrics in a format which allows for comparison over time. MoF is developing the spending review methodology at the time of the assessment. In parallel, the Ministry of Economy is leading a comprehensive overhaul of medium-term (three-year) planning by KSUs that is expected to impact planning of individual budget programmes and overarching target programmes which reflect government policy objectives and priorities.

The reporting template requires the KSUs to explain any deviations from the planned activities, outputs and outcomes but this information is at times omitted from programme budget execution reports. Additional issues are noted with the reliability of information generated by programme managers from internal, management accounting systems. Moreover, report template is missing comparable information on service delivery levels from the previous reporting period which would allow users to understand service delivery trends. Looking beyond the volume of information produced and published, the concern is with completeness, integrity and straight-forward comparability of the reported information over time. While not in the calibration, all three aspects are used as best practice benchmarks throughout the Framework and taken into consideration as an implicit requirement. Reporting remains a largely formal exercise with gaps in information to guide analysis and decision-making on programme performance against targets and over time. The current PFM Reform Strategy 2017-2020 and its Action Plan include objectives and activities related to the improvement of budget programmes' strategic orientation and introduction of efficient performance monitoring.

Since 2014, Swedish International Development Agency's Project 'Gender Budgeting in Ukraine' provided support to capacity development of programme managers to run effective gender analysis of budget-funded programmes and employ the findings for the development of an effective gender approach to budgeting. In 2018, the Project supported a gender analysis within a number of selected budget-funded programmes which resulted in some reconsideration of the programmes at the central and local levels, including the ministerial level. Additionally, the performance indicators are based on data disaggregated by gender. Resident US Treasury budget adviser is providing technical assistance for programme budgeting (KPIs in particular) and spending reviews in support of the respective PFM Reform Strategy objectives.

The pilot spending reviews highlighted in the narrative were limited to one budget programme in each KSU and there are no findings which could be generalized to provide an impression of overall spending efficiency and effectiveness. The pilot aimed to test the methodology, therefore the MoF is going to improve it and introduce the mechanisms of spending reviews further.

PI-16. Medium-term perspective in expenditure budgeting

General description of the characteristics of the indicator within the scope covered

This indicator examines the extent to which expenditure budgets are developed for the medium-term within explicit medium-term budget expenditure ceilings. It also examines the extent to which annual budgets are derived from medium-term estimates and the degree of alignment between medium-term budget estimates and strategic plans. For dimensions 16.1, 16.2 and 16.3 the assessment is based on the last budget submitted to the legislature, 2018. For dimension 16.4, it is based on the last budget submitted to the legislature 2018, and the current budget 2019. The coverage is Budgetary Central Government.

Summary of scores and performance table

Indicator/ Dimension	Scoring Method M2 Average				
	Current assessment		Previous assessment (PEFA 2016 framework)		
	2019 Score	Brief justification for score	2015 Score	Explanation of change (including comparability issues)	
PI-16: Medium-term perspective in expenditure budgeting	D+		D		
16.1 Medium-term expenditure estimates	D	Key spending units compile detailed calculations of mid-term expenditure for all budget classifications and submit them to the Ministry of Finance as part of budget requests. Estimates for the outer years are not presented in the annual budget.	D	There are no changes.	

16.2 Medium-term expenditure ceilings	D	The Ministry of Finance has calculated both preliminary expenditure ceilings for key spending units and final ones for compiling budget requests. However, the Government has not approved them.	D	There are no changes.
16.3 Alignment of strategic plans and medium-term budgets	C	17 out of 58 ministries, national agencies, academies, other CG authorities (29.3%) in 2018 had approved strategic plans of their activities. Plans of 15 of them (25.9%) contained the amounts of expenditure needed to achieve the goals and planned performance indicators. In addition, the State Debt Management Strategy for 2018-2020 covered expenditures for the debt service. Some expenditure policy proposals in the annual budget (more than 25% of total expenditures) aligned with the strategic plans.	D	Due to the above, the situation with discipline regarding the approval by key spending units of strategic plans also improved, which influenced the change in the score of indicator 16.3 from D to C.
16.4 Consistency of budgets with previous year's estimates	N/A	No medium-term budget has been adopted during the assesed period.	D	This dimension is not applicable. There is no change from the previous PEFA as the circumstances are the same

16.1 Medium-term expenditure estimates

Performance level and evidence for scoring the dimension
In drafting the State Budget the key spending units make detailed
medium-term estimates of expenditures. These are for all budget
classifications: departmental, programmatic (showing the relationship with the functional one) and the economic classification at the
level of the third digit. Such a requirement is in place following the
Order of the Ministry of Finance dated No. 687 dated June 6, 2012
"On Approval of the Instruction for Preparing Budget Requests".
According to that order, medium-term estimates of expenditure are
part of the budget request, which each key spending unit submits to
the Ministry of Finance when drafting the budget. Estimates for the
outer years are not presented in the annual budget. The score for
the dimension is D.

16.2 Medium-term expenditure ceilings

Performance level and evidence for scoring the dimension
While drafting the State Budget for 2019 the Ministry of Finance
sent key spending units both preliminary and final ceiling amounts
of expenditure. Based on these ceilings, the key spending units
determined their budget requests. However, ceilings were not
approved by the Government. Such ceiling limits are based on the
medium-term forecast of revenue, financing, expenditure, lending,
debt obligations, and inter-budgetary transfers, but they are indicative and not hard. The score for the dimension is D.

16.3 Alignment of strategic plans and medium-term budgets

Performance level and evidence for scoring the dimension
All key spending units shall develop strategic plans of their activities for three years.[59] These plans are prepared on the basis of
forecast amounts of expenditure and provision of loans from the
budget for the two budget periods following the planned one, as
communicated by the Ministry of Finance along with guidelines

---

59   According to part two of Article 21 of the Budget Code of Ukraine.

on compiling budget requests. Key spending units shall annually align such plans of activities with the State Budget indicators for the planned budget period and a forecast of the State Budget for the next two budget periods following the planned one, which in fact was approved only once in 2012 for 2013-2014.

The Ministry for Development of Economy, Trade and Agriculture[60] approved the guidelines for development of key spending units' plans of activities. This was according to budget assignments determined by the law on the State Budget for a relevant budget period for the planned and two budget periods following it.

In 2015, the Ministry of Finance adopted orders that provided for changing an approach to compiling a budget request and a budget programme passport. These orders stipulated the consistency of the distribution of expenditures for the medium-term perspective with the ministries' strategic plans of activities (Orders of the Ministry of Finance No. 553 dated 15 June 2015, "On Approval of Amendments to the Order of the Ministry of Finance No. 1536 dated 10 December 2010" and No. 554 dated 15 June 2015 "On Amending the Instruction on Preparing Budget Requests").

Despite the lack of a forecast of the State Budget, which is required by the Budget Code, only 17 out of 58 ministries, national agencies, academies, other CG authorities (29.3%) had approved strategic plans of their activities in 2018. Fifteen (25.9%) contained the amounts of expenditure needed to achieve the goals and planned performance indicators. Expenditures of the draft State Budget for 2019 correlated with the 15 strategies. The strategies are used in the preparation of annual performance plans (PI.8.1) for service delivery by KSUs after annual budget approved. According to the MoF's order No. 1098 dated December 29, 2002 "On budget programme passports" the budget programme passport should be prepared using the information provided in the budget request and be consistent with the strategy of the KSU. In addition, the State Debt Management Strategy for 2018-2020, approved by the Cabinet No. 883 dated August 22, 2017, covered expenditures for debt service.

Some expenditure policy proposals in the annual budget (more than 25% but less than 50% of total expenditures) aligned with the strategic plans. The score for the dimension is C.

---

60   Order No. 869 of 25 July 2012.

16.4 Consistency of budgets with previous year's estimates

Performance level and evidence for scoring the dimension
A medium-term budget has not been adopted during the assessed period as only the budget year is presented. Thus, this dimension is not applicable.

Performance change since the previous assessment
The Ministry of Finance had issued in 2015 orders requiring the consistency of the mid-term allocation of expenditures with the strategic plans of the ministries' activities. As a result, the situation with discipline regarding the approval by key spending units of strategic plans improved. This has influenced the change in the score of indicator 16.3 from D to C.

Recent or ongoing reform activities
The recently adopted amendments to the Budget Code[61] have established a legal basis for the introduction of MTBF. This is both at the level of the State Budget and at the level of local budgets. In accordance with the amended part three of Article 20, key spending units will now form budget programmes while formulating proposals for the Budget Declaration and drawing up a budget request, taking into account medium-term plans of activities, forecast and programmatic documents on economic and social development. The observance of this norm should help improve the score under both indicator 16.1 and indicator 16.3 to A.

The Government will in future approve the maximum amount of expenditure for the planned and the two budget periods following it for key spending units (part 9 of Article 33 of the Budget Code) as part of the Budget Declaration, which is going to be passed. This replaces the Key Areas of Budget Policy for the Planned Year and the State Budget Forecast for the Two Budget Periods following the Planned One (now repealed). This may allow for a further improvement of the score under indicator 16.2 up to A.

Part 2 of the amended Article 33 will ensure consistency of medium-term indicators by defining indicators in the Budget Declaration. This will take into account relevant indicators for previous years, as stipulated in the last year's Budget Declaration. The same

---

61   2646-VIII of 6 December 2018.

rule establishes a list of cases when the said indicators may differ, namely: (1) deviation of the estimated main forecasting macroeconomic indicators of Ukraine's economic and social development from the forecast, which was factored in as part of the Budget Declaration and approved in the previous budget period; (2) deviation of the budget indicators determined by the law on the State Budget from those specified in the Budget Declaration approved in the previous budget period; and (3) adoption of new legislative and other regulatory acts influencing State Budget indicators in the medium-term.

PI-11. Public investment management

This indicator assesses the economic appraisal, selection, costing and monitoring of public investment projects by the government, with emphasis on the largest and most significant projects. The assessment is based on the fiscal year 2017 and covers subnational government.[62]

Indicator/ Dimension	Minimum Requirements (Scoring Method M2 Average)	
	2018 Score	Brief justification for score
PI-11 Public investment management	B+	
11.1 Economic analysis of investment proposals	A	Economic analyses have been conducted to assess the investment project that dominates the Batumi investment portfolio.
11.2 Investment project selection	C	Prior to their inclusion in the budget, the major investment projects are prioritized but not on the basis of standard criteria.

---

62   This was the first PEFA in the municipality.

11.3 Investment project costing	B	Projections of the total capital cost of investment projects for the implementing timeframe, together with the collective recurrent costs for the forthcoming years annually, are included in the budget documents.
11.4 Investment project monitoring	A	The monitoring of cost and physical progress of investment projects are outsourced and monitored by the Supervisory Unit. Information on implementation of projects is prepared quarterly and annually and reported to the Sakrebulo.

An investment projects management guide was developed in 2016 and was approved by the Decree No.191 of April 22, 2016 of the Government of Georgia for the purpose of establishment of mechanisms for developing and implementing Single Cycle Management of capital / investment projects. Detailed methodology for Investment Projects Management (Decree No.165 of July 22, 2016 of the Minister of Finance of Georgia) was approved on the basis of this guide.

11.1 Economic analysis of investment proposals

Batumi municipality has been implementing a large multi-year capital improvement plan funded by KFW[63] and the municipality itself. This investment plan is responsible for virtually the municipality's entire investment portfolio. The KFW funded element is related to water and sewerage upgrading for the city and the city is responsible for funding related ancillary above ground (repairing roads etc) work. Detailed economic analysis has been carried out for the KFW element by the lender with the municipality implemented element wholly consistent and complementary to it. Score A.

----

63   Kreditanstalt Fuer Wiederaufbau (KFW) operates as a German state-owned development bank.

11.2 Investment project selection

Investment projects are prioritized in line with the municipality's strategic objectives by the Infrastructure Development Department before their consideration in the budget. Project ideas can come from spending units or from the population. There are, however, no standard criteria to guide the process.[64] However, there is a structured process which includes project identification, development of a technical document and an evaluation of urgency/progress. Nominated projects are proposed to the Mayor and an investment task force. The final selection is based on how these projects fit with the municipality's programme priorities that have been established at the start of the budget formulation process based on alternative use of the available funds and impact on the residents of alternative locations. For a project to be included in the budget a design study has to be completed and a full costing proposal prepared. Score C

11.3 Investment project costing

Investment / Capital Projects in the budget documentation are provided for the year to be planned and for the next 3 years, annually. The recurrent costs implications are factored into the budget by programme/subprogramme annually but are not broken down by individual projects. The investment documents do however include running costs as well as capital costs of a given project. Score B.

11.4 Investment project monitoring

The municipality has a special supervisory division for projects. Monitoring of project implementation including both physical such as volumes and quality[65] of inputs like concrete and cost, is outsourced to appropriate consultancy/companies that produce a monthly report. There are standard procedures for monitoring such as keeping of journals, photos and reporting on a daily basis. Physical progress is monitored against an implementation sched-

---

64   Adjara Government is currently developing standard criteria.
65   Using laboratory analysis, if necessary.

ule.[66] Costs are monitored against budget in order to flag up cost overruns so that any issues are known and can be addressed in a timely manner. There is a template for payment related to verified inputs against the contractual unit costs. All documents relating to invoices have to be verified before submission to the Finance Department and the Mayor has to issue a Payment Certificate before payment can be made. Post completion quality assurance is maintained by retaining a warranty percentage of the contract (2.5%) for 2 years after completion. Projects under Georgian Lari 100,000 are monitored by the Infrastructure Department using similar but simpler procedures.

Both quarterly and annual financial performance reports are provided to the Sakrebulo. The annual report, produced by the Infrastructure Development Department, has performance indicators related to the implementation of capital projects. This report goes to the Mayor who then submits it to the Sakrebulo (Assembly) who reviews it and calls staff to attend the meetings. Score A

PEFA and PFM Action Plans

Given the format and structure of the PEFA and the objectives of the Strengthened Approach, the indicators and their scoring are ideal for developing a PFM Action Plan. The scores of the latest PEFA establish a SMART baseline and the reform programme can be assessed against target scores over the timeframe of the PFM Action Plan. I have been involved in using the PEFA reports in this way to work with the governments of Kosovo, Serbia (SN), Barbados, Jamaica, BVI, Georgia, and Uzbekistan along with interested development partners.

The PEFA Secretariat has now produced Volume IV of the PEFA Handbook- using PEFA to support PFM improvement. Volume IV provides guidance on how to use PEFA assessments as part of a stakeholder dialogue to develop and sequence PFM reform initiatives. It focuses on the issues that need to be considered in developing effective reform improvement strategies or action plans that are designed to address each country's unique situation.

As an example, the Subnational and the Central Government PEFAs were used to prepare Georgia's PFM Strategy for 2018-2021. This PFM strategy is supporting the 2019-2025 Decentralization

---

66   The Head of Finance Department has a colour coded map of the city showing projects by contractor and progress.

Strategy, which has one of its aims, to introduce reliable, accountable, transparent and result-oriented local self-governments.

Subsequently MOF and Ministry of Regional Development and Infrastructure decided to use top-ups to capital grants for public investments as an incentive to stimulate PFM reforms amongst municipalities. The transfer of these grants would be conditional on the municipalities making improvements over the medium-term (2020-2022) in critical PFM areas of weakness identified in PEFA assessments. Over 2020-22, participating municipalities could receive on average 34 percent of the capital grant transfer they received in 2019, which should be sufficient to incentivize improvements. Transfers are pro-rated to the progress of the municipality on the indicators agreed with the MOF.

Common areas of weakness, as identified in the 2018 PEFA Municipality Synthesis Report, include the following: i) failure to timely submit annual financial statements for audit by the State Audit Office (based on the 2018 PEFA Municipality Synthesis Report, only three municipalities submitted their financial statements to the State Audit Office for external audit within three months of the end of the fiscal year); and ii) limited scrutiny of Sakrebulos (local councils) over both internal audit and external audit reports. Beyond these, additional PEFA-related actions have also been included, covering areas such as budget planning and preparation (through stronger compliance with program budgeting methodology), reporting, controls and transparency. The objective of the reform is to ensure that municipalities: i) can plan and prepare more realistic budgets in accordance with the program budget methodology; ii) are subjected to stronger internal and external scrutiny and iii) are more transparent and engaging with their citizens.

In order to implement these reforms, the Government, through Decree No. 2735, dated December 30, 2019, introduced a mechanism to support PFM improvements by municipalities, by providing additional financing for capital investments for 27 municipalities, conditional upon the municipalities improving identified areas of weakness as per PEFA assessment reports. The Municipalities then signed Memorandums of Understanding (MoU) with MOF to comply with the decree. These Memorandums of Understanding have a set of indicators based on areas of weakness identified using PEFA assessments which the municipalities should achieve by 2022 in order to get more capital grants for public investments. The

World Bank supported these policy changes under the Economic Management and Competitiveness Development Policy Operation. In addition, the Bank will support the implementation of these reforms under the Economic Governance and Fiscal Accountability Trust Fund financed by the European Union. Other Development Partners will also provide implementation support too.

The results for 27 municipalities are stipulated in the Memorandum of Understanding to be achieved by 2022. By then, it is expected that more than 50 percent of participating municipalities will have their financial statements submitted for audit. Once audited, the reports will also be scrutinized by local councils (Sakrebulos) who are expected to use the findings to ensure more efficient and transparent operations of local governments. Furthermore, improved citizen engagement in PFM processes should support delivery of better-quality services. A growing number of municipalities implementing the program budgeting methodology should also result in more gender-sensitive budgeting at the local level. According to the program budgeting guidelines, gender sensitive programs should include at least one indicator (at both program and activity level) to assess the gender performance of programs. Progress towards the achievement of these results is underway and the first measurement will be done towards the end of 2020.

Giorgi Kakauridze, Deputy Minister of Finance of the Government of Georgia has said the following: "PEFA has been very useful to the Government of Georgia as a tool for monitoring PFM reforms over time. It's allowed us to have a systematic approach for assessing progress and identifying shortfalls of the reform. PEFA findings have been guiding the PFM reform agenda for central government of Georgia since the first assessment in 2005 and we continue to actively use the tool for further reform plans for local governments. Since the tool is accepted as one of the most effective assessment mechanisms worldwide, it has also helped us to better communicate our progress and further needs to international institutions and the donor community. This has allowed us to mobilize more tailored Technical Assistance."[67]

---

67   PEFA's contribution to Georgia's PFM reform at subnational government level stimulated by capital grants By Patrick Umah Tete, Senior Financial Management Specialist and Mariam Dolidze, Senior Economist, World Bank https://www.pefa.org/news/pefas-contribution-georgias-pfm-reform-subnational-government-level-stimulated-capital-grants

PEFA and being SMART

Indeed PEFA indicators can be useful in the application of a Programme Tree for a programme such as Budget Preparation.

- Long term policy goal-outcome?
- Budget that contributes to stable economy, economic growth, low inflation and reduced inequalities measured against a baseline
- Policy objective-outcome
- Annual budget is reliable against a baseline. Use of PEFA indicators PI 1 -3?

Outputs

- Macro-economic and revenue forecasts (2 within a year?)
- Debt Report
- Budget Circular and ceilings
- Budget Hearings
- Draft Budget submitted to Legislature
- Final Budget passed by Legislature

Standards based on PEFA

- PI-5: Budget Documentation
- PI-14 Macroeconomic and Fiscal forecasts and functional allocations
- PI-15 Fiscal Strategy
- PI-17.1 Budget Calendar

The creation and development of PEFA as an assessment and diagnostic tool and input into developing a PFM reform action plan cannot be overestimated in my opinion. It would be nice to see it used in "developed" countries! Perhaps they have used PEFA but have not reported on it or maybe they think that all their 31 indicators would score $A+$[68] so there is no need. Perhaps they should watch this video which describes the use of PEFA in four municipalities in Germany.[69]

---

68   An impossibility!

69   https://www.youtube.com/watch?v = 6hFlyqnDJCI&feature = youtu. be&list = PLsEnL3PmbjXk5lxHs0PEIlWOMygqW1BK-

7 TAX POLICY AND TAX ADMINISTRATION, PRIVATE SECTOR DEVELOPMENT

The economic principles governing tax policy and private sector development policy as well as subsidies in a market economy contain the same maxim: ensure markets are efficient by eliminating distortions from market failure and imperfections and minimise distortions from policy. In his article "The Economics of Development" in *The Economic Journal*[70] Nick Stern lists nine reasons for market failure[71] and eleven problems of state intervention in the market. The boxes list these reasons and problems and they are very useful in guiding reform.

Reason for Market Failure

(i) Markets may be monopolised or oligopolistic.

(ii) There may be externalities.

(iii) There may be increasing returns to scale.

(iv) Some markets, particularly insurance and futures markets, cannot be perfect and, indeed, may not exist.

(v) Markets may adjust slowly-or imprecisely because information may move slowly or marketing institutions may be inflexible.

(vi) Individuals or enterprises may adjust slowly.

---

70   No 397 Volume 99 September 1989

71   These maxims have underpinned the approach I have adopted on work on the incidence and impact of the removal of subsidies on petroleum products, wheat and flour in Sudan in 1988 as well as the work on taxation and private sector development presented in the rest of the chapter.

(vii) Individuals or enterprises may be badly informed about products, prices, their production possibilities, and so on.

(viii) Individuals may not act so as to maximise anything, either implicitly or explicitly.

(ix) Government taxation is unavoidable and will not, or cannot, take a form which allows efficiency

Some Problems of State intervention

(i) Individuals may know more about their own preferences and circumstances than the government

(ii) Government planning may increase risk by pointing every-one in the same direction –governments may make bigger mistakes than markets.

(iii) Government planning may be more rigid and inflexible than private decision-making since complex decision-making machinery may be involved in government.

(iv) Governments may be incapable of administering detailed plans.

(v) Government controls may prevent private sector individual initiative if there are many bureaucratic obstacles.

(vi) Organisations and individuals require incentives to work, innovate, control costs and allocate efficiently and the discipline and rewards of the market cannot easily be replicated within public enterprises and organisations.

(vii) Different levels and parts of government may be poorly co-ordinated in the absence of the equilibriating signals provided by the market, particularly where groups or regions with different interests are involved.

(viii) Markets place constraints on what can be achieved by government, for example, resale of commodities on black markets and activities in the informal sector can disrupt rationing or non-linear pricing or taxation schemes. This is the general problem of "incentive compatibility".

(ix) Controls create resource-using activities to influence those controls through lobbying and corruption often called rent-seeking or directly unproductive activities in the literature.

(x) Planning may be manipulated by privileged and powerful groups which act in their own interest and further, planning creates groups with a vested interest in planning, for example bureaucrats and industrialists who obtain protected positions.

(xi) Governments may be dominated by narrow interest groups interested in their own welfare and sometimes actively hostile to large sections of the population. Planning may intensify their power.

Applying the Principles

My first taste of taxation in a development context was not really from the perspective of taxation at all. It was really centred around trade policy and the dialogue Governments had with the World Bank on reducing the number of import tariffs and narrowing their range as part of the dialogue relating to Structural Adjustment Credit policy. Effective Protection and Domestic Resource Cost analyses were the backbone of this work. Effective protection measures how value added is affected by the combination of tariffs on inputs (raising costs so decreasing value added) and by tariffs on production (outputs) (raising revenues from increases in prices charged so increasing value added). This differs from nominal protection which just looks at the tariff on traded goods.[72] Domestic resource cost calculation removes tariffs from the cost and revenue structure and assesses whether there is intrinsic value added in a company so it is a measure of efficiency. I have carried out such an analysis in Nigeria, Sierra Leone, Uganda, Kenya, Papua New Guinea, Seychelles, and The Common Market for Eastern and Southern Africa (COMESA) countries which are addressed below.

72　In the whole debate on BREXIT only nominal tariffs had been mentioned without any discussion of effective protection! But only "Experts" might be expected to understand the difference and they were a disallowed species.

However, it is also important to put all of this into the overall policy context of the time: hugely overvalued exchange rates, foreign exchange allocation by administered means and import and export licensing. Private sector investment was also permission based through licenses and discretionary tax holidays were the norm to compensate for the overall policy distortions that were in place to manage and guide development. Non project donor support was provided in the form of foreign exchange for balance of payment support which was used to import a predetermined basket of goods or from a country where support was bilateral. The vast majority of revenue often came from imports so clearly any reduction in tariff rates would have a negative impact unless the exchange rate changed (devalued). The existing domestic tax base typically was not robust enough to make up any shortfall so reform in this area was also necessary. The resultant local currency from the sale of the donor balance of payment support to private companies boosted the budget. The IMF focused on managing deficits and budgeting and public expenditure management as discussed in previous chapters were rudimentary in terms of current approaches to PFM.

Private Sector Development

Uganda in early 1990s under the guidance of Emmanuel Tumusiime-Mutebile[73] (Permanent Secretary Planning and Secre-

---

73   When I told Dick Morley (University of Durham) that I was going to Uganda on a World Bank mission in 1989, he told me to make sure I made contact with Emmanuel Tumisiimi-Mutebeli (https://en.wikipedia.org/wiki/Emmanuel_Tumusiime-Mutebile) whom he said would be either running the country or in jail as a dissident! At the first meeting between the Bank team and the government, the chair was the man himself as Permanent Secretary of the Ministry of Planning and Economic Development. After the meeting I went up to him and said that I brought greetings from Dick Morley and his eyes lit up and he was beaming the widest smile. He had been forced to flee Uganda in 1972 after he gave a speech publicly criticizing the expulsion of Asians from the country by Idi Amin as president of Makerere Unversity students union. Walter Elkan of Durham University met him and telephoned back to Durham to say that he had accepted Emmanuel as a student and he then completed his economics degree before doing postgraduate studies at Oxford. Dick Morley and Walter Elkan lived next door to each other in Shincliffe Village and Emmanuel lived 6 months of the year in one house and six months in the other, I was told. In April 1992 he became Permanent Secretary/Secretary to the Treasury of the merged Ministry of Finance and Economic Planning and in December 2000 he became Governor of the Central Bank of Uganda and is still in that position. Emmanuel was the

tary to the Treasury now Governor of the Bank of Uganda) took great steps in eliminating many of the policy distortions by removing trade licenses and introducing foreign exchange bureaus. There had been a Private Sector Assessment that I had carried out along with Raoul Ascari commissioned by the World Bank and Overseas Development Administration (now DFID).[74] The Report Developing the Private Sector Though Supporting Markets had identified policy distortions as constraints to development. The report examined the Regulatory System in Uganda covering in detail:

(i) requirements for starting and operating a business;

(ii) exchange rate and foreign trade;

(iii) internal trade and price control;

(iv) land tenure and land planning;

(v) labour market regulations;

(vi) financial sector functioning and performance; and

(vii) tax structure and administration.

The overall theme of the solutions to the analysis and findings was that effective measures for positive change should include the adoption of an overall policy framework with the basic hypothesis that movements towards a market economy had not gone far enough. There was a need to extend the move to leave productive activities in the hands of the market and the private sector, and largely reserve such services as health, education, infrastructure and social security to the government.[75] The need to encourage private companies who saw themselves as part of the long term development process was seen to be an essential element of change. The Report made specific recommendations relating to:

(i) foreign exchange

(ii) customs administration;

---

driving force behind economic reform in Uganda – one step ahead of everyone else.

74   And now no longer.

75   One state owned manufacturer of uniforms for the police and army received subsidy though the budget that was greater than that allocated to the health sector.

(iii) business finance;

(iv) rebuilding confidence in the financial system;

(v) taxes;

(vi) investment climate;

(vii) investment code;

(viii)land tenure; (

(ix) licenses and certificates;

(x) civil service reform;

(xi) creation of a Ministry of Enterprise;

(xii) private sector organisations and relationship with government; and

(xiii)support for disadvantaged businesses.

The report[76] contained a policy matrix that outlined the objectives, measures already introduced, action programme and timing which covered 6 main areas:

I Exchange rate and foreign trade reform;

II Credit and Financial transactions;

III Tax Structure and Administration;

IV Investment;

V Enterprise Operations; and

VI Institutional Framework.

Policies in these areas were grouped around action on:

1. Removal of market distortions, and

2. Compensation for market imperfections.[77]

---

76   An antidote to the depressing Chapter 8 Why Poor Countries are Poor in Tim Harford, *The Undercover Economist.*
77   Chapter V in the report uses the Stern analysis op.cit. as the basis for recommendations.

The private sector assessment conducted a survey of 20 senior civil servants who set and administer government policy in areas that impinge on the private sector to solicit their views on the role of the private sector and how government and the private sector should interact. The assessment also conducted a survey of 59 enterprises termed as small and informal but operating in the market place and 36 enterprises termed formal and following all the regulations. In addition 12 foreign related companies were interviewed. As well 30 civil service business persons – civil servants who also had a business to supplement their income – were surveyed. This ensured that any recommendations were evidence based and would likely have the support of the business community. Such endorsement may not always be the case in such work particularly if consultation is not part of the process – improving the public good has got to be the primary result of public policy if it has to be of any use and such improvement needs to be demonstrated rather than dictated. The Report included a section on the responses.[78]

The Report was well received. Indeed the Permanent Secretary pre-empted some of the recommendations in the report by taking action on foreign exchange by allowing the setting up Foreign Exchange Bureaus as he had come to the same conclusion himself.[79]

Tariff and Tax Policy

In order to carry out an adjustment of tariffs, the Permanent Secretary commissioned follow up work focusing on effective protection from the existing tariff structure and how imports by certain organisation were duty free and free from sales tax (including the government and donors). I led the team that carried out work. While import duties had been streamlined at the time of the study there were 6 rates starting at 0% and increasing by 10 percentage points to a top rate of 50%. With the help of the Uganda

---

78   This survey and my early work in Uganda were fortunate to have the support of the Chairman the Uganda Manufacturers' Association (UMA) James Mulwana who was a founding member of UMA.

79   After the production of the Private Sector Development report, he invited me to go with him to the Round Table lunch meeting at the Kampala Club to give a short presentation. He introduced me by taking out the report and saying that it was the best he had ever had. Was I embarrassed?! We developed a good working relationship and his door was always open to me whichever post he had.

Manufacturers Association a questionnaire was distributed to 80
companies which requested detailed information on input costs
and revenue from sales which allowed the calculation of effective
protection rates and domestic resource cost. A timetable of appoint-
ments was also organised and 62 companies were visited. The
company visits served two purposes. Firstly, they ensured that the
questionnaire already received could be filled in and any assistance
required could be given. Secondly, an assessment of strengths and
weaknesses could be made at the enterprise level through discussion with management on constraints and problems across the
whole spectrum of business operations. This could be backed up by
the interviewer's own assessment of the company in terms of best
practice given the constraints. The report made recommendations
on streamlining tariffs, removing exemptions, adjusting sales tax
to a VAT type structure and increasing the rate to compensate for
revenue loss and to strengthen customs to combat smuggling which
was impacting on domestic competitiveness.

Reform followed in Uganda as part of the Structural Adjustment
Process. There was a period of adjustment of tariff reduction and
the development of domestic taxation to fill the gap with sales tax
changing to a VAT with Justin Zake becoming VAT Commissioner.
The Uganda Revenue Authority was created in 1991 by amalgam-
ating Inland Revenue and Customs Departments and the strengthening of the Tax Policy Department in the Ministry of Finance
under Lawrence Kiiza supported by Gerry Cawley. One of the most
dramatic impacts on tax administration was when the Minister of
Finance in Uganda removed his ability to grant discretionary exemptions in the early 1990s. The substantial and daily queues outside
his office disappeared and officials were freed up to do other (more
important) work. Any exemption that was not in the tax code had
to be approved by Parliament so transparency was improved. This
applied to NGOs and when, and only if, approved the expenditure
equivalent to the tax paid was treated as a government contribution
to the project. Public expenditure prioritisation became a factor in
decision making. Similarly, the discontinuation of duty free shops
in Kampala ended significant leakages as there has been evidence
of abuse and goods being sold in the local market, even if it meant
diplomats had to go to the airport at Entebbe! Other related work
in Uganda followed. In 1993 I reviewed the Regulatory Framework as part of Structural Adjustment Credit II negotiations for the
World Bank. In 1995 I carried out an assessment of the taxation and

incentive structure leading to detailed recommendations for the 1995/96 and 1996/97 budget with detailed work on policies for private sector development and an examination of role and responsibilities of the Uganda Investment Centre. In 1996 I was a member of the World Bank team preparing the third Structural Adjustment Credit with responsibility for taxation issues and the anti export bias. I examined the duty drawback scheme and made proposals for its revision.[80] In 2001 I assessed the impact of the UMA proposals to import raw materials duty free on effective protection and revenues.

I had been invited to join the UK DTI Tropical Africa Advisory Group (TAAG) after working in Nigeria, and on a visit to Uganda the team met with President Yoweri Museveni at State House in Entebbe in the garden under a shade tree. He did not have any aides or advisors with him and discussed the economic reform programme in Uganda in general and barriers to investment specifically.

Sierra Leone[81] followed a similar path working with a World Bank team which I was part of. It was led by Pirouz Hamidian Rad,

---

80   Where import duties paid are rebated on exported items (as in a VAT).

81   My early work in Sierra Leone was after the coup, led by Valentine Strasser. Pirouz Hamidian-Rad, as mission leader, occasionally met him but the team worked with the Ministry of Finance. While I was in Freetown, there was a "palace coup" led by Julius Bio and all of us in the World Bank office were just told to go back to the hotel. Life resumed as normal. Over the years, the political situation in Sierra Leone was extremely unstable even with civilian rule and a further coup by JP Koroma and always the threat of insurgency from Foday Sankoh. There were times when soldiers with mounted machine guns were stationed at intersections. Peace and democracy was only restored with the help of external military assistance particularly from Britain. During the insurgency my colleague Stuart Kane was evacuated as the situation was deemed to be unsafe. However all of the time I was there I never felt unsafe and was able to walk to meetings and walk the long Lumley beach at Aberdeen next to the hotel. A similar situation faced me in Liberia when I first went there with mounted machine guns outside key buildings after Charles Taylor had taken control. I have been back in both counties after the return to democracy and peace. There are no soldiers on the streets, no mounted machine guns and people get on with their lives as best they can. In contrast my visits to Kabul were when it was possible to walk around the city. The only visible sign of soldiers was the UN ones and when a heavily protected Minster of Finance was present at a meeting. However it all became very different and three of the hotels that I visited, one that I stayed in, were all attacked by the Taliban at a later date. Since August 2021 the country has changed again with the Taliban takeover. Similarly in Yemen, Sana'a was safe to wander around the old city and walk to and back from the UNDP offices from the hotel. I was driven to Aden and back via Hodeida and walk around the two towns. Nowadays, these are no-go areas.

and collaborated closely with John Karimu, Secretary of State for Finance, Development and Economic Planning and his Deputy Mike Conteh. In the Budget for the 1993/94 financial year, duty free importation by external agencies was removed unless a procurement plan was agreed. In those cases, duties would be paid and the government would disburse the equivalent as its contribution to the project. For incorporated companies business taxes were changed to assessment based on profits rather than 10% of turnover provided businesses submitted an audited account. For unincorporated businesses, withholding tax based on 2% of the cost including freight (c.i.f.) value of their imports was collected as advance payment of income tax. The threshold for personal taxation was increased. The most significant change was in the area of indirect taxation where excise duty, sales tax and import duties were reformed. For rice and baby food there had been a sales tax on domestic production and imports and no import duties. The sales tax on both was removed and an import duty applied thus providing an incentive for increased domestic production. Import duties ranged from zero to 65 percent with 6 tariff bands with the practice of allowing the importation of "raw materials" (whatever their nominal tariff) at 5 per cent. This practise encouraged importing in bulk (such as sugar) and repackaging as manufactured items (sugar cubes in consumer packs). This treatment of classification of imports was ended and the customs tariff was based on the item rather than end use with the adoption of the international harmonised customs tariff code. The 6 rates were reduced to 3 rates of with 5, 20 and 40 per cent. The 5% was applied to the type of import typically classed as raw material but as specified in the Customs Code and to capital goods and spare parts in a similar fashion. The 20% rates was applied to intermediate goods and certain agriculture and food products with the 40% levied on finished goods produced locally and non essential consumption. This required the Customs Department and the Ministry of Finance to go through the Coding System and apply the new tariff structure to each and every item based on the principles set out in the budget.

Excise tax and sales tax were also addressed. Excise tax had been seen as general tax in addition to sales tax and applied at 10% on all domestic manufactured goods. The type of item subject to excise tax was reduced to alcohol and tobacco products and some luxury items such as jewellery and perfumery and levied at 30% on ex-factory price of domestic production and c.i.f. value plus import duty on imports. Sales tax was increased from 15 to 17.5% to maintain revenues but adjustments were made. For domestic manufactures an offsetting scheme was set up for sales tax applied to inputs (akin to a manufacturer VAT) and no sales tax was applied to capital goods and spare parts. As all investment costs had been codified against company tax in the previous budget, the existing tax holiday regime was repealed. The budget announced that the establishment of an Investment and Promotion Agency was being examined.

The background work on the budget proposals was extensive. Meetings with individual companies and private sector associations were held to understand how they operated and the constraints they faced as well how the existing incentive and tax structure impacted on their operations.

I have carried out work and led teams on tariff reform in many countries notably Kenya, PNG and the COMESA countries. A similar approach to that described above on Uganda was adopted using company questionnaires and visits. In Kenya, all members of the Kenyan Association of Manufacturers were sent the questionnaire and 75 companies returned usable ones (12.5% of the total). Thirty companies were visited and meetings were held with Kenyan Association of Manufacturers sectoral committees to get a full understanding of the issues. In PNG 43 companies covering agriculture, fisheries and manufacturing supplied the cost and revenue information to allow the effective protection calculations from the questionnaire information. In addition ninety companies were interviewed – 70 in manufacturing and 20 in agriculture and related products by Tom Dolan, Denis Gallagher, Mike Bolam, Paul Harnett and myself. These companies were located across the whole of PNG. A structured survey questionnaire was completed during 3 – 4 hour interviews which included detailed information on the internal and external environment facing the companies.[82] The report detailed the economic and business environment affecting company performance and the strengths and weaknesses of the company in terms of ability to response to a more competitive tariff regime and business environment. A summary of the Tariff Review Study Report (3 volumes) was presented in an Indirect Tax Summit and has been published in 'PNG Tariff Review Protection and Economic Efficiency and Survey of Productive Sectors' Indirect Tax Summit

82   This work benefitted from the support of Wayne Golding the president of the Manufacturing Council PNG who endorsed the tariff work.

Papers Institute of National Affairs Discussion Paper No 68 Port Moresby November 1996. For the COMESA study there were 365 fully completed and usable questionnaires covering 17 countries covering 54 sectors. While there were no individual company meetings, meetings were held with private sector organisations, national trade development organisations and relevant government department particularly Finance, Customs and Trade. These meetings were important for discussing the implications of a common external tariff, the transitional process and for examining the best ways of getting acceptance of the principle of a common external tariff within the country. As Project Director I attended the plenary session of all the COMESA countries at a conference in Lusaka that discussed the report and its finding. Examining the impact of tariffs on the textile sector was also carried out in Nigeria and Bangladesh.

Nigeria provides an interesting illustration of policy distortions at that time. Textile manufacturing was a big sector and had a big export market in the surrounding countries for traditional clothing. Yet to encourage the production of cotton by farmers, cotton carried a tariff of 60% which impacted on the cost of production of garments that could be exported but were uncompetitive. Coupled with the overvalued exchange rate of the Naira this stymied the efforts of companies to export. In addition foreign exchange was rationed and allocated administratively so companies could not access necessary foreign exchange easily particularly for spare parts. Most of the machinery in the textile companies that I visited was second hand (often from the Yorkshire/Lancashire mills that had closed down) and the repair of broken spinning and weaving machines was done by taking parts from other machines. One large international heavy machinery company told me that, given its size, it was easier to get foreign exchange for new machines than for parts. As a consequence there were many machines in the country not working for the lack of a few hundred dollars to import spare parts.

I also visited the NAFCON Fertiliser Plant in Onne near Port Harcourt whose location indicated why it was export based rather than supplying the domestic market. It was located near the raw material supply, natural gas, often flared; it had its own port facilities and loaded product straight on to the ships. The main domestic market was in the north of Nigeria and the roads could not manage the incessant throughput of lorries needed to move product. To get domestically produced fertiliser to the North a gas pipeline would need to have been built and a similar plant built near the domestic market at the end of the pipeline. In Tanzania I visited Zanzibar on two separate occasions travelling by the ferry from Dar-es-Salaam and stayed in the Stone Town. I was able to see why it is often called the Spice Island as cloves was one its biggest exports to Indonesia which was an input into Kretek cigarettes.[83] The fact that Indonesia now produces its own cloves is a good example of economic import substitution and how Zanzibar failed to adjust to keep its export market.

The removal of policy distortions and particularly the dependence on high import tariffs led the way for the development of wider tax policy in most countries. Expanding a limited sales tax to a VAT has been an almost universal change. Addressing income tax at personal and company levels has also been a notable development.

Excise Taxes

Getting an understanding of excise taxes and an appreciation of the views of domestic manufacturing companies whose products were subject to excise taxes – usually breweries and cigarette producers – was important. These contribute to both employment and government revenues as sales tax/VAT and excise tax are levied on domestic production and they are afforded protection by import tariffs. Getting to understand their management and competitiveness were crucial to any reform of the tax system and also their views on ad valorem or specific duties as well as excise stamps.[84] As a result I visited San Miguel in the Philippines where I was helicoptered up from Manila to San Fernando visiting two plants in one go. In Nigeria, I visited the Guinness Lagos brewery. In Sierra Leone the Star Brewery was part owned by Heineken and one of the few local manufacturers and a significant employer. It was an important sounding board as was the Monrovia Breweries adjacent to Monrovia in Bushrod Island. In Uganda I met with the

---

83   https://en.wikipedia.org/wiki/Kretek

84   An excise stamp is a type of revenue stamp affixed to some excisable goods to indicate that the required excise tax had been paid by the manufacturer. They are securities printed by the finance ministry of the relevant country. Some multinational producers are often ambivalent to them as they are a means of stopping their own products produced in lower taxed countries from being smuggled into a country where they are manufacturing!

management of the Uganda Breweries at Portbell which produced Bell beer. It is interesting to read its history which mentions the impact of foreign exchange liberalisation in the company's growth and survival.[85] In Rwanda, Bralirwa produced Primus and **Mützig** in **Gisenyi** but the headquarters was in Kigali and was majority owned by Heineken which shows that it was not necessary to have to visit the actual brewery to learn the facts. After visiting the headquarters I was also put in touch with the company headquarters in Holland which was a useful source for understanding a multinational company. In Zimbabwe it was the Castle Brewery which was owned by South Africa Breweries and when I was routing through Johannesburg to Mauritius from Zimbabwe, it was arranged that I visit the brewery there as I had a relatively long transit. In Curacao the Amstel brewery used desalinated water, but it looks like the brewery is now closed and Amstel is imported only. In PNG I visited the South Pacific Brewery in Port Moresby.[86] Cigarette manufacturers were not as many, but spending time with BAT in Sierra Leone was important for not only in understanding how it operated in the country but then being invited to its office in the UK to get a worldwide perspective. This also opened the doors to its operations in PNG which the tariff study team was able to visit.

Tax Administration

Looking back as I am doing now it is quite staggering to see the changes in tax policy that have taken place. However as Richard Bird[87] has written "tax administration is tax policy" so the accompanying developments in tax administration cannot be ignored. He has provided an excellent critique of both tax policy and tax administration which I am using here.

In addition to the maxim that tax administration is tax policy, there is a second quite relevant adage: the pursuit of the perfect is the enemy of the good. If the administration is not up to the

---

85   https://www.ugandabreweries.com/info/history

86   I have an attractive empty (unused!) can featuring a Bird of Paradise on my desk as a penholder.

87   For those interested in readable articles on taxation I recommend Richard Bird's articles which are available on the web. I was fortunate to be in Belarus at the same time as him and hugely benefited from his wit and wisdom as well as discussions on taxation (over a beer or two). It was 1993.

job, then taxes will not be collected. If taxes are too complex, they cannot be administered efficiently. A critical aspect of any tax review then is to ensure that any recommendations for reform are consistent with the ability of the administration to carry them out. In other words, even if a country accepts a set of recommendations regarding changes in policy, one also needs to ask whether the administration is in sufficiently good shape to meet the demands placed upon it. If not, then effective tax policy suffers as a result.

The primary function of the tax system is to generate revenue; its first goal is to ensure that this function is discharged effectively. A second goal is to raise the economic efficiency of the taxation system. This requires that, for a given level of revenue, it interferes as little as possible in decisions made by firms (about production, trade and investment) and by households (about consumption and savings). A third goal is to lift the tax burden off the poorest households and to ensure that actual tax structures are both horizontally and vertically equitable. This is likely to be carried out with some degree of progression.

Reform or redirection of the tax system is likely, as its main aim, to simplify tax policy and strengthen tax administration to achieve these objectives in the most efficient manner. The design of the tax system is thus critical to achieving the objectives set out for taxation. In this regard, it is perhaps easier to indicate what a "good tax" should not be:

- It should not be complex, difficult and costly to administer.

- The number of rates should not be many (they should be kept to a minimum);

- It should not provide strong incentives for evasion so that enforcement costs are increased. This mainly argues for avoiding excessively high rates, but would also encompass the relationship between ease of evasion and severity of penalties;

- It should not introduce serious economic distortions;

- It should not treat taxpaying individuals and businesses in similar circumstances differently – horizontal equity;

- Its administration and enforcement should not be selective or skewed in favour of those with the wherewithal to defeat the system – elements of vertical and horizontal equity;

- The system should <u>not</u> be heavily dependent on one or two particular taxes, as changes in the tax base will have serious implications for revenue collection; and

- A "not-not": the scope for granting or receiving exemptions should be minimised.

Avoiding all of these "<u>nots</u>" will ensure that the tax system will be elastic – that is responsiveness to growth in the economy. As GDP becomes larger and particularly as the formal cash economy grows, the absolute amounts of revenue collected will increase.[88]

The "good" tax rules are complemented by the "good" tax administration rules. The following are indicative of these rules:[89]

- organise the tax machinery to get the most returns by concentrating scarce resources on the major issues;

- see that the law is properly drafted and codified and changed if necessary to support sound administration;

- see that the administration is properly organised, staffed, and trained, and has sufficient numbers and the wherewithal to do their job;

- locate the tax payers, place them on rolls (computerised where appropriate), and examine returns and audit them;

- obtain relevant information from government departments and elsewhere and use it to back up the tax collection process;

- ensure that taxes due are collected; and

- ensure that appropriate penalties are set and are properly applied.

The combination of the "good" tax and the "good" tax administration provides the basis for an evaluation of the way taxation is conducted in any country.

---

88   As illustrated in Chapter 3.

89   Richard M. Bird, The Administrative Dimension of Tax Reform in Developing Countries in Malcolm Gillis, ed. Tax Reform in Developing Countries, Durham: Duke University Press, 1989. P. Shome (Ed) Tax Policy Handbook Fiscal Affairs Department IMF 1995 provides a wealth of material on both policy and administration.

There is also one important feature of a tax system that has to be added to the above: that of stability. Unfortunately, a stable "bad" tax system is not desirable. Stability can only be justified when the system has been adequately established and/or reformed. Once the system has been through an appropriate and adequate reform process, then it should be left substantially unchanged.

I carried out reviews of taxation in Seychelles (1998), Rwanda (2002), and Tanzania (2003) as well as Uganda as already mentioned and applied these principles. I also used them in Mozambique in 2013 when I mentored a team of international and local consultants on the Domestic Resource Mobilisation study carried out for the African Development Bank.

The Seychelles work was very interesting. The context of this assessment of taxes in Seychelles was the country's obligations under the COMESA Treaty (consistent with the proposed measures under the Cross Border Initiative) which I was familiar with given the COMESA tariff study that I had managed. The COMESA agreement was to implement a Common External Tariff by the year 2004 and the proposed tariffs were to be 0%, 5%, 15% and 30% on capital goods, raw materials, intermediate goods and final goods respectively. Although these rates had been put forward, their allocation to individual Harmonised System codes had not been. With respect to trade between COMESA members, the agreement was the establishment of a free trade area by the year 2000. The overall framework included removal of non-tariff barriers to trade, adoption of a common customs bond guarantee scheme, establishment of rules of origin and co-operation in trade and customs administrative procedures.

My task was to produce a report based on a study on implementation of COMESA tariff reductions and alternative revenue collection which entailed

i.   Review options for implementing Seychelles tariff reduction obligations under COMESA Treaty and as agreed under the Cross Border Initiative, while taking account of Government policies and objectives at the national level, also taking account of implications from membership of the World Trade Organisation.

ii. Present projections of losses of revenue resulting from implementing COMESA tariff reductions, Based on current trade levels and revenue collection by commodity and country.

iii. Present different scenarios/proposals for reform of the existing external and internal tax system ensuring revenue neutrality (this would imply identification of compensatory measures (e.g. introduction of a consumption tax, VAT at source, excise duties, etc.) addressing clearly the time-frame and mechanisms by which this would operate.

iv. Based on the options presented in iii above, provide projections of trade levels and revenues for Government, including an assessment of the costs of generating/collecting such revenue.

As a route to the establishment of an intra-COMESA free trade agreement, all COMESA countries were committed to have reduced tariffs by 80% as at October 1996 and by 90% by October 1998. While the Cross Border Initiative tariff proposals were similar in spirit to COMESA there were some minor differences. The Cross Border Initiative tariff proposals were based on:

- a modestly cascading tariff structure linked to the stage of processing;

- a tariff structure that was simple and transparent;

- all customs duties and other border duties and charges should be unified to one single tariff structure;

- pre-announcement of tariff reform;

- four rate structure with the lowest (0% or 5% applying to raw materials and capital goods, the intermediate rate (10% or 15%) applying to intermediate goods and the highest rate (20% or 25%) applying to final goods;

- to avoid an overly protective tariff regime and a large variation in rates of protection, the difference between the lowest and the highest rate would be restricted to 20 percentage points.

- The Cross Border Initiative and COMESA proposals differed with respect to the last two points above as the maximum under the Common External Tariff is 30% and the variation is 25% or 30% depending on the bottom rate.

For the purposes of simulating the impact of changing tariffs in Seychelles on Government revenue the following Common External Tariff was adopted for the study: 5% on raw materials and capital goods, 15% on intermediates and 30% on final goods. With respect to intra COMESA trade the implication of reductions of 80%, 90% and 100% (free trade) on existing tariffs was calculated.

The tax system in Seychelles at the time of the study was fairly unique (as far as I was aware). In the 1998 budget some 62% of revenue was planned to be collected from taxes with the remainder from fees and other income. Trade taxes accounted for the dominant share of tax revenue representing some 53% of total receipts in 1993. They were projected to decline as a share to 38% in 1998. Within trade taxes, taxes on imports were the most important. Business taxes remained in the region of 10-11%. The contribution to the Consolidated Fund from the Social Security Fund had declined from a high of 17.3% in 1995 to 8.8% in 1998. Other direct taxes representing licence fees (as a presumptive tax) amounted to just over 3% in 1998. Non tax revenue as a proportion of total Government revenue was high and was dominated in 1998 by three categories: fees and fines, administrative fees, charges and sales, and dividends and interest. Expected dividends and interest jumped considerably in 1998 and were expected to contribute over 15% to total receipts (compared to 5% in 1993)

Trades taxes (which was the collective name used for all taxes on sales) on imports combined the protective element (tariff), consumption influencing element (excise) and revenue raising element (sales/VAT) in one unified tax rate. There was a limited application of trades taxes on domestic manufactured goods that were of the excise nature. The application of trades taxes on services was of the revenue raising nature. Trades taxes on imports were levied on the c.i.f. value of imports into the Seychelles. The ad valorem tariffs ranged from a rate of 0% to 200% with a mean of 28%, a mode of 25% and a median of 25%. There were 50 categories of specific rates. There were no COMESA tariffs; however, tariff on imports from other Indian Ocean Commission countries enjoyed a 5 percentage point reduction on the standard nominal tariff on rates as shown in the table below, but not including 5% rate on imports as classified in the regulations. There were also additional levies on imports of cans of all beverages of Rupee 2 per can, on beer in non metal containers of Rupee 4 per container, and all alcoholic beverages of non glass containers of Rupee 10 per immediate package. Imports of cigarettes carried an additional levy of Rupee 100 per 200 cigarettes. Satellite dish imports had an additional Rupee 15,000 levy each. The structure of trades taxes was not very "Bird-like" in terms of their simplicity.

Nominal Tariffs					
Categories					
Rate %	0	5	10	15	25	75
Number	45	932	49	2,223	805	3

Nominal Tariffs				Specific Tariffs
Categories				
Rate %	100	125	150	200	
Number	156	2	3	64	50

In reality, the structure of nominal tariffs that applied was somewhat different from the standard rate which complicated and confused the situation even further. This was because of concessions and exemptions. For example, there was a 3% rate that applied as a concession to raw materials irrespective of the standard rate. Un-manufactured tobacco carried a rate of 200%, but if imported by the domestic cigarette manufacturer at 3%. Other non standard (unpublished) rates include 8%; 13%; 23%, 30%; 35%; 36%: and 40% as well as 45%; 95% and 195% under the Indian Ocean Commission countries concession.

There were certain prohibitions with respect to imports and a wide range of items imported with a licence issued by the relevant authorities. Essential food items could only be imported by the State-owned Seychelles Produce Marketing Board (SMB). The monopoly power of the state owned SMB was unlikely to be consistent with COMESA and WTO. As well, it was the sole importer of certain items such as sugar which was an input to soft drinks (in direct competition to a division of the local brewery). It was claimed that the cost of sugar via SMB was 50% higher than it would have been if imported directly adding some 10% to the selling price of a bottle of soft drinks. The monopoly of SMB and its general status would have to be examined as part of the reforms resulting from COMESA membership. This was likely to require enactment of competition policy to regulate monopoly and oligopoly. In addition, there was strict control of the wholesale and retail mark-up on the landed cost of imports. The permissible amount was specified in the Trades Tax Regulations for each and every HS Code. The bill of entry had this mark up on it and retail (and wholesale) prices were determined with reference to this. Application of the pricing system was monitored by the Consumer Relations Division of the Ministry of Finance who visited shops randomly on a daily basis and followed up on specific complaints. Likewise, the application of rigid mark ups would have to be reconsidered in the context of COMESA and be replaced by competition policy.

The implications of COMESA membership required that the tariff element be separated out from the other two components of the trades tax construct (sales and excise). It was recommended that as part of this exercise that the following indirect tax structure be adopted:

- a tariff that applies to imports only

- an excise tax that applies to imports and domestic manufacturing

- a value added tax that applies to imports and domestic sales.

- the term trades tax would be discontinued

These proposals were to be applied as follows: Import duties would be ad valorem rates leading to the adoption of a COMESA Common External Tariff by the year 2004. Other levies on imports that are not applied to domestic production should be discontinued. If a levy is to be applied, it should be applied to both domestic production and imports. Excise tax rates would apply specific rates to preserve existing policy such as deterring low value high alcohol content drinks. Excise rates would be applied equally to imports and domestic production. A value added tax would be applied at the point of entry and at the point of sale in Seychelles. Typically, VAT should be applicable to all sales, but for administrative cost saving there is normally a threshold whereby VAT is not charged at low levels of turnover. However, as VAT is paid on inputs the only element of turnover that escapes the imposition of VAT is the immediate value added. In the case of Seychelles, it is likely that this could be approximated by applying VAT at the following levels: all imports, existing services subject to trades tax, manufacturing companies and wholesale traders (including the retail element if there was one). The only element that would avoid the imposition of VAT would be the retail sector and it is this sector that is likely to be eliminated on traditional turnover grounds anyway. By administering VAT in this way, it should not add too many agents to the existing system. All imports were currently taxed, and all services and the major manufactures were subject to trades taxes. The extension to wholesalers and the rest of manufacturing would not cause much additional burden as the number was few.

There would be considerable benefits in adopting a modified VAT. Firstly, Seychelles suffered from not having a tax that can easily be adjusted to respond to fiscal needs. The suggested VAT would meet this need. Secondly, a VAT is superior to a sales tax as it eliminates the cascading impact of taxes as would be more beneficial to those that are subject to domestic trades tax at that time. It was recommended that exemptions be kept to a minimum, a zero rate be applied for exports and one positive rate for domestic sales.

The application of four rates of business tax allowed manipulation of the system by those that could organise their business affairs to ensure that they were taxed at the lowest rate. This meant operating different enterprises and spreading business between them to reduce profitability in them to the lowest tax rate. Not all enterprises could manage to do this, but the possibility afforded a competitive advantage to those that could. While the provision for loss carry-over was important, it should be ring fenced between businesses. It was recommended that a single business tax rate be introduced on taxable profits instead of the structure that was in operation. This should be set at a rate to generate the existing revenue from business tax. As business tax is a tax on surplus rather than on costs, it would be based on what is affordable. Nevertheless, it should not be set at a penal rate to discourage investment and a rate in the region of 20 % to 25% would still give Seychelles a competitive edge within the COMESA countries. A higher rate would be self-defeating.

There was no personal tax in the Seychelles at the time of the study but one had been in place once previously. Its absence made the taxation system lopsided and removed the element of redistribution from the fiscal system. It placed a heavy burden on the indirect tax system where both poor and rich have to pay on consumption.

To be sure, zero rating the items of the poor's consumption basket eliminated some of the tax element, but the rich also benefited as most of this was on food items. Consideration of an income tax at modest rates based on the existing Social Security payments with a threshold to eliminate low income earners from paying this tax was suggested as being worthy of consideration. There could be, say two rates of 5% and 7.5% as well as a zero rate. Care would have to be taken to ensure that the possibility of switching from business tax to personal tax was minimised.

Many licence fees were presumptive taxes on the hard to tax (or hard to quantify earnings). Given that they were not taxes on surpluses they can be very regressive. They are thus inequitable. In the long-run, it would be desirable to bring these into the more formal tax net and do away with the licences that were only in place for revenue raising purposes.

The proliferation of exemptions is a condemnation of the basic principles underlying the tax that is being exempted. The granting of exemptions creates a culture of expecting and seeking exemptions. It is better to reform the system rather than continue to allow the undermining of good tax administration by creating the conditions for the continuation of an exemption culture. The value of imports that were granted concession represented 56% of imports by value. What was collected in actual revenue from concessionary imports represented only 13.6% of what should have been collected in the absence of exemptions. The difference between what should have been collected and was collected represents almost 59% of actual recorded revenue collected. This was the cost that had to be borne by other taxpayers. Almost 90% of the concessions granted were related to discretionary rather than statutory concessions (representing international conventions and practice). These included concessions on raw materials and investment goods. The value of revenue forgone by category and the rational for the exemption are classed as tax expenditures by the spending programme they relate to best. Tax expenditures are addressed in the next chapter.

The introduction of the COMESA Common External Tariff would provide an opportunity to eliminate such exemptions as the tariff would reflect the use of the import in a way the existing Seychelles trades tax did not. However, it was important to limit the extent of exemptions to remove the culture of exemption seeking. Exemptions should not be extended to government and parastatal imports.

Removal of exemptions would also require re-thinking on investment promotion.

Tax Administration: Tax administration was spread over four major entities. Trades Tax Imports Division was responsible for collecting revenue from imports. Business Tax and Trades Tax on services and local manufactured goods were administered by the Taxation Division of the Ministry of Finance. Social Security was administered by the Social Security Section. License Fees were collected by the Licensing Authority. The Consumer Relations Division of the Ministry of Finance was responsible for checking prices. The Investment Promotion Act was administered by the Investment Division of the Ministry of Finance.

Implementing the changes in taxation suggested in the report required re-organisation of tax administration. As mentioned it was expected that the term trades tax would disappear as such taxes would be replaced by import duties, excise tax and value added tax.

Tax administration could be divided into two separate divisions covering Indirect Tax and Direct Tax. Along with the Licensing Authority, these would form the basis of revenue collection, with Seychelles International Business Authority continuing to handle off-shore licensing.

The Indirect Tax Division could be subdivided into Imports Division and Domestic Tax Divisions. The Import Division would assess and collect all three indirect taxes on imports while the Domestic Tax Division would administer VAT and domestic excise collections. Direct Tax would have a Social Security Collection Division that would collect social security payment and personal income tax (if re-introduced) and a Business Tax Division responsible for business tax. This organisational structure would facilitate tax collection as the information requirements for each subdivision would be based on similar data on tax paying units.

Imports would continue to be a focal point for tax revenue even though import duties would not. The importance of imports required the collection of data to be both timely and accurate. The Government should go ahead with the installation of ASYCUDA to ensure that information on imports and associated revenue would be of benefit to decision makers. The added advantage was that ASYCUDA was compatible with other COMESA countries and the system already had all the initial teething troubles ironed-out in the latest version.

The study also examined the revenue loss from the COMESA tariff and other gains and losses from the recommendations. Overall, the adjustment to tariffs and taxes including the reintroduction of an income tax was estimated to show a revenue loss of 8.1% of GDP which would have to be met by the introduction of a VAT or cuts in expenditure, which was high at 56% of GDP. An estimate based on an approach taken by the IMF in introducing a VAT in Uganda suggested that a VAT of 10% would fill the gap but another estimate based on a cross sectional VAT analysis also by the IMF suggested that 20% would be needed. These estimates were provided for illustrative purposes to show that a VAT would be within acceptable levels.

The Seychelles report had a separate annex that examined policies to support investment and export promotion with a critique of the law and regulations and recommendations for changes given the overhaul of the taxation system. Indeed the report made the point that what Seychelles would be undergoing was a self-imposed structural adjustment process without the support of the Bretton Woods institutions. This would enact an appropriate policy framework conducive to balance and growth relating to the country's internal and external economic environment which countries such as New Zealand, Ireland and the UK had carried out.

Exemptions

My experiences in observing these principles in action and indeed in applying the good tax principles are varied. Codifying legitimate exemptions in the tax laws was a principle that gained traction with improvements in tax policy. Doing away with tax holidays and reducing the level of high company tax rates and "earning" tax holidays through depreciation allowances and loss carry over freed up officials in the Investment Promotion Agencies to promote rather than vet applications for an investment licence that provided tax holidays. Indonesia did this in the 1980s and many other countries followed suit in the 1990s onwards. Investor surveys had shown that fiscal incentives such as tax holidays are not so important to the investment decision. Investors were unlikely to turn them down if offered but other criteria were given greater importance. However if the overall tax regime was unfavourable and rates too high relative to other countries this would be a deterrent to investment and compensating incentive would have to be offered. This is a debate that is still current in the context of the European Union and Brexit (level playing field) but also within the European Union particularly in relation to Ireland relative to the others in terms of corporate tax rates. The Organisation for Economic Cooperation's announcement in October 2021 of a multilateral agreement of a minimum corporate tax rate of 15% and that multinational enterprises pay a fair share of tax wherever they operate is a huge step in establishing a new framework for international tax reform.

As well as Uganda, I was involved in assessing investment promotion in Sierra Leone (along with Ali Alikhani), Tanzania, Yemen and Ghana.

As part of the reforms of taxation, import tariffs began to be seen as a tool for protection rather than a significant revenue generator that a country was dependent on, so items such as machinery became zero rated, and tariffs were lowered to spur economic efficiency. General Sales Taxes and Excise Tax started to fill the revenue gap that this caused. The introduction of VAT became a feature of most taxation regimes given the cascading nature (tax on tax) of existing sales tax regimes and the narrowness of their coverage – on imports and domestic manufacturing. The reform in Sierra Leone, which I was involved in, was to allow sales tax on inputs to be offset against sales tax on outputs for domestic manufacturers (a manufacturing level type VAT) with an increase in the nominal rate to make the change revenue neutral. A "proper" VAT followed at a later date once the Sierra Leone Revenue Authority was firmly established. Most countries now have a VAT.

Collection of domestic taxes – direct and indirect. The solution in many countries was to create a Revenue Authority that merged Customs and Domestic Tax Administrations: Uganda, Tanzania, Zambia, Rwanda and Sierra Leone were some of the first to be set up. I worked with all of these on various projects. The good tax administration rules were the basis of the Revenue Authority development albeit at times slowly and unevenly. Large Tax Payer Units were established, Tax Identification Numbers adopted, self-assessment introduced; audit and tax information departments created and computerisation adopted. Customs Departments had been typically the first users of focused computer software through the use of ASYCUDA and adopted it though with some difficulty at first due to its less than user friendly software. But with the development of the successive versions and the associated hardware and use of the internet, most tax administrations now use it or a similar software package successfully. One of – if not – *the* most important developments in the creation of Revenue Authorities was the recognition that professional management and staff are crucial to their success. Tax administration is a career in its own right and does not depend on rent seeking opportunities.

Bilateral and multi lateral support for improvements in tax administration was triggered by the creation of the Revenue Authorities. I had the good fortune to work with David Child in carrying out progress reports on DFID's support to Uganda Revenue Authority and Sierra Leone Revenue Authority and benefited greatly from his experience in UK Customs and the development of the combined UK Revenue and Customs but also his experience working with South Africa Revenue Authority and Uganda Revenue Authority amongst others.

Tax policy formulation and tax administration are best carried out by separate bodies to ensure the necessary skills are in the correct institution and to avoid potential conflict of interest. However, it is essential that they speak to each other and that tax policy must recognise the ability of the administration to implement. Two examples illustrate this important point. In The Gambia I was tasked with assisting in the creation of the Development Act. The team developed an incentive structure that encouraged backward linkages to encourage hotels to source supplies from within the country (Gambia is a tourist country). On returning years later I was told that the part of the Act had to be rescinded. The tax authorities could not administer it as companies were abusing the provisions by falsifying documentation and generally using the provisions as loopholes. Nothing changes it would seem! The second example was more positive. In Zambia the design of a duty drawback system was developed alongside the Zambia Revenue Authority and used the existing VAT refund procedures to implement the drawback system.

Reform of tax policy and tax administration as illustrated above along with other policy reforms such as ensuring access to foreign exchange have been key to promoting private sector development. Improving information flows about a country through investment promotion agencies can then be effective. One of the tasks when I was working in the Ministry of Trade and Industry with Darcy McGaurr in the Philippines was to produce a Development Strategy for Fruit, Vegetable and Fish Processing. This was carried out with

Max Grosser, a food specialist who supplied the technical expertise. Together, we visited 38 companies operating 42 plants in 8 regions. The visits gave us the opportunity to talk to processors at first hand and obtain their views relating to government policies. The meetings informed us of their assessment of any growth inhibiting factors and any insights which they considered useful and appropriate. From the visits we were able to assess management skills, technical skills employed and technology used, quality control and quality of product, suitability of plant location and plant layout, diversification prospects and marketing. Discussion also allowed the management to raise issues relating to raw material supply, and packaging, the role of government, infrastructure and marketing. The report contained recommendations relating to all of the specific issues uncovered separately. It also contained a chapter on opportunities for the sector and a chapter on implications for the investment priority plan that could promote private sector investment. The report has an annex analysing effective protection and domestic resource cost for the sector.

Other countries where I have been involved in taxation and private sector development in general and in specific sectors can be seen in the Annex. One of the more interesting was the two visits to Belarus in 1993 which was emerging from the influence of the Soviet Union. Two companies stood out. The first had developed fingerprint recognition software which it was using to develop locking devices and the second was a heavy machinery manufacturer where much of the assembly line was controlled by robots. I had not experienced such sophisticated technology on my travels elsewhere. As well as Minsk, I visited a cranberry manufacturer in Brest which sourced wild forest cranberries. Two other memories have remained: the continued fear of the fall out of Chernobyl and the frequent printing of ever smaller in size ruble and kopek bank notes with wild animals on the lesser value denominations.

PEFA and Taxation

PEFA in the 2005/2011 methodology had three indicators (nine dimensions) dealing with tax administration. These have been collapsed to two indicators (seven dimensions) though essentially covering the same content in the revised 2016 methodology. These dimensions reflect the principles outlined above with respect to administration. From my own experience of PEFA assessments, the tax administration indicators scores have improved over time which reflects the efforts in addressing weaknesses and improving tax administration. However one area that appears to be standing still is in tax arrears. Often the reason for that is the lack of a legal basis for writing off uncollectable debts so the debt plus accumulating penalties and interest remains on the books. PEFA does not assess tax policy in a country. In nearly all of the PEFA field work that I have been involved in, I have been tasked with assessing the tax indicators.

To illustrate the PEFA approach to assessing tax administration the following is from a recent PEFA in Fiji.

PI-19. Revenue administration

PI-19 relates to the entities that administer central government revenues, which may include tax administration, customs administration, and social security contribution administration. It also covers agencies administering revenues from other significant sources such as natural resources extraction. These may include public corporations that operate as regulators and holding companies for government interests. In such cases the assessment will require information to be collected from entities outside the government sector. The indicator assesses the procedures used to collect and monitor central government revenues. It contains four dimensions and uses M2 (AV) method for aggregating dimension scores.

PI-19 Summary of scores and performance

Indicator/Dimension	Score	Brief justification for score
PI-19 Revenue Administration	B+	
19.1 Rights and obligations for revenue measures	A	The legal basis for all revenues is up-to-date and available with redress processes and procedures. There is an active taxpayer education system with outreach programmes that is delivered throughout all the islands that comprise Fiji and easy to follow supporting documents.
19.2 Revenue risk management	A	Fiji Revenue and Customs services and Fiji National Provident Fund have well researched and implemented risk management strategies that include data sharing, Tax Identification Numbers, Tax Compliance Certificates and a penalty regime for law breaking that is pursued and enforced through the Courts.
19.3 Revenue audit and investigation	A	There is a detailed and well specified annual audit plan of tax payers. Evidence supplied by the FRCS shows that the annual audit plan is implemented as intended.
19.4 Revenue Arrears Monitoring	D	The available evidence shows that the stock of arrears is 9.1 per cent of total revenue collected but some 80% of the arrears are older than 12 months

The total revenues assessed in this indicator are those administered by the Fiji Revenue and Customs Service which is responsible for direct and indirect taxes and the Fiji National Provident Fund which collects 8 per cent of employee's wages and a further 10 percent of wages as employers' contribution to the Fund. Direct and indirect taxes and FNPF contribution amounts to 89.3 per cent of total revenue assessed in this indicator.

Table 19.1 Revenue Composition 2017-18

	$000	%
Tax revenues	2,831,550	73.7
Direct Taxes	826,768	21.5
Indirect Taxes		
Value Added Tax	788,804	20.5
Customs Taxes	668,629	17.4
Service Turnover Tax	97,872	2.5
Water Resource Tax	64,290	1.7
Departure Tax	147,495	3.8
Stamp Duty	85,266	2.2
Levies	152,426	4.0
Non-Tax revenue	412,782	10.7
Total revenue	3,244,332	84.4
National Provident Fund	599,855	15.6
Employers Contributions	328,081	8.5
Members Contributions	271,774	7.1
Grand Total	3,844,187	100.0

Sources: Data Annex (Tax and Non-Tax Revenue) and FNPF Annual Report 2018

19.1 Rights and obligations for revenue measures

Dimension 19.1 assesses the extent to which individuals and enterprises have access to information about their rights and obligations, and to administrative procedures and processes that allow redress, such as a fair and independent body outside of the general legal system (ideally a "tax court") that is able to consider appeals.

All taxes administered by Fiji Revenue and Customs Service are backed up by specific laws that are up-to-date and are available on the FRCS website as well as in hard copy.[90]

In addition, FRCS publish Practice Statements which are prepared to provide direction and assistance to taxpayers alike on interpretation and application to take when performing duties or dealing with practical issues arising out of the administration of the Revenue and Customs laws. This ensures consistency and certainty on the interpretation and application of tax laws which requires clarification. Practice Statements can be relied upon by taxpayers in the conduct of their tax affairs.[91] A further service is the development of published binding ruling or standard interpretation guidelines and these are listed on the website according to their current status.[92]

FRCS has a Directorate that is responsible for International and Stakeholder Engagement which has a Tax Education Unit and Call Centers. FRCS sees taxpayer education as an important enabler in achieving an efficient tax administration with stakeholders able to understand the tax rules that are simple and clear in order to enhance tax compliance. It conducts Tax Education programmes though workshops and seminars with associations throughout Fiji and uses social media. A series of Tax Talk documents are produced on a regular basis highlighting specific issues and guidance.[93]

The Fiji National Provident Fund is governed by the 2011 Decree No 52. Like the FRCS, the FNPF engages with its stakeholders through education programmes. FNPF publishes fortnightly articles in the local dailies, on general but important Fund matters[94] and also The Member Quarterly e-Newsletter is distributed online via email.[95]

Both FRCS and FNPF have legal procedures for addressing complaints. For the FRCS the first stage is a review by the Objections Review Team which is internal to the organization but independent from the matter under review. If there is no agreement,

---

90   https://www.frcs.org.fj/our-services/taxation/taxation-laws-and-regulations/ https://www.frcs.org.fj/our-services/customs/customs-laws-regulations/

91   https://www.frcs.org.fj/our-services/practice-statements/

92   https://www.frcs.org.fj/our-services/practice-statements/standard-interpretation-guideline-2018-02/

93   https://www.frcs.org.fj/tax-talk/

94   https://myfnpf.com.fj/index.php/corporate-2/bi-weekly-featured-articles

95   https://myfnpf.com.fj/index.php/corporate-2/member-e-newsletter

there is provision for referral to a Tax Tribunal and eventually a Tax Court. Schedule 2 of Decree 52 Review of Decisions and Determinations is concerned with complaints. These are deal with in-house by a senior member of the FNPF or by the Board although there is provision for referral to the Courts. The latest FNPF annual reports states that there were 96 complaints in 2017-18 of which 55 were resolved within a month, 37 resolved later in the year and 4 carried over to the following year.

Discussion with the Chamber of Commerce indicated that work carried out by FRCS in terms of taxpayer information and education was good and there was a positive response. Concern was raised regarding the capacity of the Tax Court (only one judge who was not full time) which could be a cause of delays should there be multiple complex cases.

Based on the analysis and supporting evidence the score for this dimension is A.

19.2 Revenue risk management

Dimension 19.2 assesses the extent to which a comprehensive, structured and systematic approach is used within the revenue entities for assessing and prioritizing compliance risks.

FRCS has a strategic plan that guides its operations. Aligned to the Strategic Plan, is its Compliance Improvement Strategy that is designed to enhance voluntary compliance by addressing risk factors in different sectors of the economy: Large and International Customers, Construction Industry, Real Estate, Supermarkets, High Wealth Individuals and VAT and Customs as focus taxes. The actions developed in the Strategic Plan have been based on research on how the tax system works and how it can be improved. Compliance Risks have been identified and addressed in the areas of Registration, Filing, Payment and Reports. The most recent Compliance Plan covers the period from 2019 to 2021.

To better improve data on taxpayers, FRCS has signed Memorandums of Understanding with various organizations. These include Fiji Immigration Department, Fiji Police Force, FNPF, Registrar of Companies, Land Transport Authorities and has access to data from Municipal Councils, Car Dealers, Fiji Electrical Company and Insurance Companies. FRCS also operates a Whistleblower policy and conducts Door-to Door projects to detect non registration and non-issuance of tax receipts.

The Tax Identification Number (TIN) became compulsory for a number of purposes following an announcement in the 2010 Revised Budget. This was initially for those wishing to create a new bank account, register a vehicle, obtain a driving licence, or register a business. The TIN can be obtained from Fiji Revenue and Customs Authority by filling a registration form which has to be accompanied by a valid Birth Certificate and photo identification such as FNPF card, driver's licence or Passport. An official letter will then be issued by FRCA. There is also a joint FRCA/FNPF card which has the holder's TIN and FNPF details along with photo identification. A TIN is required for

- Renewing or applying for a license or permit with Land Transport Authority

- Registering a used or new vehicle of any description with the Land Transport Authority

- Applying for a new business licence or renew of their business licence with the local municipalities

- Applying for Charitable Trust

- Non-Government Organisations and Religious Bodies

- Registration with the Registrar of Titles

- Registering a company, partners in partnership businesses whether jointly or severely registered with the Registrar of Companies

- Opening and operating a third party's bank account together with the Taxpayer Identification Number of the third party

- Opening or operating a bank account of any description with any financial institution, from within or outside of Fiji

- Complying with Employer Payroll requirements by any person who is a new or existing employee Identification Number of the third party

- Complying with other organisation's requirements not specifically stated but requires TIN in their process.

FRCS also operates a Tax Compliance Certificate (TCC) system. A TCC is issued with a validity of one year from FRCA to a person (or persons in a company) as proof that the person is compliant with the lodgements of tax returns and payment of taxes in accordance with relevant tax law. A TCC is required for the expression of Interest or tender to supply goods and services for any government or public sector business contract; or applies for any registration, permit or license from any government ministry or entity; or Exporter/Importers License; Bank Loan, Financing or Asset Transfer; Vehicle Registration or transfer with LTA and for Visa/ Travel and Migration.

FRCS uses the ASCYUDA World system at the ports to facilitate imports assess duties and other taxes applicable taxes. It operates the risk module and inputs data on type of good, countries and importers which determines which channel an import is assigned to: Green 46.4%[96] (no inspection), Yellow 29.0% (document inspection), Red 5.3% (document and physical inspection) and Blue 14.3% (post clearance audit). Only accredited Customs Brokers can use the system which is also a risk mitigating factor.

FNPF also adopts a risk mitigation strategy. The Board has an Audit and Risk Committee that Provides assurance on the effectiveness of the Fund's internal controls, compliance and risk management. It has conducted a detailed compliance check which indicated a reasonable degree of compliance and improvements have been implemented on an on-going basis. In an effort to strengthen compliance monitoring, a compliance register was developed to increase efficiency and reduce the risk of non-compliance. A MOU was signed with the Fiji Revenue and Customs Services and is pursuing similar partnership with other key stakeholders.

The Tax Laws and the FNPF Act has penalties for non-compliance. In 2017-18 FNPF total of 52 employers' cases were registered in the criminal jurisdiction with Magistrates Courts. The total debt for all prosecution cases in court was $1.34 million. Cases prosecuted were initiated based on a) failing to pay contributions for workers; b) failing to produce documents on demand; c) giving false or misleading statements to FNPF and d) deduction of 8% from workers without remittance to FNPF. At the close of the year, 74 court cases that included some new cases were completed. This enabled the recovery of $1.7 million in outstanding contributions. In addition to its powers of enforcement, the Fund also actively

---

96   In 2018, 4.9% of imports used a simplified system that reflected the nature of the import (personal effects and non-commercial imports).

pursues civil recovery against directors. FRCS has issued a Tax Talk- Tax and Duty Evasion where it highlights several cases where legal steps have been taken to successfully prosecute offenders.[97] It also publishes the names of defaulters.[98] It also highlights how offences are dealt with.[99]

Based on the analysis and supporting evidence the score for this dimension is A.

19.3 Revenue audit and investigation

Dimension 19.3 assesses whether sufficient controls are in place to deter evasion and ensure that instances of noncompliance are revealed.

FRCS has an Intelligence Compliance & Investigation Division that is responsible for tax audits. It produces an annual audit plan which outlines the work plan, combination of strategies, different audit approaches, methodologies, risk analysis and resource allocation for the fiscal year. This plan will also include the high-risk sectors and industries from where auditors select cases.

The primary role of the audit programme is to promote voluntary compliance of taxpayers with the tax laws. It seeks to achieve this by reminding taxpayers of the risks of non-compliance and by engendering confidence in the broader community that serious abuses of the tax law will be detected and appropriately penalized. It guides the activities to detect non-compliance at the individual taxpayer level: By concentrating on major areas of risk (e.g. unreported cash income) and those individual taxpayers most likely to be evading their responsibilities, audits are planned to address significant understatements of tax liabilities, and additional tax revenue collections.

The Division gathers information on the "health" of the tax system (including patterns of taxpayers' compliance behaviour): The results of normal audit activity are designed to provide information on the general well-being of the tax system. Audits conducted on a random basis are also used to assist overall revenue administration by gathering critical information required to form judgments on overall levels of tax compliance—that over time can

---

97   https://www.frcs.org.fj/wp-content/uploads/2019/08/Tax-Talk-Fraud-Issues.pdf.

98   https://www.frcs.org.fj/wp-content/uploads/2018/04/defaulters.pdf

99   https://www.frcs.org.fj/wp-content/uploads/2018/02/69.Talk-Customs-on-Customs-Offence-and-its-Consequences-CEOs-amendments.pdf.

be used to identify trends in overall organizational effectiveness—and to gather more precise information that can be used to inform decision-making on future compliance improvement strategies, to refine automated risk-based case selection processes, and even support changes to tax legislation. Audits are also used to gather intelligence to bring to light information on evasion and avoidance schemes involving large numbers of taxpayers that can be used to mount major counter-abuse projects. The audit process supports Taxpayer Education as they assist to clarify the application of the law for individual taxpayers and to identify improvements required to record-keeping and thus contribute to improved compliance by taxpayers in the future.

The execution of the audit plan is driven by the achievement of performance objectives that are measurable and follow a defined set of audit principles around determined deliverables. Risk profiling and assessment are used to select audit cases. The audit plan specifies different audit types and allocates staff hours to carry them out.

Table 19.3.1 FRCS Tax Audits

Type of Audit[100]	Coverage	No of hours
SPECIFIC ISSUE VERIFICATION	This may constitute simple desktop verifications that can be performed by an auditor to ascertain the correctness and validity of information and documents submitted by taxpayers, accountants or agents.	7.5
SIMPLE AUDIT-SINGLE ISSUE	This type of audit covers a single issue that is not complex in nature. This can relate to specific issues such as VAT desk audits, 1st VAT refund audits or an audit on the Outputs or Reports from the VAT Monitoring System	37
COMPLEX AUDIT/MULTIPLE	These are audits where more in-depth examinations of the technical tax issues are required and it can include more than one tax type. In certain cases, it would require the inputs from the legal team on interpretation issues with respect to certain elements of the tax laws.	120

100   There are also transfer pricing audits.

FULL INTERGRATED AUDIT [3YRS or more]	These are more comprehensive audits that would cover a period of 3 years or more depending on the risks identified at the risk profiling and audit planning stages. It is possible that such cases have been under audit examination in the past and there is a higher risk of non-compliance.	250
FORENSIC AUDIT	These types of audits require more in-depth examination of the tax affairs covering the business processes, source documents, electronic information systems etc. A forensic audit can be conducted in order to prosecute a party for fraud or tax evasion.	250
SIMPLE INVESTIGATION	A simple tax investigation can focus on a specific issue and does not require prior information on what is going to be investigated. It can be based in suspicion, information from an informant or by following the money trail or flow of transactions.	37
COMPLEX INVESTIGATION	Complex investigations would require more time and resources and can be prolonged in order to gather all substantial evidence. The process allows investigation officers to take possession of records, documents and computers and to conduct interviews with third parties. The outcome could lead to prosecution or heavy penalties.	120

The scope of the audit required is defined by the risks identified within the case selection process. The Risk Assessment and Planning Team identify and issues high risk cases to the audit managers and team leaders. Audit Managers also identify certain medium to high risk auditable areas for their teams. Once the teams have set the scope of the audit, the auditor can use limited discretion to alter the scope during the audit. During the audit, additional or new information may be acquired that needs to be examined by the auditor. Other pre-audit factors are recognized in audit selection. In particular, these factors concern assuring the public that the burden of audits will not fall disproportionately on any segment. Also, there are controls that prevent individual auditors from repeatedly auditing the same business, and to require an auditor to exclude themselves from taking up an audit where they are acquainted with the taxpayer selected for audit.

Audits are conducted by teams such as Large & International Audit Team which manages and audits taxpayers with gross annual turnover of above $15 million or other cases approved by Executive Management. Large & International taxpayers have complex finance & business structure, multiple operating entities & international business dealings, cross border and tax transactions with related parties, high volume of transactions and contribute a significant portion of tax revenue. The Small & Medium Team manages and audits taxpayers with annual gross turnover of less than $15 million or other cases as approved by Executive Management. Small & Medium taxpayers comprise of the majority number of taxpayers with high risk cash transaction, deficient document & record keeping and internal control operating structures.

Evidence supplied by the FRCS shows that the annual audit plan is implemented as intended.

Table 19.3.2 Fiji Revenue and Customs-Planned Audits vs Actual for August 2018-July 2019

Audit Classification	Planned Audits	Actual Audits	Variance
Large and International Businesses	50	58	16%
Small and Medium Businesses	650	886	36%
Individual Taxpayers	150	237	58%
VAT Audits	1200	1013	-16%
Customs Compliance Audits	130	197	52%
Totals	2180	2391	10%
Additional Work Undertaken by Audit for 1st VAT Refund Audits, New Dwelling House Audits, VAT Project verification and VAT Deregistration Audits [Not Full Audits]		3033	
		5424	

Based on the analysis and supporting evidence the score for this dimension is A.

19.4 Revenue arrears monitoring

Dimension 19.4 assesses the extent of proper management of arrears within the revenue entities by focusing on the level and age of revenue arrears.

The available evidence shows that the stock of arrears is 9.1 per cent of total revenue collected but some 94% of the arrears are older than 12 months. The FRCS is managing to ensure that taxes dues are being collected during the year but there is a historical overhang of arrears greater than one year in age.

TABLE 19.4 Total Arrears as of 31 July 2019	$ m
Total FRCS Arrears	204.1
Arrears Older Than 12 Months	204.1
Total FRCS Revenue Collected	2,818.0
Stock of Revenue Arrears as % of Revenue Collected	7.24
Arrears older than 12 months as % of Total Arrears	100%
Total non-tax revenue Arrears	79.0
Arrears Older Than 12 Months	62.1
Total non-tax Revenue Collected	298.0
Stock of non-tax Revenue Arrears as % of Revenue Collected	26.5
Arrears older than 12 months as % of Total Arrears	78.6
Total Revenue Arrears	283.1
Arrears Older Than 12 Months	266.2
Total Revenue Collected	3,116.0
Stock of Revenue Arrears as % of Revenue Collected	9.1
Arrears older than 12 months as % of Total Arrears	94.0

Source: Ministry of Economy

Based on the analysis and supporting evidence the score for this dimension is D.

PI-20. Accounting for revenue

PI-20 assesses the procedures for recording and reporting revenue collections, consolidating revenues collected, and reconciling tax revenue accounts. It covers both tax and nontax revenues collected by the central government. This contains three dimensions and uses M1(WL) for aggregating dimension scores.

PI-20 Summary of scores and performance

Indicator/Dimension	Score	Brief justification for score
PI-20 Accounting for Revenue	A	
20.1 Information on revenue collections	A	Information is available on all tax and non-tax revenues on a monthly basis.
20.2 Transfer of revenue collections	A	Over 90% of payment of revenues are paid directly into the CFA on a daily basis
20.3 Revenue accounts reconciliation	A	Reconciliation of payments made by a taxpayer are made monthly against assessments. With respect to reconciliation of FRCS payments and MOE General Ledger receipts these are done on a monthly basis.

20.1 Information on revenue collections

Dimension 20.1 assesses the extent to which a central ministry, i.e. MoF or a body with similar responsibilities, coordinates revenue administration activities and collects, accounts for, and reports timely information on collected revenue.

FRCS prepare a monthly report on tax revenues collected in that month and year to date (by month and cumulative). It includes an analysis of collections including variance of collections against forecast as well as a comparison with the previous year collection on the same basis. This report is submitted to the FRCS executive board and the Ministry of Economy. The Fiscal Department in the Ministry of Economy uses this report as an input into a monthly overall revenue report which is submitted to management. This report also includes an analysis of revenue performance.

Based on the analysis and supporting evidence the score for this dimension is A as all revenues are reported monthly.

20.2 Transfer of revenue collections

Dimension 20.2 assesses the promptness of transfers to the Treasury or other designated agencies of revenue collected.

All payments of tax and non-tax revenues types are paid directly into the consolidated fund accounts. The FRCS accepts walk-in payments at all of its 10 offices throughout Fiji. Payments made by internet are transferred on a monthly basis to the CFA account which allows reconciliation and reduction of transfer fees. Payments using the internet accounts for some 7 to 10 per cent of tax revenue payments. Based on the analysis and supporting evidence the score for this dimension is A.

20.3 Revenue accounts reconciliation

Dimension 20.3 assesses the extent to which aggregate amounts related to assessments/charges, collections, arrears and transfers to (and receipts by) the Treasury or designated other agencies take place regularly and are reconciled in a timely manner.

Reconciliation of payments made by a taxpayer are made monthly against assessments which generates a report by the Debt management Team. When payments are made the format allows the tax payers to select the tax that is being paid. Misclassification errors are picked up during the reconciliation process. New taxpayer accounting software is being rolled out and will be fully operational by June 2020. This will replace the Fiji Integrated Tax System. With respect to reconciliation of FRCS payments and MOE General Ledger receipts these are done on a monthly basis. Based on the analysis and supporting evidence the score for this dimension is A.

Annex: Tax policy and World Basic Income

I have produced a short note on The Concept of Basic Income and Taxation which is annexed to this chapter on Taxation as it addresses policy issues.[101]

---

101   https://pfmboard.com/index.php?topic = 9099.0.

Following discussions on Basic Income with my colleague Paul Harnett who is a Director of World Basic Income I looked at the tax issues in the UK that I felt would need to be addressed if such a policy could become a reality. This is my analysis of why if Universal Basic Income is to become policy and be implemented, personal tax taxation reform is essential.

With the COVID-19 pandemic, governments have intervened to provide income support to companies and their employees and those that are self employed. In the United Kingdom of Great Britain and Northern Ireland the amount payable under Universal Credit has also been increased. The concept of Universal Basic Income (UBI) has gained traction: even the Pope has entered the debate.

There is a growing literature on UBI across the world and also in the UK. Guy Standing has produced Basic Income as Common Dividends: Piloting a Transformative Policy which was presented to the (then) Shadow Chancellor of the Exchequer.[102] The Green Party has also produced its proposals.[103] Stewart Lansley and Howard Reed have authored Basic Income for All: From Desirability to Feasibility.[104] Anthony Painter and Chris Thoung have produced (T)he principled and pragmatic case for a Universal Basic Income[105] for the RSA. How We Could Fund a World Basic Income by World Basic Income[106] looks at a funding mechanism "through new global mechanisms, which would aim to harvest a share of the of the wealth that our ancestors have built up over the centuries, and that the earth naturally yields now, which is known as 'the commons'". I am grateful to my colleague Paul Harnett for pointing me in the direction of these articles.

There is no agreed estimate of the value that UBI should be set at but the documents cited have set out models which point to various sums of money. There is no agreed concrete proposals with respect of how much UBI in the UK should be nor who should receive it:

---

102 https://progressiveeconomyforum.com/publications/
basic-income-as-common-dividends-piloting-a-transformative-policy

103 https://www.greenparty.org.uk/news/2019/11/15/
green-party-announces-plan-for-fully-costed-universal-basic-income-for-everyone/

104 https://www.compassonline.org.uk/wp-content/uploads/2019/03/
Compass_BasicIncomeForAll_2019.pdf

105 https://www.thersa.org/discover/publi-
cations-and-articles/rsa-blogs/2015/12/
in-support-of-a-universal-basic-income--introducing-the-rsa-basic-income-model

106 http://www.worldbasicincome.org.uk/funding-a-world-basic-income.
html

adults / adults plus children? The Universal Credit monthly sum of £409.89 is available for a single person over 25. The current single person's pension is £134.25 per week.

Whenever there is any discussion of UBI in the media, a common interjection relates to the rich receiving it. However there is also very little mentioned, if at all, that UBI forms part of a recipient's taxable income. Indeed it is difficult to ignore the taxation side of the public finance equation in addressing UBI not only from the perspective that UBI has to be paid for but how it benefits all citizens alike. In this regard introducing tax reform at the same time as UBI needs to be an essential part of the package. This is not to soak the rich to pay for it but to clean up the taxation of personal income so that the simplicity of UBI is matched by a much simpler personal taxation system.

UBI, properly designed, should be replacing welfare payments such as universal credit but also over time part of the state pension once the workplace pension scheme has started to become effective. But these are not the only aspects of the welfare system that UBI should replace. All personal incentives, credits and allowances that are built into the personal income tax system (as tax expenditures) should be rolled into the UBI. This would then produce a much more simplified taxation and benefit system. There may be very specific support to individuals such as those suffering from invalidity that UBI could not cover where top ups may be necessary. The one tax incentive that would make sense to retain would that for pension contributions as it encourages pension savings. It defers tax payments to a later date when the pension income materializes so there is no loss of tax revenue over time apart from the impact of inflation which hopefully is offset by returns on the invested contributions.

Table 1 is taken from HMR&C website.[107] It shows that different types of income are taxed differently taking into account income from employment, allowances and different rates at different income bands, national insurance, taxes on dividends with rates and allowances, capital gains tax allowances and the impact of pension contributions.

---

107   https://www.gov.uk/government/organisations/hm-revenue-customs

Table 1 Tax rates[108] on different income streams and national insurance on earned income				
		Basic rate	Higher rate	Additional rate
Income Tax allowance	£12,500	20.00%	40.00%	45%
No Personal Allowance over £125,000				
Dividend allowance	£2,000	Basic rate	Higher rate	Additional rate
		7.50%	32.50%	38.10%
Capital gains allowance	£12,300			
Rental Income Allowance[109]	£1,000			
National Insurance	£9,515 to £50,024		12%	
	Over £50,024		2%	

Table 2 applied these rates to four different income levels and applies different constructs of how the income is earned along with allowances and rates. The result is differences in total tax payable depending on the sources of income. The source of income can impact on tax and national insurance payments made by the tax payer.

Table 2 Tax and national insurance due from all income earned from employment				
	£12,500	£20,000	£50,000	£60,000
Tax	£0	£1,500.00	£7,500.00	£9,500.00
NI	£358	£1,258.20	£4,858.20	£5,057.72

---

108   Scotland has one percentage point more than the rest of the UK on income tax rate.

109   Replaces wear and tear.

Tax and national insurance due from all dividend income				
	£12,500	£20,000	£50,000	£60,000
Tax	£0	£412.50	£2,662.50	£14,787.50 if all at 32.5% or £5,912.50 if at marginal rate[110]
NI	£0	£0	£0	£0

Tax and national insurance dues from Capital gains of £12,300 and rest earned income				
	£12,500	£20,000	£50,000	£60,000
Tax	£0	£0	£5,040.00	£7,040.00
NI	£0	£0	£3,382.20	£4,582.20

Tax and national insurance dues from earned income with £40,000 pension allowances				
	£12,500	£20,000	£50,000	£60,000
Tax	£0.00	£0.00	£0.00	£1,000.00
NI	£0.00	£1,258.20	£4,858.20	£5,057.72

The brief analysis here poses important questions not only for the introduction of UBI but also for the personal taxation system that complements it. There are questions that need addressing:

- Why should different sources of income be taxed differently?

- Why should National Insurance be separated from income tax as its rationale linking payment to pensions and benefits no longer holds? This still holds even though an increase in National Insurance is to be enacted in April 2022 as well as an increase in personal tax as a Health and Social Care Levy to be apportioned to fund health care.

- Why should higher rate income tax payers receive a higher pension allowance?

---

110   It is not clear from the information on the HMRC website whether the higher rate is applied to all dividends above £2,000 or is progressive i.e. above £52,000.

Addressing these questions and simplifying the tax system with respect to allowances and tax rates should be an essential element of the policy reform that UBI would be part of. It would simplify the administration of both that tax and benefit system and improve their rationale. Even without the introduction of UBI reforming the personal taxation system with respect to tax rates and a single tax exempt allowance needs to be addressed. Of course this would require work into tax incidence – pre and post reform to come up with the zero rate allowance and subsequent bands. This would give the platform for UBI to be introduced.

Could the UK government's response to COVID-19 have provided that platform?

It is interesting that the UK government's support schemes for companies and their employees and the self-employed have not been extended to those company directors who receive their income though dividends. Has the Treasury woken up to the distortion in the tax system from the treatment of dividends relative to other sources of income?

8 TAX EXPENDITURES

Tax expenditures link public expenditure reviews (as standalone or as part of an MTBP review) and tax policy. They are often ignored. PEFA indicator PI-5 on Budget documentation has quantification of tax expenditures as one of the 8 additional elements to the 4 basic elements required to be counted to score. If it is missing and the other 10 elements are present (including all the 4 basic elements) an A score is still achieved. It is not mentioned as part of the guidance for PI-10.3 Contingent liabilities and other fiscal risks or for PI-15.1 Fiscal impact of policy proposals or for PI-16.3 Alignment of strategic plans and medium terms budgets or for PI-17 Guidance on budget preparation. Of the 12 Central Government PEFAs that I have been involved in using the 2016 methodology, only Ukraine reports on tax expenditures although Jamaica does but with a time delay that negated its usefulness. Georgia and Fiji are reported as working on the production of a tax expenditure report whereas the remaining 8 do not consider the topic. I suspect that this sample over represents the recognition of tax expenditures. The IMF's Fiscal Transparency Handbook also emphasises the importance of measuring and including tax expenditures in the budget process.

If and when tax expenditure reports become the norm, a revision of the PEFA scoring for PI-16.3 could include tax expenditures in the context of assessment of sector strategies and medium term budgets. Given the PEFA methodology, it can only be included in one indicator/dimension so as not to penalise or reward more than once in the overall scoring so PI-16.3 would seem to be the most appropriate relative to the other indicator candidates noted above.

The Climate Responsive Public Financial Management Framework (CRPFM) addresses tax expenditures more specifically than the standard PEFA. However there is scope to expand the assessment of tax expenditures in the Climate PEFA beyond the coverage in the pilot assessment methodology. Tax expenditures in the context of climate change policy is important from two perspectives: the potential use of tax expenditures as a positive policy tool to encourage green usage; and the use of tax expenditures as a redundant policy tool that encouraged carbon usage in the past, but also the present. Both of these aspects need to be assessed.

Indicator CRPFM-9: Climate responsive revenue administration is concerned with climate related tax management, audit and investigations. The guidelines state that indicator measures the government's capacity to implement tax policies aimed at reducing greenhouse gas emissions and increase resiliency. It also evaluates the extent to which revenue collection generates arrears. The intention is to assess whether carbon taxes are being administered as intended. It has two dimensions: dimension CRPFM 9.1 the management, control and audit and dimension CRPFM 9.2 the arrears of climate related taxes. The guideline state that the alignment of tax policy with Climate Change strategies is covered by CRPFM-1: Budget alignment with climate change strategies. The evaluation of the impact of the whole fiscal policy on climate change is assessed in CRPFM-13: Climate related evaluation with dimension CRPFM-13.1: Climate related evaluation of expenditure and dimension CRPFM-13.2: Climate related evaluation of taxes which includes evaluation reports on tax policy; evaluation reports on climate change related taxes and evaluation reports on tax expenditure. CRPFM-4: Legislative scrutiny assesses the extent to which the legislature takes Climate Change impact into consideration when scrutinizing the budget.

Tax expenditures are excluded from the scope of CRPFM-4 but are implicitly captured by the other tax related indicators but these are not as specifically as strong as they could be given their importance in the climate change context. The standard PEFA does not address tax policy but it is much more relevant for the Climate PEFA. Given that the implementation of tax policy related to climate related matters is included in CRPFM-9, tax expenditures related to climate change could then be included as a third and fourth dimension of indicator CRPFM-9: CRPFM-9.3 covering enhanced investment and other allowances against tax for green investment and usage and CRPFM-9.4 potentially harmful tax expenditures for coal-based electricity and the fossil fuel industry in general. The criteria could include whether these are costed as often tax expenditures are not costed and are not aligned with sector expenditures and subsidies. Scoring of these dimensions would be related to the degree of positivity in CRPFM-9.3 (higher score) and degree of negativity in

CRPFM-9.4 (lower score). Their evaluation would still be included in CRPFM 13.2 which covers evaluation reports on tax policy; evaluation reports on climate change related taxes and evaluation reports on tax expenditure.

Guidance Material

There are two documents on tax expenditures which are very useful in fleshing the topic out. The IMF FAD has produced a How To Note on Tax Expenditure Reporting and Its Use in Fiscal Management: A Guide for Developing Economies prepared by Christopher Heady and Mario Mansour.[111] It provides the definition as "tax expenditures are alternative policy means by which governments deliver financial support to individuals and companies". The UK National Audit Office (NAO) Report The Management of Tax Expenditures[112] examines the economy, efficiency and effectiveness of how the exchequer departments used their resources with regard to the design, administration, monitoring, evaluation and management of tax expenditures. It defines "two broad categories of tax reliefs: structural tax reliefs that are largely integral parts of the tax system and define the scope and structure of tax (such as the personal tax allowance); and non-structural tax reliefs where government opts not to collect tax to pursue social or economic objectives (such as relief on contributions to pension schemes). Non-structural tax reliefs are often referred to as 'tax expenditures' and we use this description in this report".

The figures in the report are quite informative

- The UK tax system had 1,190 tax reliefs as at October 2019.

- 828 structural tax reliefs of which

  - 85 are costed by HM Revenue & Customs.

  - £271 billion sum of the estimated costs of structural reliefs.

- 362 tax expenditures (tax reliefs supporting government economic and social objectives) of which

---

111 https://www.imf.org/en/Publications/Fiscal-Affairs-Department-How-To-Notes/Issues/2019/03/27/Tax-Expenditure-Reporting-and-Its-Use-in-Fiscal-Management-A-Guide-for-Developing-Economies-46676

112 https://www.nao.org.uk/report/the-management-of-tax-expenditures/

- 111 tax expenditures that HM Revenue & Customs has costed.

- 23 tax expenditures with a forecast cost of more than £1 billion in 2018-19.

- 63 tax reliefs HM Treasury assessed for value for money as part of a monitoring exercise by 2019.

- 15 tax expenditures with published evaluations since 2015.

- £155 billion sum of the estimated costs of 'tax expenditures' in 2018-19 (tax reliefs supporting government objectives).

- 5% real increase in summed estimated cost of tax expenditures, 2014-15 to 2018-19.

- £11 billion estimated 2018-19 cost of tax expenditures with published evaluations since 2015.

One of the observations of the report was the identification of tax expenditures as a fiscal risk. Fiscal risk from tax expenditures has been commented on by the Office of Budget Responsibility in its Fiscal Risks Report, July 2019 and the International Monetary Fund's United Kingdom Fiscal Transparency Evaluation of November 2016. This is likely to be true of most countries that have tax expenditures and suggests that the guidance for PEFA indicator PI-10.3 Contingent liabilities and other fiscal risks should include tax expenditures in the list of fiscal risks covered by the dimension (although it may not impact on the score as currently configured). Indeed the NAO report has a chart taken from the IMF Fiscal Transparency Evaluation Report which shows the cost of tax expenditures as a percentage of gross domestic product for 26 countries ranging from less than 1 per cent to greater than 8 per cent with 8 less than 2 per cent, 9 between 2 and 4 per cent and 9 greater than 4 per cent of GDP.

In addition to this international comparison Appendix 5 of the NAO report presents an International comparison of good practices in the administration of tax expenditures: Financial Management. This covers 11 countries and includes in excess of 1,803 tax expenditures of which at least 1,362 are costed. This compared practices for measurement, reporting, and evaluation of tax expenditures. The analysis used government publications and information on government websites, publications by academic researchers and independent institutions. The key questions the research carried out by the Tax Administration Research Centre[113] sought to answer are:

- How do countries other than the UK administer and monitor tax expenditures?

- How does administration differ between countries and between different tax expenditures?

- What does good administration look like?

The aggregated results compare the extent of good administrative practice for the countries studied. It reveals the extent to which the quality of administration varies among the countries and emphasises what can be achieved with the current best practice.

There are slightly more cases of good practices undertaken (104) relative to it being lacking (102). This perhaps indicates how tax expenditures are not treated in the same manner as public expenditure as conventionally defined.

The NAO conducted case studies of nine established tax expenditures. It selected these expenditures based on criteria including: relevance to government objectives; cost; cost increase in recent years; whether action has been taken on abuse in recent years; and whether a tax expenditure has been covered by previous NAO work. The nine tax expenditures selected on this basis were:

- Research and Development tax reliefs for small- and medium-sized enterprises;

- Research and Development expenditure credit (primarily claimed by large companies);

- Entrepreneurs' relief on Capital Gains Tax;

---

113   https://tarc.exeter.ac.uk/. It has also produced a report for the NAO The Definition, Measurement, and Evaluation of Tax Expenditures and Tax Reliefs which can be found at https://tarc.exeter.ac.uk/media/universityofexeter/businessschool/documents/centres/tarc/publications/reports/TARC_Tax_Expenditures_and_tax_reliefs_09-07-14.pdf

International comparison of good practices in the administration of tax expenditures: Financial Management

	Categorisation		Alignment with public spending	Costing techniques				Budgetary controls on Tax Expenditures			Monitoring
	By Objective	By Tax		Revenue foregone	Behavioural assumptions	Present Value	Combined effect	Annual cap on individual tax expenditures	Overall limit on public spending		
y	8	6	7	11	1	.	2	3	2	6	11
x	3	5	4	0	10		0	8	9	5	0

	Transparency			Triggers for review			Parameters for evaluation			Sunset clause
	Published analysis	Highlighted changes	Use of external evaluation	Regular cycle	Change in legislation	Size	Serves purpose	Cost efficiency	Public Interest	
y	9	6	5	5	5	2	4	4	3	4
x	2	5	6	6	5	6	7	7	7	7

y demonstrates this example of good practice is undertaken

x reflects where good practice is lacking

where totals do not add up to 11 information on one country is not available

- Zero-rated Value Added Tax on the construction of new dwellings;

- Relief on employer National Insurance Contributions for employees under 21;

- Relief on employer National Insurance Contributions for apprentices under 25;

- Film tax relief;

- Agricultural property relief from Inheritance Tax; and

- Patent box relief.

For each of the tax expenditures the NAO assessed the effectiveness of the management of the tax expenditure by HM Revenue & Customs and HM Treasury, considering issues such as monitoring arrangements, cost forecasts, management of risks such as abuse, and consideration of the impact of the tax expenditure. NAO undertook these assessments through a series of structured meetings with HMRC and HM Treasury officials and reviewed documents.

In addition, NAO conducted further case study examinations of three more recently designed or revised tax expenditures. These tax expenditures were selected based on criteria including their age, the amount of revenue forgone, and the extent to which their success was dependent upon behavioural change. The three cases studies covered:

1. First-time buyers' relief from stamp duty land tax which is part of a package of housing measures;

2. Structures and buildings capital allowance which is part of a package with other changes to capital allowances to support business investment and

3. Risk to capital condition for venture capital schemes relief which is one option in a package of options to encourage high-risk business investment

While the NAO have assessed that many the objectives set out for these tax expenditures are specified none of them are SMART[114] and

---

114   This would appear to be the case for the 9 others examined as it is noted that when designing tax expenditures, HM Treasury has not given enough

for only the third a comparison is made to spending alternatives. However the case studies, HM Treasury had considered most of the factors that the NAO would have expected. But the absence of SMART negates the principles established for full inclusion in an MTBP alongside conventional expenditures.

Given that tax expenditures appear to be an area that merits attention in all countries the IMF FAD How to Note (op cit.) is a useful guide not just for developing countries.

A key step identifies in the Note is the benchmarking of the tax system as a basis for identifying tax expenditures. The Note states that "it is desirable to define a simple benchmark tax system, grounded in the principles of neutrality, efficiency, and equity. Such a benchmark system implies that—despite possible tension among these principles—the system should be limited to the key features of the main taxes. The benchmark should include (subject to country-specific attributes) the general personal and business income tax rates, a simple consumption tax (such as a single-rate VAT), excise taxes consistent with the objectives of addressing externalities, tariffs, and other more minor taxes. The benchmark tax systems typically include such aspects as the actual rate structure of taxes and the concept of income or spending that is used in the actual law. The benchmark tax system should be chosen to exclude tax provisions that favour (or disfavour) particular groups of people (such as homeowners) or business activities (such as profits from exports). This kind of benchmark ensures that the cost of such provisions is calculated and included in decisions on budgetary priorities. Ideally, the benchmark should also exclude tax features designed to promote particular actions by taxpayers, even if such actions are in the public interest.

The Note discusses benchmarking for (i) Personal income tax; (ii) Corporate income tax; (iii) VAT-style consumption tax; (iv) Excise taxes; (v) Import tariffs; (vi) Social security contributions and (vii) Property taxes. In general the benchmarking advice follows the good tax principles outlined in the chapter on tax policy.

The Note has a table that guides the process of specifying and costing tax expenditures. However given the discussion on specification and quantification, objectives and beneficiaries (equivalent to outputs) should be made SMART as well as being described.

---

consideration to how it will measure impact.

The Note has a section on estimation of the cost of tax expenditures. This requires several steps: choosing the methodology, identifying and collecting data, and the estimation of revenue forgone. With respect to the methodology it advocates the approach that quantifies the direct revenue loss associated with the provision under consideration, relative to the benchmark system, which has no such provision. This benchmark is the equivalent to structural tax reliefs of the NAO two-stage classification. The benchmark tax yield will be based on what is normally collected adjusted for inflation and any other changes such as tax rates, tax-paying population and taxable category. The revenue forgone will be based on the changes to the normal structure due to what is not being taxed relative to what would have been collected.

This makes certain assumptions. Firstly the revenue-forgone method assumes no change in behaviour following the removal of a tax expenditure. It is important, however, to understand that a tax expenditure estimate can differ from the additional tax revenue from removing a specific tax provision if it causes a behavioural response. This assumes no dynamic tax effects. Secondly the cost estimate of a tax expenditure should be based on the amount of income or consumption actually taxed, rather than on the total value of incomes or consumption on which taxes should be paid. The difference between these two tax bases is noncompliance. Tax expenditure estimates assume that compliance remains constant at its level in the current system (not in an ideal system with full compliance).

In practice, of course, the removal of a tax expenditure can change compliance. For instance, removal of a tax expenditure could motivate taxpayers to be more aggressive in their tax avoidance strategies, which would in turn reduce collections elsewhere in the tax system or increase the cost of other tax expenditures.

The Note explains that the removal of one tax expenditure may alter the revenue forgone from other tax expenditures. For example, removing Company Income Tax, tax expenditure would be expected to increase profits, and therefore the room available to use larger amounts of other tax expenditures—for example, accelerated depreciation. This is not a change in real behaviour or compliance; it simply reflects certain mechanical interdependencies between tax expenditures. These properties of the revenue-forgone method are essential to appropriate interpretation of the numbers in a tax expenditure review.

Preparing an Inventory of Tax Expenditures

Dimension	Description and Guidance			
Title and Description	Assign a meaningful title and a short description of how the measure functions (key design features).			
Legal Reference	Indicate the date the measure was introduced, main provisions, and the corresponding law.			
Type of Tax	Indicate the taxes the measure affects—for example, personal income tax, corporate income tax, value-added tax, excise tax, customs tariff.			
Type of Measure	Attribute one of the following categories to the tax expenditure (other categories could be developed based on national circumstances): preferential tax rate, surtax, legislated exemption, discretionary exemption, rebate or refund of tax, zero-rate under value-added tax, tax credit			
Objectives	Indicate the objectives pursued by the tax expenditure as officially stated by the government when the tax expenditure was introduced and subsequently amended.			
Beneficiaries	Describe beneficiaries—for example, families with minor children; seniors; businesses grouped according to sector, size, or other attributes.			
Reason This Measure Is Not Part of the Benchmark Tax System	Indicate the manner(s) in which the tax expenditure departs from the benchmark tax system. For example, "this measure may permit the depreciation of a capital asset faster than its useful life."			
Data Sources	Indicate data sources used in estimating the cost and projections—for example, "corporation income tax return."			
Estimation Method	Provide a short description of the method used to calculate the cost estimates for the tax expenditure.			
Cost Estimates (if more than one tax base is affected, report on each in a separate row)	Year t	Year t + 1	Year t + 2	Year t + 3

The Note points out that under the alternative revenue gain method, a tax expenditure is estimated taking into account behavioural changes and the revenue effects on other taxes. While this provides a better approximation of the revenue effect of repealing a certain tax provision, it differs from a pure tax expenditure estimate. For instance, when determining expenditures of ordinary government spending, dynamic behavioural effects on tax revenues are typically ignored in the cost estimate. Estimating dynamic effects requires an understanding of taxpayers' behaviour, including tax evasion and the elasticity of demand and supply of the goods and services/ incomes associated with the tax provision, as well as the effects on the revenues raised in other markets that might be affected by the removal of the tax expenditure.

The simpler revenue forgone methodology for calculating tax expenditures would appear to be a pragmatic approach given the current absence of reporting on tax expenditures in many countries. It also would allow an assessment of the fiscal risks that the existence of open ended tax expenditures may generate.

9 TRAINING AND OTHER PRESENTATIONS

My recollection of my first presentation was back in Aberdeen. I had been invited by David Greenwood to present the research I had been carrying out since I departed the Granite City in 1974 some five to six years earlier. My abiding memory was David waving his arms at the back signalling to me to slow down! While as a research fellow at both Aberdeen and Durham I took first year tutorials (which were great for reminding me of the economics I had forgotten) but I did no lecturing nor had I made any presentations while at the NRST. So it could be said that, in one sense, I did not possess some of the skills needed for my next journey.

Acquiring Training Experience

The company that I was with – and had worked with in The Philippines and Nigeria – was contracted to carry out an Engineering Subsector Study in Indonesia. This was essentially a development strategy. Its aim was to assess which subsectors had comparative advantage; what could be done to promote investment in them; and identify constraints and solutions to the development of weaker subsectors. Part of the work programme was the development and delivery of a training programme on investment for the BKPM (The Investment Coordinating Board) of Indonesia. I went out to Jakarta to input into the work, but the training component was not going well and it was put to me that I would have to take it on. After discussions on trips home for myself and family visits to Indonesia during school holidays I was reasonably confident that the logistics were sufficient to make it work.

The next step was the design and delivery of what turned out to be a three week training programme on the identification, selection and evaluation of investment opportunities which would be given in Medan in Sumatra, Ujung Pandang in South Sulawesi and just outside of Jakarta on the way to Bandung in Java. While I was OK with the content, I still did not really know much about its presentation or delivery in the context that I found myself. However help was on hand. Tony Koop who specialised in education and training at Macquarie University was roped in to guide me. Together with others specialists from the subsector work a training programme was put together that covered:

1 Principles

    Use of Economics as tool for decision-making

    Opportunity Cost – a measurement methodology

2 Information requirements and data generation

    Identifying the benefits and costs

    Market studies

    Estimating demand

    Technical and cost studies

3 Techniques of analysis

    Effective protection rates

    Domestic resource cost

    Discounted cash flow analysis

    Evaluating a hypothetical project

4 The generation of projects

    Investment planning

While I managed the programme and delivered the training, Geoff Walton, Mark Reynolds, Les Johnson and Jim Harland prepared material in their own technical areas. David Pearce produced a presentation on Cost Benefit Analysis (CBA) on VHS which supplemented the training manual that was produced. Jan Daud and Budi Harsono supported the presentations and materials by converting everything into Bahasa Indonesia. One thing I am sure about after all of this was my understanding and appreciation of the economics of investment identification, appraisal and selection was significantly more advanced than when I started.[115]

The presentations in Indonesia were without the aides that are available now and the recent past such as PowerPoint. To be sure I cannot remember what aides we had, but I assume that there must have been an overhead projector and slides containing the main points of the presentation. The danger of this, of course, is that the presenter just reads what is on the slide rather than using them as a reference point. I think I have moved on from the reading of slides stage. The training was also organised given the time available so that there were group discussions as part of sessions so that there was interaction in the training. It was not all presentations, which would soon lose the participants.

Any training in countries where English is not the lingua franca needs to be supported by translation which can come in two forms depending on the facilities available – simultaneous translation while the presenter is speaking and participants have headphones and hear the translator or continuous translation where the presenter speaks and then the translator repeats in the participants' language. Time can also be a factor as continuous translation needs more time for a course presentation. The benefit for the presenter is that there is an inbuilt breathing space.

Presentations

Presentations, as opposed to training, tend to be focused on providing information on what has taken place and the conclusions of a visit to a country by the World Bank or the IMF. Usually at the end of a PEFA field visit there would be a presentation which would outline what has been achieved in terms of provisional scores and what the next steps would be particularly if there was still information outstanding. At the conclusion of a PEFA when the report has been finalised there would be a presentation of the results and if an Action Plan has been developed this would be also presented.

---

115 I converted the manual and training material while "resting" after Indonesia into a manuscript "Planning for the Market: The Identification, Selection and Evaluation of Investment Opportunities" that had the aim of presenting the standard appraisal rules in a way that could be understood by non-economists but at the same time not offend economists. However it did not see the light of day beyond the manuscript.

A good example of this was after the completion of the PEFAs in Georgia, the results were presented to all the involved parties and staff including the Minister and Deputy Minister of Finance and the development partners. In the development of the budget manual work in The Philippines I started off with a presentation workshop to 46 participants across 8 government agencies on what the objectives were to solicit inputs and feedback. At the end, I presented the outlines of the resultant manual to 47 participants across 7 government agencies. I remember one presentation in Addis Ababa vividly. I was asked to make a short presentation to a small group on the work on budgeting on capital projects that the World Bank mission was doing. When I got to the venue, which was a large lecture theatre, it was full to the brim. After swallowing hard, I got my breath back. Fortunately I was well prepared and delivered what was a lecture. Perhaps lessons learnt!

In contrast, an evening presentation in Amman on export competitiveness and private sector development to companies was tense. That day a terrorist stabbed foreign tourists on a bus tour that had stopped in downtown Amman. There was a protest march related to the Iraq situation targeted at the hotel where the seminar was being held. The march had to be circumvented to reach the venue and clearly the event itself was impacted. What it did demonstrate was the difficult operating conditions in a country which was trying to pursue peace and stability and I am sure that was not lost on the participants. The hotel we were staying at was opposite the US Embassy. We found the area was closed down temporarily, but fortunately there was a suitable venue behind the hotel to wait until it was all clear.

Training

Training usually takes two forms – formal and on-the job, almost informal – both equally important but depend on the circumstances and situation. Formal training is usually planned and follows a timetable for the delivery of presentations. One of the more interesting training two days that my colleagues in Albania put on in Durres was for the Public Accounts Committee members on the new PFM system and the role of the PAC in conducting scrutiny. I remember making a presentation on the ODI study on MTEFs and the lessons for Albania which was too long and boring! However, there was a superb role playing session by Sotiraq Guga and Simon Stone on "interrogation" of witnesses summoned to the PAC. This was later followed by a trip to Parliament in London with meetings with members of the PAC and other Parliamentarians there and attending a PAC session. The Albania team were fortunate to have John Butcher who had been undersecretary in Education and Trade and Industry. He worked with parliamentarians in Albania under the project and made all the contacts in London. I was also involved in the delivery of a seven-session three day training workshop which Kit Nicholson had arranged for Endrit Lami's Macro Department (on a separate project) where I was able to discuss the revenue forecasting model for Albania that I had developed. Other training that I was involved in Albania was on Expenditure Analysis.

Informal training tends to be ad hoc and discussion based. It is usually linked to technical assistance projects where there is day to day support such as the work in Albania and Palestine on MTPB where technical issues would be discussed with the departmental staff in an informal manner. Colleagues were adept at this. This format was very useful when I was providing a help-desk for the Kosovo central government PEFA, led by Azem Reqica, and sharing an office space room in the Ministry of Finance with the team. In Palestine there was a nice almost halfway house where a presentation could be organised at lunch with a question and answer session combining the informal and formal. I used that time and opportunity to present the revenue forecasting model.

PEFA Training

I have been involved in PEFA training on most of the PEFAs that I have been involved in. These have ranged from three days training in Antigua to three hours in Grenada. The length often depends on the scheduling. Antigua was well before the actual PEFA fieldwork. The objective was to ensure that the data needs as well as the structure and composition of PEFA was understood so that when the field work took place the assessment team would hit the ground running. Shorter presentations focused more on the data needs with a briefer coverage of the PEFA format itself.

The PEFA Secretariat has invested in the production of training modules which are readily available. I have presented with members of the Secretariat on a regional training event in Barbados for all the Caribbean islands organised by CARTAC and on subnational PEFAs in Georgia and Ukraine. When carrying out training as part of an actual PEFA I add a section onto the PEFA Secretariat slides on data and sources for each of the indicators. The purpose in this training circumstance is not to train participants to carry out a PEFA, but to understand what a PEFA is and what data and information they need to produce so that the PEFA can be realised within the timeframe.

Examples of Training Delivered

A PEFA training programme that was delivered for the subnational PEFAs in Serbia which were conducted by me, Paul Harnett, Siniša Jovanović and Stefan Teodosić, is shown below. While these PEFAs were conducted using the 2011 methodology I have modified the schedule to the 2016 format to be consistent with the overall presentation of material on PEFA previously.

One of the countries that I delivered PEFA training over two days was in the Federation of St Kitts and Nevis. Both St Kitts and Nevis have separate PFM systems. The training was organised by the Fiscal Management in the Caribbean (FMC) project[116] implemented by the IMF and supported and funded by the Government of Canada as part of its work on PFM in the islands in which I was involved. There were 28 attendees. The actual PEFA was conducted by the EC at a later date.

Serbia Subnational PEFA training programme

The purposes of the training is to provide an overview of the PEFA objective, methodology (including rating methods) and to raise awareness on the necessary preparation for the PEFA that will take place in the 6 municipalities.	
Day 1	
10.00	Welcoming Remarks and Introductions
10.30	The PEFA Initiative
11.30	Break

---

116 Successor to SEMCAR.

11.45	Indicators PI-1 to PI-4
12.15	Guidance on Evidence PI-1 to PI-4
13.00	Lunch
14.30	Indicators PI-5 to PI-10
15.15	Guidance on Evidence PI-5 to PI-10
15.45	Case Study PIs-1, 5 and 10
16.45	Organisation of Field visits
Day 2	
09.00	Recap of day 1
9.15	Indicators PI-11 to PI-12
9.30	Guidance on Evidence PI-11 to PI-12
9.45	Indicators PI-13 to PI-15
10.00	Guidance on Evidence PI-13 to P-15
10.15	Indicators PI-16 to PI-21;
10.45	Guidance on Evidence PI-16 to PI-21;
11.15	Break
11.30	Case Study PIs-11, 17 and 19
13.00	Lunch
14.00	Indicators PI-22 to PI-25;
14.30	Guidance on Evidence PI-22 to PI-25
	Break
15.00	Indicators PI-26 to PI-28
15.15	Guidance on Evidence PI-26 to PI-28
15.30	Indicators PI 29- PI-31 HLG-1
15.45	Guidance on Evidence PI 29- PI-31 HLG-1
16.00	Case Study PIs-25, 28
16.30	2007 and 2010 Central Government PEFA Scores

As well as the PEFA training in St Kitts, which was at end of August 2015 I delivered training workshops on programme budgeting a year earlier in July 2014 and on budget planning in January 2017. These training workshops have to be seen in the context of a SEMCAR mission in 2012 to both St Kitts and Nevis islands which had identified problems in budgeting resulting from the misspecification of the software in St Kitts (referred to in footnote 34). All of the SEMCAR missions had focused on the move to programme budgeting and what needed to be done. All reports made the same recommendations. While there was a long gestation period, a revised version of SIGBUD was eventually commissioned supported by FMC under Than Lwin and later Suhas Joshi which also included a new Chart of Accounts. The coverage of the training is below and 13 senior staff in budget and finance departments from Ministries of Finance, Health, Home Affairs, Foreign Affairs, Agriculture as well as the Office of the Prime Minister and the Audit Office.

In addition to the 2012 SEMCAR mission, there was a CARTAC mission I undertook to Nevis in 2013 for Matthew Smith (following up a previous visit by Martin Bowen in 2011). While on SEMCAR/FMC missions visits were made to Nevis and informal training was provided that followed up on the analysis and recommendations in the CARTAC reports. Nevis had abandoned the SIGBUD software and developed an in-house solution using a readily available software programme.

St Kitts and Nevis
Workshops on Programme Budgeting
Each session allows for a presentation (by John Short) and group discussion

Day 1 11 July, 2014	Focus on Reform and Conditions for Strategic Budgeting
9.00 -9.15	Introduction
9.15 – 9.30	Structure and Content
9.30 – 10.45	Programme Budgeting in context of Fiscal Reform

11.00 – 12.15	MTEF – key features
12.15 – 13.15	Lunch
13.15 – 14.30	Links between Planning and Budgets
14.45 – 16.00	Forecasting fiscal aggregates and production of ceilings
Day 2 14 July 2014	Focus on Strategic Budgeting
9.00 – 9.15	Recap
9.15 – 10.15	From Policy and Plans to Strategic Budgeting
10.15 -12.15	Group work
12.15 – 13.15	Lunch
13.15 -14.30	Group work
14.45 – 16.00	Expenditure Analysis
Day 3 15 July 2014	Management Tools for Strategic Budgeting
9.00 -9.15	Recap
9.15 – 10.30	Budget Calendar
10.45- 12.15	Budget Manuals and Guidelines
12.15 – 13.15	Lunch
13.15 – 14.00	Software
14.15 – 16.00	The way forward

Budget Planning Workshops St Kitts January 2017

Each session will consist of a presentation and group discussion.

The focus will be on what is required to be done/put in place based on good practice.

18 January 2017 (Half Day)

For Senior Management

Session 1 Public Financial Management – evolution of steps to Performance Budgeting.

Presentation John Short

Discussion

Where is St Kitts at today?

What are the next steps?

What does your staff <u>need to</u> implement this successfully?

- From your own Ministry
- From the Centre of Government?

Session 2 Medium term Budgeting – a Framework for successful implementation

Presentation John Short

Discussion

What does St Kitts need to do to get there?

What are the next steps?

What does your staff <u>need to</u> implement this successfully?

- From your own Ministry?
- From the Centre of Government?

Day 2 (Full day)

For Budgeting and Planning Departments

Session 1 Public Financial Management – evolution of steps to Performance Budgeting.

Presentation John Short

Discussion

Where is St Kitts at today?

What are the next steps?

What does your department <u>need to</u> implement this successfully?

- From your own Ministry?
  - o From senior management?

- o   From other Departments in your Ministry?
- From the Centre of Government?

Session 2 Medium terms Budgeting – a Framework for successful implementation

Presentation John Short

Discussion

What does St Kitts need to do to get there?

What are the next steps?

What does your department <u>need to</u> implement this successfully?

- From your own Ministry?
- o   From senior management?
- o   From other Departments in your Ministry?
- From the Centre of Government?

Session 3 From Policy and Plans to an MTEF and Budget – the Programme Tree Approach

Presentation John Short

Discussion

Where is St Kitts at today?

What are the next steps?

What does your department <u>need to</u> implement this successfully?

- From your own Ministry?
- o   From senior management?
- o   From other Departments in your Ministry?
- From the Centre of Government?

Session 4 Policy based Multi-year Budgeting: The Mechanics of Rolling over policy and plans into expenditure and the creation of fiscal space

Presentation John Short

Discussion

What does St Kitts need to do to get there?

What are the next steps?

What does your department <u>need to</u> implement this successfully?

- From your own Ministry?
  o From senior management?
  o From other Departments in your Ministry?
- From the Centre of Government?

The training was well attended and the participation of 13 Permanent Secretaries or equivalent ensured that it was targeted at the decision makers. In all there were 73 participants including: 7 staff members from Ministry of Public Infrastructure, Post, Urban Development and Transport. 3 staff members from Ministry of Community Development, Gender Affairs and Social Services. 2 staff members from Ministry of Youth, Sports and Culture. 9 staff members from Ministry of Finance, 3 staff members from Accountant General Department, 3 staff members from Inland Revenue Department and 3 staff members from Audit. 3 staff members from Ministry of Foreign Affairs and Aviation. 7 staff members from Ministry of Agriculture, Human Settlement, Cooperatives and Environment. 6 staff members from Office of the Prime Minister. 3 staff members from Ministry of Health. 3 staff members from Ministry of Education. 4 staff members from Ministry of Tourism. 5 staff members from Ministry of Justice, Legal Affairs and Communications. 6 staff members from Ministry of Sustainable Development. 4 staff members from Ministry of International Trade. 1 staff member from Ministry of National Security. 2 staff from Ministry of Nevis Affairs, Labour, Social Security and Ecclesiastical Affairs.

In Kosovo workshops and training were a major focus of the work programme supporting the activities outlined in Chapter 2. Given that an overall aim of the programme was to learn from the Albania experience, the very first training workshop was on "Public Finance Management – Albania Experience" to exchange information on Public Finance Management Reform, and more specifically the government-wide and individual ministries integrated planning processes

Workshop with Line Ministries Kosovo – PFM and Albanian Experience 10 June 2010

10:00 – 10:10	**Introduction and Welcome** Mr. Bedri Hamza, Deputy Minister, MEF Mr. John Short, PFM Consultant
10:10 – 10:50	**The role of decision-makers in establishing the planning system and Strategy Review and Coordination** *(40 minutes)* *Mr. Sherefedin Shehu, former Deputy Minister of Finance, currently Member of Parliament* *Ms. Arjana Cela, Advisor to the Prime Minister*
10:55 – 11:35	**Medium Term Planning Processes and Structures at Government-wide and line ministry level, and the Role of MF and Budget Department** *(40 minutes)* *Ms. Arjana Cela, Advisor to Prime Minister, former Budget and Policy Director* *Mr. Genti Opre, Head of Budget Analysis* *Mr. Saimir Sallaku, PFM Expert*
11:35 – 11:55	**Discussion** *(20 minutes)* (Questions and Answers)
12:00 – 13:15	**Lunch Break and Coffee**
13:15 – 14:30	**Integrated Planning System Calendar and Software Tools** *Mr. Saimir Sallaku, PFM Expert*
14:30 – 15:00	**Discussions** (Questions and Answers)

The attendees were: Permanent Secretary and Head of Strategic Planning Unit Office of the Prime Minister; Acting Permanent Secretary and Head of Budget and Finance Ministry of Finance and Economy; Deputy Minister, Acting Permanent Secretary and Head of Budget and Finance Ministry of Education, Science and Technology; Deputy Minister, Acting Permanent Secretary, Head of Budget and Finance Ministry of Justice; Deputy Minister. Acting Permanent Secretary, Head of Budget and Finance Ministry of Health; Deputy

Minister, Acting Permanent Secretary, Head of Budget and Finance Ministry of Public Administration; Deputy Minister, Acting Permanent Secretary, Head of Budget and Finance Ministry of Agriculture, Forestry and Rural Development; Acting Permanent Secretary, Ministry of European Integration; Chairman and Head of Budget and Finance Kosovo Judicial Council; Chairman, Public Procurement Regulatory Committee; Head of Budget and Finance, Public Procurement Agency

Following this initial workshop there was a series of events in support of an Improved Planning and Budgeting Process and Support to Training and Capacity Building on Public Financial Management. These were all tied into the technical assistance that the DFID funded team was implementing to transfer the knowledge from the Albanian experience. Where possible the Albanian consultants were used for delivery with me being on hand to support them which made Albanian the lingua franca! The various workshops are presented to indicate the coverage.

Strategic Expenditure Review Workshop 16 August 2011

10:00 – 10:20	Opening of Workshop *Naim Baftiu,* *General Secretary, MoF* *Lum Mita,* *Chairman of SER Working* *Group*
10:20 – 11:30	*1. Public Expenditure Management – A Case study(15 minutes)* *2. Policy, strategy and financial planning – (45 minutes)* Saimir Sallaku *Advisor to SER Working Group, REPIM (DFID)*
11:30 – 11:50	*Discussion, Q&A (20 minutes)*
11:50 – 12:20	Break *(40 minutes)*
12:20 – 13:10	Budget Planning Process – Linking Budget Policies *(45 minutes)* *Arjeta Abazi, Advisor to SER Working Group, REPIM (DFID)*
13:10 – 13:30	*Discussion, Q&A (20 minutes)*
13:30 – 14:00	Conclusion

Initial meeting on the implementation of public finance management across municipal governments

Meeting objectives:

1. Summary presentation of strengths and weaknesses in municipal PFM practices.

2. Discussion of reforms measures toward improvement of municipal practices in public finance management.

3. Discussion of priority measures, stakeholders and timeframes for reform implementation.

The meeting is designed for Mayors and Municipal Team Leaders who in future will be the contact point with the Ministry of Finance, representatives from the Ministry of Finance – the relevant units, the Ministry of European Integration, Office of the Auditor General, Procurement Agency of Kosovo, Association of Kosovo Municipalities, representatives of donors who support this process – USAID and DFID.

29 February, 2012

Time	Agenda
10:00-10:30	Reception
10:30-10:40	Welcome address and opening Mr. Ramadan Avdiu, Deputy Minister of Finance
10:40-10:50	Support for public finance management reforms to local governments in Kosovo William Lawrence, USAID
10:50-11:15	Improved approach to public finance management and related reforms John Short, Adviser, DFID
11:15- 11:45	Implementation of the Municipal PFM Reform Action Plan in Kosovo Besa Gashi, Adviser, GFSI/USAID
11:45- 12:00	Open discussion
12:00 – 13:00	Lunch

Follow up conference on municipal budget practices

The conference aims at addressing the importance of sound mid – term budget planning as well as existing disconnect between policy making, planning, and budgeting, with local authorities. Additionally the event will highlight the importance of better understanding of national medium term expenditure strategies and policies primarily in education and health, focused on the link with local authorities in Kosovo. Finally the occasion will mark the potential municipal MTEF progress achieved in some areas from last year and improvements further needed.

Strengthening municipal medium term expenditure framework, March 14, 2012

AGENDA

	MORNING SESSION
10:00 – 10:10	Welcoming Remarks Mr. Driton Qehaja, Advisor to the Minister of Finance
10:10 – 10:20	USAID Support to Local Government in Kosovo William Lawrence, USAID
10:20 – 10:40	General observations on municipal MTEFs from the PEFA exercise : progress achieved and areas to be improved USAID/GFSI Team
10:40 – 11:05	MTEF Best Practices John Short, DFID Advisor
11:05 – 11:30	Albania's MTEF Experience Ms. Arjeta Abazi, Lecturer at Faculty of Economics – Tirana University
11:30-11:45	Strengthening Approach to Municipal MTEF Practices during the 2013 Budget Process Mr. Petrit Popova, Municipal Budget Director, Ministry of Finance

11:45-13:00	Lunch Reception
	AFTERNOON SESSION
13:00-13:20	Recent MTEF central budget strategies Ruzhdi Halili, Director of Office for Strategic Planning – PM Office
13:20-13:40	National MTEF on Education and impact towards local authorities Fehmi Zylfiu – Ministry of Education, Science and Technology
13:40-14:00	National Health Sector Strategy Mr. Arsim Cavdarbasha & Mr. Musa Rexhaj- Ministry of Health
14:00-14:20	Medium Term Budget Planning of Social Services Mr. Laurie Joshua, Team Leader – DFID-KSSD Project
14:20 -14:40	Discussion – Questions and Answers Session
14:45	Adjourn

The project that DFID supported and I managed produced two manuals each with its own self-development workbook.

- Guidelines for the preparation of sector strategies for the Strategic Planning Office which was prepared by Martin Johnston

- Manual for costing new policy initiatives for the Ministry of Finance which I prepared.

Training on Costing and Strategic Planning based on these were produced and delivered as follows:

10 and 11 July 2012 (OPM Strategic Planning Office, OPM Government Coordination Secretariat, MF Central Budget Department)

30 and 31 July 2012 (MoF Central Budget Department 2nd Group)

13 and 14 Sep 2012 (Ministry of Economic Development, Ministry of Agriculture, Forestry and Rural Development, Ministry of Environment and Spatial Planning, Ministry of Trade and Industry)

19 and 20 September (Ministry of Labour and Social Welfare, Ministry of Health, Ministry of Education, Science and Technology, Ministry of Justice)

25 and 25 September (Ministry of Return and Communities, Ministry of Public Administration, Ministry of European Integration, Ministry of Finance, Ministry of Security Forces, Office of Prime Minister, OPM Veterinary and Food Agency, OPM State Archives Agency, Ministry of Internal Affairs, Kosovo Judicial Council)

No. of Training events: 5

Participants:

PMO Strategic Planning Office: *4*
PMO Government Coordination Secretariat: *2*
MF Central Budget Department: *18*

Total Centre of Government   24

Line Ministries and Agencies   *57*

Total Government-wide Participants   83

Budget Institutions (Line Ministries and Agencies)   16

The training schedule was as follows:

First day		
8:30 – 9:00	Registration of Participants	
9:00 – 9:10	Opening of Training, Ministry of Finance	
9:10 – 9:20	Training Opening, Office of Prime Minister	
9:20 – 9:30	Training Opening, REPIM	
9:30 – 9:40	Presentation of participants	
9:40 -12: 30	First Session:	Introduction Costing of New Policy Initiative *Decision making tree for the New Proposal-Policy*
10:30 – 10:45	Break for Coffee	

		Summary of Costing Methodology
		The process of calculating the cost "bottom-up"
12:15 -13: 15	Lunch	
13:15 – 15:30	Second session:	Elements Key to Costing
		Programmes
		Programme Tree
		Overall goals of policy
14:30 – 14:45	Break for Coffee	
		Policy Objectives
		Policy Standards
		Projects
		Products
		Activities
15:30	Completion of the first day	
Day Two		
9:00 – 11:00	Third session:	Determining Costs
		Introduction
		People-related Expenditures (Code 111)
		Goods and Services inputs (Code 130)
		Transfers and Subsidies (Code 20)
10:30 – 10:45	Coffee Break	
		Capital Expenditure Treatment (Code 30)
		Treatment of Quasi Fixed Costs and Marginal Costs in Specifying inputs to Activities to deliver Outputs
		Apportionment
		Minor Items
		Reserve Funds (Contingencies)

		Distinguishing between Unit Input Costs and Unit Output
11:00 – 12:15	Fourth session:	Costing of Legislation through a Bottom-Up Approach in the Government of Kosovo
12:15 – 13:15	Lunch	
13:15 -14:15	Work in groups:	Compilation of a budget request using the structure in the presentation *Work in group* *Instructions to the participants*
14:15 – 14:30	Break for coffee	
14:30 – 14:50	Presentation by participants	
14:50 – 15:10	Course evaluation	
15:10 -15: 30	Discussion	
15:30	Completion of training	

Trainers: Saimir Sallaku, REPIM
                                      Arjeta Sallaku, REPIM
                                      Alban Kaçiu, REPIM

The final training material that was produced under the DFID supported projects was a Training Manual for the new budget officers that would be joining the Ministry of Finance. Jolanda Trebicka prepared the module assisted by me. This was supported by the design of a 5 day training programme that consisted of 5 PowerPoint presentations.

- Overview of the State Budget (16 slides)

- Strategic Planning (20 slides)

- Medium Term Expenditure Framework (31 slides)

- Annual Budget (24 slides)

- Budget Monitoring Financial Control and Auditing (22 slides)

Each of the sessions was designed to take three hours and it was intended that it would be delivered by the Kosovo Institute of Public Administration the Government's training agency.

All the materials in the training programme were in Albanian (although there was an initial English language version so I could review it).

Given the training materials and presentations that I have been involved in as outlined in this Chapter, I also have gained an appreciation of what presentations and training is all about. I would not say that after Indonesia I enjoyed standing up in front of an audience and that I was proficient in delivery – but better than my Aberdeen experience and have become better over time. Perhaps practice ensures better results as well as the passage of time! I also appreciate the need for teaching qualifications for teachers and the significant input of time and effort and probation period that the teachers in my family have undergone as well as training the rugby coaches, physiotherapist practitioner and trainer and dog trainer and behaviourist have undergone – daughters and son-in-law and son and daughter-in-law!

As well as my induction by Tony Koop, I have attended the training that the PEFA Secretariat puts on for PEFA practitioners.

10 COMMONALITY OVER TIME: 50 YEARS OF PROGRESS?

Has there been progress in the areas that I have been involved it over my journey as an economist in almost 50 years? I do not mean the geographical areas – some 60 countries – that I have been involved in but the policy areas. To a certain extent this would require being able to compare the situation in country A in the past with the situation in the present; but that would have required me to have worked in the same policy area then and now in the same country. And that has not been the case. However, it is possible to take a generic policy area such as, say budget formulation and ascertain whether there has been progress using individual or groups of countries as a guidepost.

A second question that can be posed is: why has there been progress? What are the conditions that have been in place that has generated development in the policy areas? And a third question that I will seek to answer: are there any lessons? These questions then can be answered by using the same format of individual or groups of countries as a guidepost. I will explore these questions in relation to the topics covered which related to my experiences as far as it is practicable and possible given the timeframes involved. Responses are presented specific to a topic and where there is commonality such as Information Technology (IT), these are grouped.

Import Tariffs and Tariff Policy

Tariff reform in the 1990s was driven by economic considerations to improve efficiency and also expand market opportunities in areas that countries have comparative advantage – the ability to carry out a particular economic activity (such as making a specific product) more efficiently than another activity or in another country. Multilateral agreements such as COMESA opened up the ability of

Uganda to export its agriculture products to Kenya when it was more efficient and vice versa on industrial products without the imposition of tariffs. Indeed tariffs would have appear to be something that was no longer a topic that appeared much in the public domain once the General Agreement on Tariffs and Trade and its successor the World Trade Organisation expanded its membership and a rules based trading system was adopted.

This was until the middle of the 2010 decade where tariffs became a weapon in disputes over non tariff issues such as patents, security of equipment and allegations of misuse of state aid and whatever other disagreements countries may have had with each other. Tariffs have been moved from an economic concept to a political tool. This has ended up having economic consequences on consumers through increases in prices and indeed on producers who no longer are able to access particular overseas markets. There are bilateral and unilateral tariff wars between the USA and China, China and Australia, the USA and the EC. These appear to have by-passed the World Trade Organisation which was established to rule on such disputes.

In this context can be placed Brexit where its justification and rationale appears to be one of political sovereignty rather than economic rationality. Getting agreement on tariff free trade between the UK and the EC has been hindered by failure to see eye to eye on state aid and product standards as well as access to fishing grounds. Moreover, the removal of tariff free access and the introduction of different standards will necessitate investment in hitherto not needed costly infrastructure and document checks (with associated software and hardware). This is even without the thorny issue of the Northern Ireland Protocol with all its "unforeseen" ramifications even though it is part of a binding agreement that was signed by both parties. Political desires can have hidden economic consequences and considerable cost to the electorate.

It can be concluded that progress on multilateral trade has been reversed because of political and unilateral action. The lessons of increased trade supported by rules and adjudicated by an unbiased multilateral organisation have been forgotten.

Tax Policy and Tax Administration

Tax policy is, in general, particular to an individual country. Some countries have no income tax and where there is income tax rates of taxation vary from a single rate to different multiple rates which have divergent levels. Similarly company tax rates differ as countries try to attract mobile investment. Perhaps a common theme has been the almost universal adoption of value added tax and excise tax to replace the revenue lost by tariff reform with rates varying between countries. A second generalisation is that discretionary exemptions from tax payable have become much more infrequent as tax breaks for investment have been codified and exemptions from import duties discontinued.

Nevertheless while these changes may well be considered progress in balancing the tax system between varieties of revenue sources, the taxation of the digital economy has become an area where there is considerable debate. While the OECD is taking the lead in garnering a consensus to formulate a multilateral solution similar to that on a minimum corporate tax rate, there is still the danger of unilateral action comparable to that relating to the use of tariffs.

Tax administration has experienced significant progress over the years. Using the PEFA scores on the tax indicators as a benchmark, for the 12 PEFAs that I have been involved in (using the 2016 methodology) the average score has gone from 2.77 in the previous PEFA to 3.14 in the most recent one – a rise of 13.4% based on the 2011 methodology.[117] The mode for the taxation scores in the earlier comparable PEFAs was A while the median score was B and both mode and median are A in the most recent PEFAs. The average scores have been dragged down by generally D scores in revenue arrears monitoring where historical arrears still remain on the books even though there is no hope of collection as the companies have often been liquidated. Legislation to write off these and other uncollectable arrears is usually absent. Although a comparison with any PEFA before the one with the 2.77 average score has not been made, I am confident that this 2.77 average will have been signif-

---

117   PIs-13, 14 and 15. These numerical scores have been derived from assigning a value of 4 to A, 3 to B, 2 to C and 1 to D to each dimension and adding up all the dimensions across countries and getting an overall country average. These indicators are scored using the data from the 2016 PEFA applied to the 2011 methodology for comparision purposes.

icantly higher that a previous like for like average. This is based on my experience in carrying out many earlier assessments having assessed taxation indicators. Steady progress has been made in tax administration since the PEFA assessment has been implemented in 2005.

Why has this progress been achieved? There are many interrelated reasons. The most significant reasons perhaps have been the professionalization of tax administration coupled with the advances in information technology which placed a barrier to face to face interaction between the tax collector and the tax payer. The creation of Revenue Authorities combining Customs Departments and Direct Tax Departments was a first step in this direction with Uganda, Sierra Leone, Zambia, Tanzania and Rwanda in the precursor. The motivation came from the desire of governments to ensure that revenue was maximised to fund services and the move was supported by donors particularly by DFID. DFID supported their creation by technical assistance with short and long term consultancy and operational support. IT specific to tax administration is addressed below.

Budget Preparation

PEFA 2016 methodology relating to budgeting preparation is one of the areas that were expanded from the PEFA 2011 methodology. However it is possible to assess progress by making a comparison of the scores for PI-12 (2011 methodology): Multi-year perspective in fiscal planning, expenditure policy and budgeting and its dimensions.

For PI-12 (i) Preparation of multi-year fiscal forecasts and functional allocations the average score increased from 2.08 to 2.75 with a median and mode score of C which increased to median B/C and mode A. For PI-12 (ii) Scope and frequency of debt sustainability analysis the average score decreased from 3.25 to 2.83 with a median and mode score of A with a decrease to median B with mode staying at A. For PI-12 (iii) Existence of sector strategies with multi-year costing of recurrent costing of recurrent and investment expenditure the average score decreased from 2.08 to 1.92 with a median of C mode score of D with the median staying at C and the mode moving to C/D. For PI-12.4 (iv) Linkages between investment budgets and forward expenditure estimates the average score in earlier PEFAs was 2.08 falling to 1.83 in the later PEFAs with the earlier median and mode at C but both falling to D in the later PEFAs. Clearly a mixed picture and one of relative decline where the score for PI-12 could be said to have gone from a C+ to C.

For PI-12 (i) there has been good progress and the higher modes show that the average scores are dragged down by a few weak performers. For P12 (ii) the mode is A in both timeframes but the average has been dragged down by a few non performers not carrying out a debt sustainability analysis within three years on the assessment time period when they had done so in the previous PEFA. The weak and deteriorating scores for PI-12 (iii) and (iv) are reflective of the nature of the dimensions which require more than just a mechanical application of information supported by specific software. PI-12 (iii) and (iv) are integral to the MTBP process described in Chapters 4 and 5. Indeed this observation is supported by looking at the scores for PEFA 2016 PI-8 Performance information for service delivery which is a new indicator that has been introduced. The scores for PI-8.1 Performance plans for service delivery for the 12 PEFAs shows an average of 2.08 with a mode of D and a median of C/D: six scored D, two scored C, one score B and three scored A. Two out the three that scored A scored A for PI-12 (iii) and B for PI-12 (iv) while the third scored low on these as it did not have multi-year coverage.

Information Technology as a boon to progress

Information technology coupled with the internet has allowed significant improvements in processes and procedures. For tax administration this has been transformative. The transformation of the initial but problematic ASYCUDA programme though ++ to World has meant that import documentation can now be done online. Taxes are assessed and paid and risk assessment determined for physical and documentation checks or no checks or audits after receipts of goods with minimal face to face interaction. Similar IT development has taken place in direct taxes where segmentation of companies into Large, Medium and Small Tax Payers has improved compliance through audit selection based on risk assessment. As well linkages with government procurement and other activities such as company registration have been facilitated though tax compliance certification. IT and the internet has also allowed easier information on tax responsibilities and coverage. This has facilitated tax payer education which has become a key service that revenue authorities deliver. IT has allowed reporting on revenue collection, transfers of revenue collected to the Treasury and updating of taxpayers' records often in real time. I have been in tax administrations where I have been shown the revenue collection at the time of the meeting on a mobile phone.

These achievements appear to be universal but clearly not perfect in all countries. The diagnostic tools on taxation that have been developed – the two 2016 PEFA indicators and perhaps more importantly the drill down TADAT – have provided benchmarks and areas where improvements are required. These usually form part of an Action Plan that can be implemented with support from external agencies. The support that CARTAC provides and has provided to island countries in the Caribbean is a good example of this, but also the way that Georgia has implemented tax reform internally.

For the development of the MTBP, IT and the internet, although important, are only crucial to the process so long as the procedure is correctly specified. Chapter 4 has shown this in the discussion on PSHIP and SIGBUD. Information Technology certainly has assisted in PI-12 (i) and with programmes such as CS-DRMS,[118] IT is crucial for PI-12 (ii).

Information Technology is at present more in use for budget execution and accounting. It has been crucial to achieving high PEFA scores in the relevant indicators. A good and functioning Integrated Financial Management Information System should ensure good scores in debt data and recording (PI-17 (i)), effectiveness of expenditure commitment controls (PI-20 (i)) and stock and monitoring of expenditure payment arrears (PI-4) as well as timeliness of the issue of (in-year) budget reports (PI-24 (ii)) and timeliness of submission of the financial statements (PI-25 (ii)).[119] The average scores for PI-17 (i) have increased from 3 to 3.5 and for PI-20 (i) from 2.83 to 2.92 and the associated PI-4 from 2.29 to 2.33. However scores for PI-24 (ii) declined from 3.09 to 2.82 and for PI-25 (ii) from 3.42 to 2.75. It has to be noted that 3 of the sample did not have an IFMIS so had to use other means of controlling

---

118 Commonwealth Secretariat Debt Recording Management System an integrated tool for recording, analysing and reporting public sector debt integrating with financial systems and allows exchange of debt related data for improving efficiency and accuracy of information

119 2011 PEFA methodology for comparison purposes.

commitments and arrears but did use software to manage debt data. The scoring for PI-25 (ii) is conditional on when the financial statements are submitted for audit and not when they are completed which has impacted on scoring on some of the countries.

It is perhaps apposite to quote from the Georgia PEFA to appreciate the importance of IT and the internet to PFM: "An overriding feature of PFM in the Republic of Georgia has been the development and good use of Information Technology in budget preparation, budget execution (accounts, commitment control, and cash management), personnel and payroll, revenue services, and procurement. The application of IT has been developed in-country based on business processes in each of the subject areas (redefined as necessary) and not on the reconfiguration of business practices to suit particular software. This adoption of IT solutions combined with the internet as a vehicle for its implementation by competent and trained personnel (with appropriate control) has been fundamental to the development of strengths in PFM. The integration of IT, internet and personnel has resulted in PFM's positive effectiveness and efficiency". Georgia's Central Government PEFA scores have been one of the highest worldwide, and the application of the processes supported by IT has been applied to its municipalities where the IFMIS and other procedures such as procurement are applied to the whole of government.

Information and decision making

In Stern's article quoted in Chapter 7, information, or more precisely the lack of it, is cited as both an issue relating to market failure and government intervention. Analysis of PI-12 results have shown that existence of sector strategies with multi-year costing of recurrent and investment expenditure and linkages between investment budgets and forward expenditure estimates are relatively weak in the sample countries. The questions then are what processes and procedures are governments undertaking to try to improve their appreciation of citizens' priorities for spending other than through the election cycle and what information are governments providing to the electorate. A PEFA indicator can assist in this direction.

Public access to fiscal information (PI-9 2016 PEFA methodology) lists nine elements[120] of which 5 are deemed critical to a high score. The five are: Annual executive budget proposal documentation; Enacted budget; In-year budget execution reports; Annual budget execution report; and Audited annual financial report, incorporating or accompanied by the external auditor's report. To score an A all five must be met along with three of the four additional elements which are: Pre-budget statement; Other external audit reports; Summary of the Budget proposal or enacted budget (Citizen's budget) and Macroeconomic forecasts. The average score for the 12 PEFAs was 2.42 which would require, for a C score, 4 basic elements only. The median score was C but the mode was A and D with 4 having these scores. Of the 12 PEFAS, seven provided a citizens budget.

There are two other indicator dimensions that are relevant alongside public access to information. PI-18.2 Legislative procedures for budget scrutiny require that procedures include arrangements for public consultation to score an A. The average score for the PEFAs was 2.67. The median and mode score was B. Only two PEFAs scored A. PI-31.4 Transparency of legislative scrutiny of audit reports require that hearing are conducted in public and committee reports are published in publically accessible means to score A and B.[121] The average score for the PEFAs was 2. The median and mode score was D. Two PEFAs scored A and two also scored B

The overall conclusion on information to and ensuring participation with the public by governments is could do better with a few exceptions: only Georgia scored A in all three categories while Uganda scored A in two and B in 31.4 which met the public hearings criteria.

Information is important to people. In Port Moresby there was a general misunderstanding of the World Bank and how it was working with the PNG Government to fund education and health. There were signs of protests particularly at the university. The mission leader and country economist Pirouz Hamidian-Rad agreed to go to the university to explain that the Bank was planning to channel such support through Non Governmental Organisations to

---

120   Although the 2011 PEFA methodology has the same indicator (PI-10 Public access to key fiscal information) it is not as extensive and has just 6 elements of information deemed critical.

121   The difference in score relates to the extent of exceptions related to the coverage of the hearings.

ensure that it was effective. I volunteered to go with him to provide support. When we got to the university it was clear that the protests had taken a violent turn with cars with government number plates being attacked and some set on fire. We were led into the Senate Room which was filled to the brim with many chewing buai (a mild stimulant from the betel nut). Every time the mission leader Pirouz tried to speak there was a surge towards the stage and each time I stood up on my tip toes to accentuate my 6 foot 4 inches (at that time!) behind Pirouz! The impasse was broken when Pirouz agreed to sign a letter to the Prime Minister for a meeting with the organisers which then appeared on the front page of the paper the following day.[122]

The global public good nature of the PEFA Framework – the voluntary nature of its application with no constraints – has also increased the information on PFM to members of central and local government that are managing the processes and procedures across the whole of the budget cycle. The PEFA website states that 1,000 plus officials are trained annually on the details of the PEFA framework.

It has been noticeable that the enthusiasm over an assessment exhibited by officials has increased over time as they have become more familiar with the process with repeat assessments and have appreciated the benefits. This has also undoubtedly been helped by the evolution of PEFA itself. In the early days PEFA was seen to be more a donor tool supporting fiduciary risk assessments but now it is seen as a diagnostic tool that identifies strengths and weakness in a country's PFM processes. This is then used to formulate a PFM Action Plan with a SMART baseline and targets to be realised as presented in Chapter 6.[123]

---

122   The student organiser then said to us "you guys were good and stood up to them well – let's go for a beer"! An Iranian and an Irishman working in tandem! When we went back to the car we found that our elderly driver had been robbed. Paul Harnett had a more hair-raising experience when he was discussing the programme with a Permanent Secretary and mentioned the World Bank: the Permanent Secretary reached over the desk grabbed Paul by the collar and started to punch him and only stopped when someone from the outer office came in and pulled him off Paul. PNG was not all like that and the tariff team travelled all over and were made very welcome and enjoyed the beauty of the country. However the country has a darker undercurrent and information is important.

123   Although in *"Advice, Money, Results – Rethinking International Support for Managing Public Finance" International Working Group Report, New York University* the view is postulated that current approach treats PFM as a "closed" system, in which the PFM processes and conventions that drive operational performance are

Quality of People

Most of the work I do is with people not just with numbers so gaining respect and trust are hugely important particularly with the private sector. This can be so if you are seen as being associated with the government (working with development partners as donors were once termed). But that is also true of staff of Ministries and Government Departments as I could not be able to achieve anything without their support and collaboration. A PEFA would be impossible to carry out without them. It is hugely important never to be blasé or presumptive about carrying out an assessment as a PEFA is based on information. All of the information resides in the staff of the institutions that are being assessed. Good working relations are important but more importantly is trust. I was up in Martvilli, a rural municipality small in population but large in area, with my colleagues Lasha Gotsiridze and Papuna Petriashvili carrying out the PEFA. The deputy mayor who was organising our schedule said that the mayor wanted to invite us to dinner. My colleagues were not sure as they were concerned about probity. I said that it would be a good way to ensure full cooperation as we were aware that the municipality employees were bit suspicious of the mission thinking that we were a follow up scrutiny audit, given recent audit findings. As it was, the mayor was a retired rugby player like me and the evening was full of Georgian toasts using his homemade wine. Georgian toasts are many – celebrating family – and wine is not sipped and a great many different sized receptacles are used, including horns. The mayor did not speak English but my colleagues

---

considered to be unchanging ends in and of themselves. Viewing PFM instead as an "open" system that interacts more fluently with all aspects of public policy—namely, government policy choices, government actions (especially service delivery), and development results—offers the potential for developing a new generation of approaches to managing public finance. This broader perspective would better reflect the complex realities of context and the unavoidable nature of trade-offs in policy objectives. This "open" conception of PFM, proposed by the International Working Group on Managing Public Finance, is distinguished by a willingness to revise and expand the guiding objectives for managing public finance and to reappraise the conventions that drive the form and content of external technical advice in this area. It sees conventions about the operational performance of PFM processes as useful benchmarks, without considering them to be set in stone or remaining blind to their purpose of informing and delivering wider public policy outcomes. The Report and other material can be found on https://wagner.nyu.edu/advice-money-results/about. Perhaps getting the existing systems to work might achieve this rather than getting too excited about change for changes sake and might be more effective.

translated our discussion of rugby experiences. One of the mayor's friends was nearby and, as he was an opera singer, we were treated to arias as the flagons of wine became emptier. Culture, rugby and wine, and the full confidence of the mayor in what we were doing and what we needed from his staff for the PEFA! We were able to report in the wrap up that the visit achieved everything that we had set out to do.

In all of this, leadership and "Champions of Change" are critical. In Uganda, Emmanuel Tumusiime-Mutebile provided these and was supported by his politicians. In Albania Fatos Nano as Prime Minister pushed on integrated planning and the MTPB and after elections Sali Barisha continued the process and empowered his staff even though he was of a different political party. In Kosovo Bedri Hamza led the way in using PEFAs as a tool for diagnostic appraisal and subsequent implementation. In Georgia, Giorgi Kakauridze continued the work his predecessors had started. In Sierra Leone ever in the days of military government, John Karimu supported by Colonel Mike Conteh ensured that reforms and implementing them were at the forefront of government.

As outlined in Chapter 9 training has been an important component of the work I have carried out. I have noticed that over time the education and quality of civil servants has been on an upward curve at both central and local government across all departments and ministries. Over time individual experience has been gained. In Uganda back in the early 1990s one of Emmanuel Tumusiime-Mutebile's strategies in his approach to developing Uganda was to ensure that he had good qualified staff and got the donors to support the Ministry through funding (of supplementary salaries). He secured young and talented staff and also got overseas staff in support for his ministry. All of them reached high positions in the Ministry (up to Permanent Secretary) and the IMF and the overseas staff ended up working for the IMF (some reaching Resident Representative) and the World Bank. The foresight and investment has paid off. Countries have also invested in government training facilities such as Uzbekistan's Training Centre of the Ministry of Finance, Kosovo's Institute of Public Administration and Georgia's Academy of the Ministry of Finance, which is linked with the IMF training courses. The role out of internal audit and overall Public Internal Financial Control in Georgia was facilitated by the Academy and its training.

Triangulation

Triangulation – getting other participants' independent views – is an important, though not particularly time-consuming, element of a PEFA assessment. Meetings are held with civil society, NGOs, development partners etc, to get a more independent, perhaps jaundiced, view of how processes work. Mostly these meetings are carried out with businesses organisations such as a Chamber of Commerce and Manufacturers Association. Experiences on how the tax administration and procurement systems work as well as expenditure arrears can be related. As well, an appreciation of how the budget process works, particularly how priorities are determined, can be obtained.

Likewise understanding the constraints faced by the private sector would not be possible without speaking to and having the confidence of business men and women. Chapter 7 illustrates that point in terms of the survey work related to tariff reform. But often unexpected opportunities arise to gain greater insights. One of the businessmen I met a few times in Harare was Strive Masiyiwa[124] who was having a difficult time in setting up competition to the State owned company in the telecoms sector. He was able to provide an insight that counterbalanced others that may have more vested interests. In Ethiopia, Shiferaw Bekele General Secretary of the Addis Ababa Chamber of Commerce was a thoughtful contributor to private sector development and the issues that the sector faced. On the non business side when working in Khartoum, it was arranged for me to meet John Garang[125] who was an agricultural economist but at that time a leading proponent of the creation of South Sudan as a separate country. He clearly could not have been on a wanted list at the time, although the political climate was not stable.[126]

---

124 https://en.wikipedia.org/wiki/Strive_Masiyiwa

125 https://en.wikipedia.org/wiki/John_Garang

126 Indeed returning to Khartoum from a visit to an establishment just south of the city along the Nile we were driven to and through a refugee camp related to the conflict in the South. It was huge. It was quite sobering and made me think how fortunate I was. But also on how development is constrained by such instability. It was certainly in stark contrast to the hotel where I was staying on the confluence of Blue Nile and the White Nile.

Promoting PFM

During the Albania work, Mauro Napodano, one of the team, established the PFMBoard, postings on which have been referenced earlier. On April 7 2010 he posted[127] "The PFM Board is a community where practitioners like you MEET on-line to DISCUSS public financial management issues. Through its open exchange, the PFM Board provides access to consultants and civil servants who are responsible for the PFM reform in developing and transition countries, and to individuals entering the PFM area for the first time. There are several authoritative PFM presences on the web, among which the PEFA Secretariat,[128] and the IMF blog on PFM.[129] The PFM Board intends to complement them by providing a bottom-up approach to the PFM discussion, whereby you can decide the topics you are interested in to advance the Board content. Register for free and decide whether to use your real name or an avatar as username. If you have something to say and/or to ask in the area of PFM you are welcome to the PFM Board! How it all started? The idea to create the PFM Board was nurtured in 2008-2009. In that period I studied the business model of the community of people around the Grateful Dead, an American rock band of the 60s-70s. This business model has attracted the interest of several economists, among whom there is the Nobel laureate Paul Krugman who concluded his 2008 New York Times newspaper article by stating: 'In the long run, we are all the Grateful Dead'."[130]

The PFMBoard is something I have supported from the start and try to post on it regularly if I see something topical and relevant. I think Mauro would agree with me that, unfortunately, it has stagnated a bit and has suffered from attack by spammers (with fictitious email addresses) which has needed vigilance and frequent changes to the membership registration process. Chapter 4 points to some of the very useful and educational posts on the PFMBoard.

---

127 on https://pfmboard.com/
128 http://www.pefa.org/
129 http://blog-pfm.imf.org/
130 http://www.nytimes.com/2008/06/06/opinion/06krugman.html

Good Sound Policy

The cliché "location, location, location" has been used by **property** experts as the three most important factors in determining the desirability of a property. The equivalent aphorism in the economics of development is policy, policy, policy with the qualifying adjectives of "good sound" preceding policy. And good sound policy to be backed up with the laws, regulations, processes and procedures to make them effective. After all bad policy is more than likely to, at best, maintain the status quo if there is no change in policy or cause regression in an economy once it is introduced. The lessons contained in this and previous chapters hopefully are a pointer in the direction of good sound economic policy as applied in most of the countries I have worked in. Often the nature of the Government does not have to be a factor as the reforms in Sierra Leone have shown. But clearly a democracy works best in determining priorities and allowing citizens to express what they would like their elected government to do. But conflicts, such as in Sudan, Yemen and Afghanistan, ensure that any government cannot provide the platform for such policy to be implemented even if it is formulated.

The Beginning of the End – the Joining of the Circle

My experiences in the consultancy profession (if a profession is the correct word) have also shown changes over time. While assignments in East Africa were initially with the World Bank I also started to get contracted by the UK Overseas Development Administration (ODA) which later became the Department of International Development (DFID). ODA had a close interest in the overall policy reforms and indeed was working closely with the World Bank. For instance I was contracted by ODA led by Alister Moon on the Uganda Private Sector Assessment while my colleague Raoul Ascari was contracted by the World Bank. A similar situation emerged in West Africa particularly in Sierra Leone where most of the support to the Ministry of Finance and PEFAs was contracted by the UK Development Agency.

My company REPIM grew out of this – almost in two phases. I had been contacted by Lancashire Enterprises which had consulting operation in Eastern Europe in economic and regional development and wanted to expand into a wider market. So REPIM was formed as a joint venture between me, trading as John Short Economic Services and Lancashire Enterprises. REPIM carried out the tariff reform work in Kenya and Uganda with me and Lancashire Enterprises staff. However, given changes in the structure of Lancashire Enterprises and internal opposition from its in-house consultancy section, Lancashire Enterprises decided to pull out from the joint-venture without having given it the support that it needed. Lancashire Enterprises handed the company fully to me. Indeed, Paul Harnett had been the first employee of REPIM but had seen the writing on the wall and took the opportunity to take his family off to Namibia for a year in 1991. When he returned, he rejoined the fold. I was also getting more requests than I had time. I had been approached by Martin Johnston whom I had known when he was an ODI fellow in Uganda and we had been in Namibia at the same time on different assignments. He had just finished a long term assignment in The Marshall Islands and wanted a change. As it happened I had just been approached by Eric Hawthorn who was based in the ODA office in Harare to do consultancy in Lusaka which I was unable to do because of other commitment and Martin filled in.

REPIM had become what could be termed a niche and nimble consultancy in the PFM field and able to field small teams at relatively short notice. The biggest number in a team was 5 in PNG tariff work but often it was much smaller and often just one or two of us. Work was always short term and limited in time but often there was follow up on related assignments. The work was often based on demand from the World Bank and DFID and based on reputation and successful delivery with recommendations passed on within and between the organisations. We would be shortlisted within a limited competitive process to submit technical and financial proposals – some would be won, some would be lost.

This changed to a degree when REPIM was invited to tender for SPEM 2 in Albania. This was a considerably significant larger contract but REPIM had the technical capability to do the work, and it the end, that capability won the contract. REPIM successfully bid for SPEM 3 but just because we had won SPEM 2 there was no guarantee of success. Indeed it went down to the wire and the fact that REPIM had an excellent working relationship with the Albanian government tipped the vote in REPIM's favour. REPIM then won the competitive bid for the Trust Fund continuation project.

Would REPIM have been as successful today? The hurdles in such tenders are now so high and given the barriers to entry REPIM would not even pass the pre-selection process to be short-listed. For REPIM to be involved in such projects there would have to be a link up with a larger company. This happened in the successful bid for the Palestine PFM work where REPIM was in partnership. However, such arrangements can be fraught with problems as overall leadership and control are lost even though there is responsibility for certain technical elements. The specification of the work in Palestine was based on the previous contractor's reports which turned out to be recommendations that were neither de facto nor de jure. It took Martin Johnston a lot of time in discussions with the Budget Department to get things on track. However the project was hindered by lack of interest at DFID Jerusalem and poor project management by the lead contractor, both of which were unable to set up the steering group with the Minister of Finance which really was essential for overall buy-in, despite the great cooperation and support of the Budget Department. It was only in the last six months or so that the project was managed by someone who understood the issues and DFID's new manager took control to establish the type of structure that should have been in place from the start. The REPIM public expenditure team of Martin Johnston, John Blissett, Saimir Sallaku, Sharon Hanson Cooper and Imad Dayyah all worked incredibly hard (which I was part of), and along with the Budget Department made significant changes to the budget process in the Line Ministries and Ministry of Finance. The successor project would have found the landscape better that than it was before their inputs.

REPIM is also part of framework contracts which also reflect the way the consultancy world has changed. DFID essentially now organises most of their consultancy projects both short-term and long-term though a number of contracts organised around themes. REPIM is part of a consortium relating to Governance which is concerned with larger long-term projects. It is not part of the consortium that manages short-term work. Essentially DFID has farmed out the management of most of its technical assistance operations to companies that have the wherewithal to do this with a database of CVs. If a company is not in a consortium then it is out of the game which has removed REPIM from such short-term work.

A Sour Taste

The EC also operates framework contacts for work below €300,000 in value which generally is short-term. A number of consortia are selected after a detailed tendering process and generally the overall contract is for 3 years and is generally extended. REPIM has been a member of a consortium but has found the process frustrating. Indeed the process is to me a great example of the George Akerlof article on lemons and asymmetric information[131] which Martin Johnston often bemoans. A mix and match selection process is usually adopted by the consortium leader who selects teams from the CVs nominated and because of this overall leadership and control may be compromised and usually is. On occasions I have nominated teams but have pulled out once the mix and match approach had been applied. One of those was for a PEFA and another for PFM work in Uganda which we were well positioned given our history. The one project that we successfully bid was a two man team with REPIM taking the lead but there was no ability to control the inputs of the second person from a time and quality perspective and this caused problems. We also put in a CV for a country that the nominated person had carried out a FRA for DFID who would be backed up by myself who had worked on the PEFA and other work for the IMF in that country. The CV was rejected by the consortium leader for someone who had not worked in the country. The EC did not select that CV submitted by the consortium leader. I have tried to engage in correspondence with the Managing Director of the Framework Contract leader over how the consortium has been managed but did not get a reply!

Despite receiving many opportunities it is only recently that I have dipped my toes into the muddy waters as I wanted to be sure that there may be a chance of being considered. A project to provide training to (i) Ministry of Finance and selected line ministries to reinforce the capacities of the Ministry of Finance on Medium-Term Expenditure Framework and (ii) reinforce the capacities of the Ministry of Finance on tax policy and revenue forecasting including the tax expenditures provided that opportunity. There were two parts to each element an in-country training programmes (using selected EU member states as examples) and a study tour to

---

131 'The Market for "Lemons": Quality Uncertainty and the Market Mechanism', Quarterly Journal of Economics (August 1970).

a member state. Given my reticence but knowing I had the relevant experience I submitted my CV as I felt I would be able deliver both with others and given the specification of tax expenditures be able to link both components. Before the closing date for internal consideration I decided to withdraw my CV as I was still unsure but on being approached by the Consortium Leader to reconsider as the deadline had been extended by the client. I also submitted the CV of Paul Harnett who had worked with me on the MTBP in Albania and on similar work in Kosovo as well as numerous PEFAs and PERs. Crucially Paul had carried out PERs in the two sectors, agriculture and environment, that were specified in the ToRs. I also reiterated that I wanted to be considered for both the tax and MTEF component to work with Paul on the MTEF and "AnOther" from the submitted CVs. The training was to be in the English language and as Paul and me are both citizens (if not resident) of the only English speaking member state that might have been an advantage!

The selection criteria comprised two categories: PFM expert (covering MTEF component) and Specific requirement (which included elements such as writing sector development plans, experience in building and monitoring KPIs, experience in performance-based budgeting and budget classification and experience in gender-based budgeting). I had top score in MTEF (38 out of 40) although Paul with similar experience scored 33. I was scored 14 out of 15 for experience in developing MTEF including elaboration of training on the MTEF for the staff of the ministry of finance and some sector ministries (at least in the last 10 years). This is what the project was about.

Both of us fully fulfilled the MTEF requirement! However, when coming to the specific experience I scored 19 out of 40 and Paul 17. I scored 0 out of 10 on sector development plans (as did Paul), 7 out of 10 on performance-based budgeting and budget classification and 0 out of 5 on gender based budgeting even though my CV had stated that I had participated on training on the subject delivered by the PEFA Secretariat. So two other consultants with less MTEF and training experience, (who scored 12 and 9 out of 15 on that critical element) were selected. I was not considered for the taxation training component.

On reflection it looks like the person that created and scored the evaluation grid did not understand what an MTEF was about and where PERs linked in and what was included in both such as sector development plans and applying budget classification. It is also ironic that the background in the Terms of Reference stated that the World Bank were to be working on two public expenditures reviews for Education and Public Investment Management, the latter being one of the weaknesses in the PFM in the country and an area that Paul had been on many Public Investment Management Assessments. Looking at the website of the consortium leader, it is clear that the evaluator has no PFM experience; the supervisor has no PFM experience, and also the person that the supervisor reports to, has no PFM experience. The nescient are leading the nescient who are reporting to the nescient.

I wonder if the EU Framework people who see the tip of the iceberg – those CVs that are submitted – know about the bulk of the iceberg below the surface of the murky waters – as noted: a market for lemons!

The End?

In a real sense, my work opportunities, at my tender age, have gone full circle and I am working on World Bank and IMF missions to the extent that I want to. After a hiatus the World Bank is clearly back in the provision of PFM support to its client countries. However, what is now missing is the team camaraderie that was built up in REPIM as the "body shops" that provide the opportunities for work do not often provide that environment and control.

Nevertheless COVID-19 has changed the way we work. Missions are now being held virtual, for the time being anyway. Delivering PEFA training and being able to participate in meetings in the other side of the world from my desk in rural Northumberland with simultaneous translation is a fact. However, good internet has been essential to its realisation. Without the roll out of full fibre connectivity this would not have been possible.

ANNEX: ASSIGNMENTS AND EXPERIENCE

2021	Azerbaijan – Medium Term Budget Framework. Member of World Bank team working with the Government of Azerbaijan to develop a Medium Term Budget Framework covering Fiscal Management, Public Expenditure Analysis and Efficiency, Public Investment Management, Transparency and Accountability. Initial work used relevant PEFA indicators to diagnose the initial MTBP status and develop a baseline.
2021	Albania - Member of World Bank team carrying out a Climate PEFA.
2021	Moldova – CG and SN PEFAs. Member of a World Bank team with responsibility for assessing indicators 6, 8, 10, 12, 14-15 and 21-22 and guidance and quality control on indicator scoring and report production.
2021	Vietnam – CG and SN PEFAs. Mentoring a World Bank team with responsibility for training, guidance and quality control on indicator scoring and overall reports production
2020	Serbia – Fiscal Fisk. As part of a World Bank team producing guidelines for fiscal risk analysis and monitoring with specific responsibility relating to climate change and impact on natural disasters.
2020	Pakistan– PEFA- Quality Control review of Federal, and Sindh and Punjab provinces PEFAs with rewrites to achieve PEFA Checks. (World Bank)
2019	Fiji – CG PEFA. Member of IMF PFTAC team carrying out the CG PEFA. Responsible for assessing indicators 1, 2 3, 19, 20, 24, 25, 26, 30 and 31 and drafting the full report which received the PEFA Check using the revised PEFA report format.
2019-2020	Ukraine – CG and SN PEFAs. Acted as reviewer of Ch 3 draft and subsequently drafted the PEFA report in conjunction with the World Bank team. Worked on SN PEFA (2) from Concept Note stage to leading field work and drafting report to achieve PEFA Check.

2019	Uzbekistan – PFM Strategy and Action Plan. Worked with the Government to produce a PFM Action plan based on the 2019 CG PEFA (World Bank)
2019	Lao PDR – PEFA. Provided Quality Assurance inputs to the 2019 PEFA Assessment team to achieve the PEFA Check (World Bank)
2018	Georgia – PFM Strategy and Action Plan. Worked with the Government to produce a PFM Action plan based on CG and SN PEFAs and other diagnostic tools (World Bank)
2018	Georgia – Subnational PEFAs and PFM Action Plan. Team Leader of 3 subnational PEFAs. Managed and delivered 3 PEFA reports through PEFA Check along with two local consultants. Delivered PEFA training along with PEFA Secretariat. Dissemination workshop on SN PEFAs results. Subsequently produced SN PEFA Synthesis report. (World Bank)
2018	Georgia – Central Government PEFA. Member of World Bank team carrying out a validation of the Government's self assessment. Responsible for PI-1-3, 10-14, 16 and 19-20 as well as drafting chapter on summary, conclusion and reform programme. Responsible for collating all comments and getting final report through PEFA Check (World Bank)
2017	Uganda – Internal peer review of PEFA including revisions to draft report based on PEFA Sec comments particularly on tax indicators
2017	St Lucia – PEFA. Member of CARTAC team that carried out a PEFA using the 2016 methodology. Responsible for assessing indicators 1-3 13-15, and 19-20 and peer reviewing other indicators as well as inputting into Chs1-2 and 4.
2017	Palestine – Palestine Governance Facility. As part of the project final report carried out interviews with relevant Development Partners on their perceptions on the design and implementation of the project and lessons for a successor project. Updated the Revenue Forecasting Model.
2017	St Kitts – Budget Formulation. Reviewed progress on budget formulation and conducted workshops for senior management and planning and budget staff in Line Ministries and Ministry of Finance.
2017	Philippines – Budget Preparation Manual. Assisted the Department for Budget Management in reviewing budget preparation practices and translating them in to a manual to guide the various agencies (IMF FAD).

2016	Jamaica – PEFA. Member of CARTAC team that carried out a PEFA using the 2016 methodology. Responsible for assessing indicators 1-3 18-20 and 30-31 and peer reviewing other indicators as well as drafting Chs1-2 and 4.
2016	Dominica – Vulnerability Fund. Member of IMF FAD team that prepared proposals for a Vulnerability Fund relating to fiscal risk from catastrophic events such as hurricanes using Citizens for Investment revenues.
2016	St Kitts – Budget Formulation. As part of on-going inputs into budget formulation methodology, worked with Ministries of Education, Health, Finance, Infrastructure and Agriculture to develop performance indicators to adjust the budget process to meet the changes in Chart of Accounts and budget formulation process. Mapped out the existing budget process into a document to develop new procedures consistent with PEFA 2016.
2016	Palestine – Revenue Forecasting. Updated and tested the revenue forecast model with recent data.
2016	Dominica – PEFA. Member of CARTAC team that carried out a PEFA using the 2016 methodology. Responsible for assessing indicators 1-3 18-20 and 30-31 and peer reviewing 20-21, 27-29 as well as drafting Chs1-2.
2015	British Virgin Islands – PEFA. Delivered training on PEFA methodology and carried out an assessment on most indicators as a guide to development of a PEFA Action Plan to address weaknesses. CARTAC
2015	St Kitts and Nevis – PEFA training. As part of ongoing support on budget reform carried out training on 2015 PEFA (all 30 indicators and their 90 dimensions). PEFA budget formulation indicators used to provide workshops to senior management of Line Ministries on the changes to budget formulation methodology that are needed for PEFA compliance.
2015	UK – Peer reviewed Mozambique PEFA for SECO
2015	Grenada – PEFA. Member of team that carried out a PEFA Assessment using the 2015 methodology as well as scoring on 2005/2011 methodology to compare with previous PEFAs. This assessment was carried out using fully the 2015 methodology and has been awarded the PEFA Check. Provided extensive comments on all of the indicators and report structure to the PEFA Secretariat as part of the over review process that it carried out. Rescored PEFA to be consistent with 2016 PEFA methodology.

2015	Jamaica– PEFA training, Delivered training on 2015 PEFA (all 30 indicators and their 90 dimensions) and linked these to the revision of the PFMRAP
2015	St Vincent and the Grenadines – Programming Mission. Member of IMF Team programming PFM TA support under the Fiscal Management in the Caribbean programme funded by Canada and implemented by the IMF
2015	St Kitts and Nevis – Programming Mission. Member of IMF Team programming PFM TA support under the Fiscal Management in the Caribbean programme funded by Canada and implemented by the IMF
2015	Grenada – PEFA. Prepared the ToR and Concept Note for the Grenada PEFA carried out in 2015 using the 2015 test PEFA methodology. CARTAC
2015	Grenada – Fiscal Regulations. IMF FAD Programming Mission to assist the authorities finalise the regulations to support the 2014 Public Finance Bill and carry out a PFM diagnostic assessment.
2015	Dominica – PEFA. Prepared the ToR and Concept Note for the Dominica PEFA to be carried out in 2016 using the 2016 PEFA methodology.
2015	Barbados – Training on 2015 PEFA. Prepared and delivered training on 2015 PEFA (all 30 indicators and their 90 dimensions) for the 20 CARTAC members over 3 days. This training was the first training programme on the 2015 PEFA that was carried out and was attended by the Head of the PEFA Secretariat who presented the rational for the changes in methodology.
2015	Palestine – Revenue Forecast Model. Developed a revenue forecasting model consistent with the IMF Transparency guidelines and 2016 PEFA indicator PI-15
2014	Serbia – Municipality PEFAs. Team leader on 6 municipality PEFAs responsible for management, training and report (summary and resultant PFM action Plan) as well as leading on 2 municipalities' PEFAs. SECO
2014	UK – PEFA Carried out peer review of PEFA Concept Note and reports on Azerbaijan and Indonesia and ToR of Mozambique PEFA for SECO
2014	St Kitts and Nevis – Strategic/Programme Budgeting Training. Responsible for design and delivery of training programme on the development of strategic/programme budgeting for the Ministries of Finance in the two islands.

2014	Palestine – Ceilings and Resource Envelopes. Advised As part of the DFID Governance project on the preparation of the resource envelopes and ministerial ceilings for the 2015-2017 Medium Term Budget Programme
2014	Jamaica – PFMRAP monitoring. On behalf of CARTAC, assisted in introducing outputs and objective criteria based on PEFA Framework to measure successful implementation, in addition to the activities already being carried out. Delivered training on PEFA methodology.
2014	Barbados – PEFA and PFM Action Plan. Presentation of PEFA results and use of PEFA as input into a PFM Action Plan. On a follow up mission assisted in translating the PEFA results into a PFM Reform Action Plan. CARTAC
2014	Anguilla – PEFA Consultant on CARTAC team. Responsible for delivery of training (1 day), assessment of indicators PIs-14 -18, 20, 21 and 26, 27 and 28.
2014	Antigua – PEFA Consultant on IMF Team. Responsible for assessment of indicators PIs-13 to 18 and 20 -21.
2014	Myanmar – Assessment of PFM. As member of IMF FAD's Technical Assessment Team examined budget formulation developed initiatives for a Fiscal Unit in the Ministry of Finance assessing and recommending methods of forecasting of macro aggregates including revenue estimation and baseline expenditures. Made a presentation on revenue forecasting techniques suitable for Myanmar
2013	Mozambique – Domestic Resource Mobilisation. Mentored a team of international and local consultants on the Domestic Resource Mobilisation study carried out for the African Development Bank.
2013	Nevis – Budget analysis. Provide assistance to the Budget Department as part of CARTAC assistance. Carried out a needs assessment for PFM training in the context of the budget formulation process and procedures.
2013	Montserrat – Budget analysis. Provide assistance to the Budget Department as part of CARTAC assistance. This work included reviewing the link between strategic planning and the budget in the context of higher level national plans, commenting and making recommendations on the content of the quarterly reports, assistance in developing a budget scorecard and provides training on expenditure analysis for the analysts in the budget department in the context of the Ministry of Finance's contestability function.

2013	Barbados – PEFA Lead consultant on IADB-CARTAC team. Responsible for delivery of training (1 day), assessment of indicators PIs-5-14, 26, 27 and 28 and drafting of report.
2013	Antigua – PEFA Training. Provided training to Government Officials over a three day period on PEFA in preparation for the PEFA which is to be carried out by the IMF
2013	Albania – National Strategy for Development and Integration (2013-2020). Member of team comprising government officials and local and international consultants preparing the national strategy with primary responsibility for macro-economic and revenue issues.
2013	Palestine – PEFA. Member of Donor team (for EC) led by World Bank that carried out a PEFA Assessment with responsibility for indicators PI-6, 8, 9 and PI 13 to PI-17 inclusive.
2012	St Kitts and Nevis – Assessment of PFM. As member of SEMCAR Technical Assessment team carried out a review of PFM process and procedures in context of potential TA needs. Responsibility for budget formulation component of PFM and budget cycle.
2012	Myanmar – Assessment of PFM. As member of IMF FAD Technical Assessment team carried out a review of PFM process and procedures in context of potential TA needs. Responsibility for budget formulation component of PFM and budget cycle.
2012	St Vincent and Grenadines – PEFA member of joint IMF – World Bank team carried out a PEFA Assessment with responsibility for indicators PI-5 to PI-12.
2011-2012	Kosovo – MTEF Team leader for DFID's support to reformulation of MTEF leading inputs into the production of and training on a policy costing manual as principal author, template and manual on linking strategic planning to MTEF and impact analysis of new policy initiatives and associated training, including a training programme for inductees into budget departments.
2011	Palestine – As part of inception team reviewed progress on programme budgeting and as an input to the design and annual work programme of DFID's support programme to Ministry of Finance carried out by OPM & REPIM
2011	Kosovo – Public Expenditure Review Team leader with examination of Labour and Welfare, and Private Sector Development (Ministry of Trade and Industry) expenditures linking objectives to outputs for MTEF and annual budget.

2011	Kosovo – Municipality (SN) PEFA Assisted the Government of Kosovo's SN PEFA assessment team by providing a "help-desk" with respect to assessment methodology and scoring of the PEFA indicators. Responsibility for production of final report. This work was done in two waves covering 6 municipalities in wave 1 and 5 municipalities in wave 2.
2010	Sierra Leone – PEFA Team Leader of the PEFA assessment team (Central Government and Local councils). Carried out an initial PEFA sensitization workshop for government officials and donors. Presented the evidence requirements of the full indicator (and dimension) to the government and donors in pre PEFA workshop, as well as assessed indictors on budget credibility, fiscal risk, decentralisation, budget preparation and taxation. Principal author of CG PEFA report and presentation of results.
2010	Serbia – PEFA Assisted the Government of Serbia's PEFA assessment team by providing training and a "help-desk" with respect to assessment methodology and scoring of the 31 PEFA indicators as well as principal author of PEFA report.
2010	Zambia – As part of evaluation of PFMRAP, carried out a review of PFM reforms in various countries (Kenya, Tanzania, Sierra Leone, Albania and Kosovo) covering the full range of reform programmes, including IFMIS.
2009-2010	Kosovo – Budget Reform Assisted the Ministry of Economy of Finance with budget and MTEF reform through facilitating exchanges with the Ministry of Finance Albania in lesson learning from the reform process supported by presentations.
2009	Kosovo – Fiduciary Risk Assessment. An FRA was produced for DFID using the 2009 PEFA and surveys on corruption.
2009	Albania – Sector Guides for Budget Preparation. As part of the Supporting the Ministry of Finance, Line Ministries and the Department for Strategy and Donor Coordination for Strategic Plans Development, the Implementation of Medium Term Budget Programme, Public Investment and Monitoring Project produced Sector Guide for Ministry of Finance and coached Ministry team in budget preparation.
2009	Serbia – Fiduciary Risk Assessment of the use of the Deposit Insurance Agency for channelling DFID support to the reform process. This entailed an examination of DIA's financial management process and the overall Serbia PFM using PEFA indicators as appropriate, and producing an analysis of corruption indicators.

2009	Moldova – Annual Statement of Progress relating to Fiduciary Risk for DFID updating the PEFA analysis and review of corruption material.
2009	Kosovo – PEFA Assisted the Government of Kosovo's PEFA assessment team by providing a "help-desk" with respect to assessment methodology and scoring of the 31 PEFA indicators. This was followed up in assisting the translation of the PEFA into a PFM Reform Action Plan. As well, production of a FRA for DFID based on the How to Guidelines.
2009	Sierra Leone – Output to Purpose Review (annual assessment report) of DFID support to the National Revenue Authority.
2009	Kosovo – Economic Policy Advisor. Providing support to the inter-ministerial team developing sustainable employment policy in the context of a multi-donor budget support operation led by the World Bank.
2009	Moldova – Public Financial Management Project. Carried out a mid-term review assessment and evaluation for the Ministry of Finance of the PFM project that includes the introduction of an IFMIS, improved budget preparation and execution, introduction of internal audit and the development of related training.
2008	Moldova – Fiduciary Risk Assessment for DFID budget support for PRSP applying the PEFA analysis and review of corruption material.
2008	Moldova – Public Expenditure and Financial Accountability (PEFA). Team Leader for second PEFA assessment with responsibility for drafting and presenting the report and technical inputs into budget credibility and preparation, taxation and donor issues.
2008	Georgia – Public Sector Financial Management Reform. On behalf of DFID participation in the annual review mission of the PSFM Reform Support Project. This project covers support to the MTEF, introduction of IFMIS, development of HR in the MoF and support to the supreme audit institution. On a second mission examined progress against timetable in the light of DFID timetable for withdrawal from Georgia and un-spend financial inputs to the project.
2008	Liberia – PEMFAR Carried out public expenditure review of health and public works.
2008	Sierra Leone – Multi donor budget support Member of team assessing compliance with conditionality for tranche release of budget support and design of new benchmarks linked to PEFA.

2007	Sierra Leone – PEFA Team leader and principal report writer with responsibility for indicators covering credibility of the budget, inter government fiscal relations and oversight, taxation, legislative scrutiny and PETS
2006	Uganda – Output to Purpose Review of DFID project Modernising the Uganda Revenue Authority. This work also included a review of a new donor basket funded project in particularly linking the modernisation plan into the 5 year corporate plan for annual work plans and budget.
2006	Moldova – Fiduciary Risk Assessment for DFID budget support for PRSP applying the PEFA analysis and review of corruption material.
2006	Afghanistan – Output to Purpose Review of DFID's project Transforming and Modernising the Budget Formulation Process
2006	Serbia – Joint Project "Towards the more effective implementation of reforms". Review of pilot stage with recommendations for 2006 work programme. This involved extensive consultation with participating institutions (both commissioning and recipients) including two workshops to discuss findings and recommendations to plan 2006 programme for Yearly Operational Plan of Action in recipient ministries for all participants.
2006	Moldova – Public Expenditure and Financial Accountability (PEFA). Team Leader for multi donor Public Expenditure Financial Accountability assessment with responsibility for drafting and presenting the report and technical inputs into budget preparation, taxation and donor issues.
2006	Kenya – Public Expenditure Reviews. External consultant for the 2006 PER in Health and HIV/AIDS.
2005-2009	Albania – MTEF As part of the Strengthening Public Expenditure Management Team, reviewed the delay in applying the budget calendar and its impact on the MTEF, inputs into the macro economic background section and assisted in developing the General Directorate of Macroeconomic and Fiscal Policies. Assisted with visit of the Albania Parliamentarian Public Expenditure Committee to the UK PAC, Treasury Committee and Treasury. Produced a paper on tax administration and policy and revenue forecasting and an analysis of public expenditure from 1997 to 2007.
2005	Uganda – Output to Purpose Review of DFID project Modernising the Uganda Revenue Authority.

2005	Kenya – Public Expenditure Reviews. External consultant for the 2005 PERs in Health and HIV/AIDS. Team leader comprising MoH officials and local consultant responsible for project direction and report production.
2005	Kenya – Poverty Health Classification. Carried out a review of the classification of health expenditure to core poverty programmes, by examining Kenya's poverty policy and international best practice.
2004	Uganda – Output to Purpose Review of DFID project Modernising the Uganda Revenue Authority
2004	Palestine – Carried out fiduciary risk assessment for DFID Emergency Budget Support to Palestine Authority.
2004	Kenya – Public Expenditure Review Coordinator of REPIM team assisting the GoK in preparing options for 2004 Budget covering in detail Health, Education, Roads and Transport, Agriculture and Police. Specific input into health sector work.
2003	Ethiopia – Assessment of Incidence of Taxes on different income groups. Carried out an assessment of the changes in direct and indirect tax policy reform on different income groups.
2003	St Helena, Falklands Islands and Pitcairn – Desk study review of macroeconomic performance, public finance and public expenditure management. Carried out this review for the EC to assess viability of budget support under the agreement with Overseas Countries Territories using Public Expenditure Management Country Assessment and Action Plan methodology.
2003	Anguilla – Review of macroeconomic performance, public finance and public expenditure management. Carried out this review for the EC to assess viability of budget support under the agreement with Overseas Countries Territories using Public Expenditure Management Country Assessment and Action Plan methodology.
2003	Kenya – Public Expenditure Management Country Assessment and Action Plan. Member of World Bank and IMF team that assessed the quality of the public expenditure management systems to reflect this in the public expenditure management assessment and action plan, and the 16 key indicators

2003	Afghanistan – Assessment of TA for Budget Development reviewed the budget process and assessed the technical assistance that DFID could supply requirement to improve the budget process in the light of existing donor assistance. Retained to provide support to DFID for monitoring and evaluation and guidance to project.
2003	Tanzania – Tax Review Team leader on a review of tax policy, tax administration and the relationship between tax collection, GDP and GDP composition.
2003	Ghana and Rwanda – MTEF Review Carried out a review of each country's MTEF as part of an ODI cross country study of MTEFs in Africa.
2002	Ghana – AgSSIP Member of DFID's team on the Implementation Support Missions of the World Bank's Agriculture Services Sub–sector Investment Project and preparation of DFID's support to the sector over the 2002–2004 period.
2002-2005	Albania – MTEF Director of the REPIM's team carrying out the Strengthening of Expenditure Management. Technical inputs on training and public investment issues as well as policy programme and expenditure reviews. Drafting MTEF documents before translation to Albanian.
2002	Ghana – MTEF Assessment of the MTEF for the World Bank as input to the preparation of the Poverty Reduction Support Credit
2002	Kenya – Public Expenditure Review. Consultant to the Ministry of Finance and Planning on the 2002/3 Public Expenditure Review.
2002	Rwanda – Tax Policy and Administration. Assessment of the relationship between tax collection and GDP in an examination of the real sector and GDP composition.
2002	Rwanda – Design of methodology and implementation of costing of Poverty Reduction Strategy Programmes. Sectoral allocations based on resource envelope scenarios including HIPC and additional donor funding.
2001	The Gambia – MTEF Diagnostic Analysis. Diagnostic study of the budget process with recommendations for the design and phasing of budget reform and the introduction of a Medium Term Expenditure Framework process.
2001-2002	United Kingdom – Research into the regional dimension of public expenditure as part time research fellow in the Centre for Regional Public Finance, University of Aberdeen

2001	Kenya – Budget Process Analysis. As background to DFID's budget support to Kenya, assessed the formulation of the budget, payment control, accountancy and auditing arrangement at the head–quarter and district levels. Reviewed the transfer modalities to local authorities. Analysed Government expenditure and revenue and balance of payments.
2001	Uganda – Tax Policy. Assessed the impact of the UMA proposals to import raw materials duty free on effective protection and revenue.
2000	India – Development Strategy. Leader of a team that produced the documentation for a Donor's Forum for the State of Madhya Pradesh. This involved examination of all aspects of economic and social policy.
2000	Sierra Leone – Introduction of MTEF. As part of REPIM's support to the Budget Department, reviewed exemptions in context of tax policy, examined public expenditure system and prepared DFID programme aid submission. During further work, estimated the costs of the IMF report on indirect taxes as well as alternative scenarios compared to the existing, including the cost of exemptions and reviewed the UNDP report on direct tax. Delivery of workshop on budget reform and introduction of an MTEF
1999	Zambia – Tax and Investment Policy. Evaluation of operation of duty drawback and investment policy as part of World Bank credit conditionality
1999	Vietnam – Public Expenditure Issues. Member of DFID team reviewing financial and technical support for the structural adjustment programme with specific emphasis on public expenditure issues.
1999	Zimbabwe – Tariff Reform. Advised the Tariff Commission on Tariff Reform.
1999	Pakistan – Provisional Governments Public Finance. Member of World Bank Team examining Provincial Public Finance with primarily responsibility for revenue mobilisation issues
1999	China – Budget Procedures Design for DFID Support. Evaluation of budget procedures, and revenue and expenditure aspects of proposed DFID support to education in Province of Gansu. Development of management structure for the project.

1999-2000	Rwanda – MTEF, Sector Review Process and Budget Preparation. Assisted the Government prepare the 1999 Budget as part of a REPIM team. Managed the social sectors public expenditure review. This was extended to cover the 2000 budget and the update of the sector reviews (health, education and justice). Assisted the Government in producing its paper for the Donor Conference. Co–authored paper on linking poverty alleviation strategy to MTEF and Budget.
1999	Rwanda – DFID Budget Support. Preparation of documentation for DFID budget support to Government.
1998	Seychelles – Tax Policy Analysis. Analysis of the tax revenue implications of the country's accession to COMESA and provided recommendations for changes in tax policy.
1998	Ghana – DFID Programme Aid Design. Programme aid design for UK DFID examining budgeting, expenditure and accounting procedures and public expenditure analysis including a detailed analysis of the education sector.
1998	Liberia – Post–Conflict Reconstruction Strategy. Member of World Bank Team preparing World Bank strategy for its involvement in the reconstruction of Liberia.
1997	Malawi – Trade and Tariff Support. Prepared report on trade and tariffs as part of the SADC Trade Protocol negotiations
1997	Zambia – Duty Drawback Design. Review and recommendations for strengthening the duty drawback and manufacturing under bond scheme including a review of indirect taxes. This was followed up by implementing the recommended scheme including training, drafting procedures, regulations and legislation and public awareness.
1997	Tanzania, Uganda and Ethiopia participated on an Irish aid mission to the three countries. Worked with Irish Aid on articulating the benefits of budget support as an aid modality and delivered training to staff on budget support modalities. Served on an interview panel for Irish Aid recruitment
1997	Zambia – Public Expenditure and Budget Procedure Analysis. A review of public expenditure trends and budgetary procedures for DFID budgetary support programme.
1997	Papua New Guinea – Tax Policy Reform. Reviewing progress on tariff and indirect tax reform and preparing revenue forecasts to 2005.

1996	Netherlands Antilles – Public Expenditure and Taxation. Team leader of consultancy for Inter America Development Bank and Dutch Government on Medium Term Policy Framework and Development Strategy. Responsible for technical work on public expenditure and taxation.
1996	Malawi – Structural Adjustment Support Evaluation. Leader (of 3 plus local consultants) of the evaluation of the European Union's structural adjustment support programme with responsibility for study direction and report as well as technical inputs on macro and budgetary aspects of terms of reference.
1996	Uganda – PER Budgeting and Accounting Formats. Member of World Bank Team on Public Expenditure Review covering budgeting and accounting formats. Member of team that is preparing technical assistance project to implement budget reform programme under SAC III developing output oriented budget for agriculture.
1996	Papua New Guinea – PER Education Expenditures. Member of Public Expenditure Review team analysing education expenditure. On a separate assignment delivered a paper on tariff reform in the Indirect Tax Summit and delivered seminars and workshops on trade and industry liberalisation and tariff reform.
1996	Malawi – UK Budget Support Procedures. Evaluation of procedures for ODA budget support for the Government of Malawi.
1996	Tanzania – Social Sector Budget Procedures. Member of team evaluating the EU's support to the Government of Tanzania under its Structural Adjustment and STABEX programmes; responsible for examining budget procedures and health and education expenditure.
1996	Sierra Leone – Ministerial Restructuring. Restructuring the Department of Trade, Industry and Co operatives in context of the economic policy environment following the structural adjustment programme.
1996	Uganda – Tax Policy. Member of World Bank team preparing the third Structural Adjustment Credit with responsibility for taxation issues and the anti export bias. Examined the duty drawback scheme and made proposals for its revision.

1995	Papua New Guinea – Tariff and Indirect Taxation Review. Leader of REPIM Team that carried out a tariff and indirect taxation review as input into 1995/96 budget. Carried out a review of the duty drawback system and made recommendations for a new system. The work also included a detailed analysis of agriculture and industry.
1995	Uganda – Revenue Forecasting. Prepared a medium term revenue forecast as part of the 1996 budget preparation.
1995	Papua New Guinea – Structural Adjustment Issues. Member of World Bank team managing the structural adjustment loan.
1995	Zimbabwe – PER Public Expenditure Analysis. Member of the World Bank Team that carried out the initial Public Expenditure Review with specific responsibility for data compilation and analysis of public expenditure.
1995	Tanzania – Taxation and Incentive Review. Assessment of the taxation and incentive structure leading to detailed recommendations for the 1995/96 and 1996/97 budget. Assessment of the operations of the Investment Promotion Centre and incentives offered.
1995	Uganda – Private Sector Development. Assessment of the taxation and incentive structure leading to detailed recommendations for the 1995/96 and 1996/97 budget. Also detailed work on policies for private sector development. Detailed examination of role and responsibilities of the Uganda Investment Centre.
1995	PTA Africa – Common External Tariff. Lead consultant on study on establishing a common external tariff for COMESA. This study covered 22 countries examining the impact of tariffs on the real economy and assessing the impact of changes on employment, industry and the Government budget. Presented a paper at the COMESA members' review and discussed the study's findings. Attended the meetings of the Trade and Customs Committee and the Ministerial Committee.
1994	Tanzania – Export Development. Formation of an Export Development Strategy.
1994	Namibia – Public Expenditure and Taxation. Lead consultant of a six person team carrying out a public expenditure and taxation review. Specific responsibilities for taxation, but also covered budgeting and aggregate public expenditure.

1994	Ethiopia – Public Investment. Member of World Bank team carrying out a Public Expenditure Review responsible for the capital budgetary work, development of methodology for a 3 Year Rolling Plan and expenditure analysis, and directing sectoral specialists.
1994	Ethiopia – Indirect Taxation. Responsible for proposal for changing the structure of indirect taxes and tariffs and the rates (with revenue implications).
1994	Liberia – Taxation and Incentives. Member of World Bank mission assessing indirect taxation and incentives.
1994	Kenya – Effective Protection. Effective Protection Analysis of Indirect Taxes and Tariffs for Government of Kenya with the World Bank and UK ODA.
1993	Belarus – Two studies were carried out for the World Bank comprising an assessment of the demand for long term foreign exchange and an export development strategy. These were conducted by surveying companies and banks as well as relevant government departments.
1993	Sierra Leone – Tax Policy Advice to Minister. Retained as the advisor to the Minister of Finance on indirect taxation and the Minister of Trade and Industry on trade and investment policy. Responsible for proposal for changing the structure of indirect taxes and tariffs and the rates (with revenue implications) and new investment and export policy. Designed and implemented a duty drawback scheme.
1993	Uganda – Regulatory Reform. Review of Regulatory framework as part of SAC II negotiations for World Bank.
1993	Sierra Leone – Tax and Tax Policy. Trade policy review as part of indirect taxation reform.
1992	Bangladesh – Textile Sector Study. Analysis of competitiveness and trade policy using DRC and EPR analysis.
1992	Ghana – Investment appraisal. Regional resources investment opportunity study.
1991 – 1992	Yemen – Investment Climate Appraisal. Analysis of policy and institutional framework for investment promotion as part of Round Table Conference documentation including Free Trade Zones.
1991	Nigeria – Public Expenditure Review. Analysis of public expenditure in manufacturing industry in the Rolling Plans and Budget, and the privatisation of manufacturing enterprises.

1991	Uganda – Structural Adjustment Appraisal. Member of World Bank structural adjustment credit identification, pre appraisal and appraisal missions.
1990	Jordan – Export Competitiveness. Analysis of the competitiveness of Jordanian manufacturing in terms of the potential to export. Review of trade policy and its impact on competitiveness.
1990	UK – Defence expenditure and employment The vulnerabilities of localities to cutbacks, Research paper for Lancashire Enterprises
1990	Kenya – Agriculture PER. Analysis of Ministries of Agriculture and Livestock Development investment portfolio of development projects: design of methodology to prioritise projects for additional funding.
1989	Uganda – Private Sector Assessment. Analysis of policy environment and constraints in setting up and operating businesses leading to the creation and implementation of policies for the development of the private sector. Lead economist on World Bank/ODA team.
1989	Nigeria – Economic Review. Review of Customs and Excise rates and duties with respect to estimating yields and isolating revenue and protection aspects. Review of Federal Ministry of Industries' expenditure plans for 1990 Budget, and the operations of the Technical Committee on Privatisation and Commercialisation with respect to FMI's portfolio. Assessment of the Structural Adjustment Programme (SAP) on manufacturing industry; analysis of problems and prospects and strategies for development. Main sectors covered: textiles, wood products, food processing.
1988	Ghana – Competitiveness analysis. DRC and EPR estimation from MIST's 1987 Industrial Survey.
1988	Sudan – Public Expenditure Review. Member of World Bank Economic Mission with responsibility for analysis of subsidies on petroleum products, sugar and wheat and flour as part of review of public expenditures.
1988	The Gambia – Privatisation analysis. A development plan for the Dockyard in Banjul in the context of privatisation leading to a bid document by interested parties.

1988	Ghana – Competitiveness Analysis. Assessment of changes in industrial policy on manufacturing industry from 1985. This involved analysis of industrial survey carried out by the Ministry of Science, Industries and Technology (MIST) to estimate economic efficiency (DRC) and levels of protection (EPR)
1988	The Gambia – Development Act. Design of operational system to implement the Development Act and training of officials of departments responsible for its implementation.
1988	Zimbabwe – Manpower Planning. The demand for architects, quantity surveyors and building industry professions in the medium to long–term as part of feasibility of establishing a department at the University of Zimbabwe.
1988	Mauritius – Manpower Planning. Needs assessment study for technical and vocational training for human resource development with action and implementation plan.
1987	Nigeria – Public Expenditure Review. Member of World Bank team on 1988 Budget and Public expenditure programme–responsible for assessment of sugar, pulp and paper, fertiliser and machine tool industries. Examination of Duty Drawback Scheme for exporters; assessment of progress on trade and industry policy reform programme.
1987	The Gambia – Private Sector Development. Member of World Bank appraisal mission on Private Sector Development Project. Responsible for assessment of participating institutions capacity with recommendations for institutions strengthening and training requirements.
1987	Mauritius – Manpower Planning. Member of World Bank Mission appraising vocational and training loan, responsible for assessing industry's requirements for training.
1987	Zimbabwe – Manpower Planning. Member of World Bank team, assessing manpower development, particularly training needs for industry.
1987	The Gambia – Design of the Development Act. Design for Fiscal Incentive, Regulations and Guidelines for 1988 Development Act for Industry.
1987	Nigeria – World Bank economic mission. Responsibilities covered analysis and recommendations for industrial projects for 1987 public expenditure capital account; Analysis of impact of Second–Tier Foreign Exchange Market on private sector performance and prospects; and analysis of the investment climate, incentive and regulations. Review of duty drawback provisions.

1986	Ghana – Investment Policy. Member of IFC team to the Ghana Investments Centre to provide guidelines and regulations for the operations of the 1986 Investment Code.
1986	Niger – Debt Analysis. Preparation of paper on debt relief and concessional aid for Round Table Meeting (World Bank)
1986	Nigeria – Tariff Reform. Evaluation of protection for industries where import ban is removed and replaced by tariffs.
1986	Netherlands Antilles and Aruba. – Economic Analysis. Member of World Bank mission (on behalf of Dutch Government) with responsibilities for evaluating current industry and future employment prospects, and public expenditure and finance.
1985	Indonesia – Strengthening Investment Policy and Administration. Economist and deputy project manager (resident) on World Bank financed project on strengthening economic – decision making capability of BKPM – The Investment Coordinating Board. Developed and presented a training programme on investment selection and appraisal in three locations across Indonesia.
1984	Nigeria – Federal Capital Expenditures. Review of Federal capital expenditures as part of public expenditure review, examining major on–going projects with a view to recommending those projects to be mothballed or otherwise restructured, terminated or continued. This work involved extensive use of economic project evaluation, including CBA and DRC measure, producing a ranking of projects for budgetary presentation and financial analysis.
1984	United Kingdom Research project on the Developmental Role of Public Expenditure in Regions and Sub-regions at Centre for Urban and Regional Development, University of Newcastle
1982-83	Philippines – Structural Adjustment Support. Assigned as core consultant on the technical assistance component of the World Bank Structural Adjustment Loan to the Philippines, Ministry of Trade and Industry. One of the outputs was a development strategy for fruit, vegetable and fish processing.
1980-1981	Egypt – Pricing Policy. Petroleum Products Pricing and Gas Utilisation Studies (for the Egyptian General Petroleum Corporation, financed by the World Bank). Developed an energy related input–output table by adding a petroleum products sector to the existing input model and further disaggregating it into key energy-using sectors. PEIDA consulting

1980	Carried out some ad hoc work for PEIDA Consulting: interviewing companies in the North east relating to location and investment and also interviewing companies and institutions on the demand for a deep water testing facility.
1978-1980	United Kingdom – Inter–Regional Financial Flows. Responsible for design, development organisation and supervision of research on UK inter–regional financial flows for the UK Department of the Environment) at Department of Economics University of Durham.
1980	United Kingdom – Local Council Public Expenditure. Consultant to North East County Council Association in matters relating to public expenditure.
1974-78	United Kingdom – Regional Public Expenditure Analysis. Sole responsibility within multi–disciplinary team for development of work on public expenditure systems in the UK regions, including the relation of public expenditure costs to recommendations as part of economic strategic plan for Northern Region at Northern Regional Strategy Team. Also wrote reports on Tourism & Linkages.
1972-1974	United Kingdom – Regional Impact of Defence Expenditure. Research into the regional impact of defence expenditure including impact studies on the employment and income effects of defence bases on their local economies together with analysis of the regional incidence of defence contracts placed by the Ministry of Defence at Department of Political Economy University of Aberdeen
1971-1972	University of Lancaster MA in Economics: studied macro and micro economics, econometrics and regional economics. Dissertation: An analysis of Earning Changes in the United Kingdom, 1960-71: expectations, Union Influence and Excess Labour Demand. A Fourteen Industry Study
1967-1971	University of Stirling BA (Hons) in Economics. Final year option: Money and Public Finance Dissertation: Economic Analysis of Airport Location with Special Reference to Regional Development

PUBLICATIONS

Books and Monographs

Public Expenditure in the Northern Region and Other British Regions, Technical Report No 12, Newcastle–upon–Tyne, Northern Region Strategy Team, 1976

Public Expenditure and Taxation in the UK Regions, Aldershot, Gower, 1981

Money Flows in the UK Regions (with Nicholas, D.J.), Aldershot, Gower, 1981

Assessment of the MTEF in Rwanda, Centre for Aid & Public Expenditure, Overseas Development Institute, London, May 2003

Assessment of the MTEF in Ghana, Centre for Aid & Public Expenditure, Overseas Development Institute, London, May 2003

PEFA and Policy Management Gordon Evans John Short Martin Johnson. The PFM Board Compendium vol. 01 February 2013

Refereed Journals and Book Chapters

'The regional dimension of public expenditure in England' (with David Heald) *Regional Studies*, Vol. 36, 2002, pp. 743–755.

'PNG Tariff Review Protection and Economic Efficiency and Survey of Productive Sectors' Indirect Tax Summit Papers Institute of National Affairs Discussion Paper No 68 Port Moresby November 1996

'The regional distribution of public expenditure in Great Britain, 1967/70 – 1973/74', *Regional Studies*, Vol. 12, 1978, pp. 499–510.

'Defence spending in the regions of the UK', *Regional Studies*, Vol 15, 1981, pp. 101–10.

'The Northern Region: Borrower or Lender?', *Northern Economic Review*, No 2, 1982.

'Public expenditure in the English regions', in Hogwood, B.W. & Keating, M. (eds), *Regional Government in England*, Oxford, Clarendon Press, 1982, pp. 191–216

'Public finance and devolution: money flows between government and regions in the United Kingdom', *Scottish Journal of Political Economy*, Vol 31, 1984, pp. 113–29.

'Financial Flows in the Regional Context: the Experience of the United Kingdom in Situation and Outlook with Regard to Regional Accounts in the Community, Eurostat, 1984 (Seminar Proceedings from event held in Luxemburg, 30/11 to 3/12/1982).

Other Publications

Military Installations and Local Economies – A Case Study: The Clyde Submarine Base (with Greenwood, D. and Stone T.), ASIDES No 5, University of Aberdeen, Aberdeen, 1974.

Military Installations and Local Economies – A Case Study: The Moray Air Stations (with Greenwood, D.), ASIDES no 4, University of Aberdeen, Aberdeen, 1973

Money Flows in the Regions of the UK (with Nicholas, D.J). Department of Economics Research Paper, University of Durham, Durham, 1980.

The Developmental Role of Public Expenditure in Regions and Sub-Regions (with Howard, J.), Centre for Urban and Regional Development Studies, University of Newcastle upon Tyne, Newcastle, 1985, mimeo.